ASPEN PUBLISHERS

TORTS

5TH EDITION

NEIL C. BLOND

Wolters Kluwer

Law & Business

AUSTIN   BOSTON   CHICAGO   NEW YORK   THE NETHERLANDS

To contact Customer Care, e-mail customer.care@aspenpublishers.com, call 1-800-234-1660, fax 1-800-901-9075, or mail correspondence to:

Aspen Publishers
Attn: Order Department
PO Box 990
Frederick, MD 21705

Printed in the United States of America.
1 2 3 4 5 6 7 8 9 0

ISBN 978-0-7355-8618-5

About Wolters Kluwer Law & Business

Wolters Kluwer Law & Business is a leading provider of research information and workflow solutions in key specialty areas. The strengths of the individual brands of Aspen Publishers, CCH, Kluwer Law International and Loislaw are aligned within Wolters Kluwer Law & Business to provide comprehensive, in-depth solutions and expert-authored content for the legal, professional and education markets.

CCH was founded in 1913 and has served more than four generations of business professionals and their clients. The CCH products in the Wolters Kluwer Law & Business group are highly regarded electronic and print resources for legal, securities, antitrust and trade regulation, government contracting, banking, pension, payroll, employment and labor, and healthcare reimbursement and compliance professionals.

Aspen Publishers is a leading information provider for attorneys, business professionals and law students. Written by preeminent authorities, Aspen products offer analytical and practical information in a range of specialty practice areas from securities law and intellectual property to mergers and acquisitions and pension/benefits. Aspen's trusted legal education resources provide professors and students with high-quality, up-to-date and effective resources for successful instruction and study in all areas of the law.

Kluwer Law International supplies the global business community with comprehensive English-language international legal information. Legal practitioners, corporate counsel and business executives around the world rely on the Kluwer Law International journals, loose-leafs, books and electronic products for authoritative information in many areas of international legal practice.

Loislaw is a premier provider of digitized legal content to small law firm practitioners of various specializations. Loislaw provides attorneys with the ability to quickly and efficiently find the necessary legal information they need, when and where they need it, by facilitating access to primary law as well as state-specific law, records, forms and treatises.

Wolters Kluwer Law & Business, a unit of Wolters Kluwer, is headquartered in New York and Riverwoods, Illinois. Wolters Kluwer is a leading multinational publisher and information services company.

Check Out These Other Great Titles:

BLOND'S LAW GUIDES

Comprehensive, Yet Concise . . . JUST RIGHT!

Each Blond's Law Guide book contains: Black Letter Law Outline ·
EasyFlow™ Charts · Case Clips · Mnemonics

Available titles in this series include:

Blond's Civil Procedure

Blond's Constitutional Law

Blond's Contracts

Blond's Criminal Law

Blond's Criminal Procedure

Blond's Evidence

Blond's Property

Blond's Torts

ASK FOR THEM AT YOUR LOCAL BOOKSTORE
IF UNAVAILABLE, PURCHASE ONLINE AT http://lawschool.aspenpublishers.com

Law school is very different from your previous educational experiences. In the past, course material was presented in a straightforward manner both in lectures and texts. You did well by memorizing and regurgitating. In law school, your fat casebooks are stuffed with material, most of which will be useless when finals arrive. Your professors ask a lot of questions but don't seem to be teaching you either the law or how to think. Sifting through voluminous material seeking out the important concepts is a hard, time-consuming chore. We've done that job for you. This book will help you study effectively. We hope to teach you the law and how to think.

Preparing for Class

Most students start their first year by reading and briefing all their cases. They spend too much time copying unimportant details. After finals they realize they wasted time on facts that were useless on the exam.

Case Clips

Case Clips help you focus on what your professor wants you to get out of your cases. Facts, Issues, and Rules are carefully and succinctly stated. Left out are details irrelevant to what you need to learn from the case. In general, we skip procedural matters in lower courts. We don't care which party is the appellant or petitioner because the trivia is not relevant to the law. Case Clips should be read before you read the actual case. You will have a good idea what to look for in the case, and appreciate the significance of what you are reading. Inevitably you will not have time to read all your cases before class. Case Clips allow you to prepare for class in about five minutes. You will be able to follow the discussion and listen without fear of being called upon.

"Should I read all the cases even if they aren't from my casebook?"

Yes, if you feel you have the time. Most major cases from other texts will be covered at least as a note case in your book. The principles of these cases are universal and the fact patterns should help your understanding. The Case Clips are written in a way that should provide a tremendous amount of understanding in a relatively short period of time.

EasyFlow™ Charts

A very common complaint among law students is that they "can't put it all together." When you are reading 400 pages a week it is difficult to remember how the last case relates to the first and how November's readings relate to September's. It's hard to understand the relationship between different torts topics when you have read cases for three or four other classes in between. Our EasyFlow™ Charts will help you put the whole course together. They are designed to help you memorize fundamentals. They reinforce your learning by showing you the material from another perspective.

Outlines

More than one hundred lawyers and law students were interviewed as part of the development of this series. Most complained that their casebooks did not teach them the law and were far too voluminous to be useful before an exam. They also told us that the commercial outlines they purchased were excellent when used as hornbooks to explain the law, but were too wordy and redundant to be effective during the weeks before finals. Few students can read four 500-page outlines during the last month of classes. It is virtually impossible to memorize that much material and even harder to decide what is important. Almost every student interviewed said he or she studied from homemade outlines. We've written the outline you should use to study.

"But writing my own outline will be a learning experience."

True, but unfortunately many students spend so much time outlining they don't leave time to learn and memorize. Many students told us they spent six weeks outlining, and only one day studying before each final!

Mnemonics

Most law students spend too much time reading, and not enough time memorizing. Mnemonics are included to help you organize your essays and spot issues. They highlight what is important and which areas deserve your time.

EASYFLOW™ CHARTS

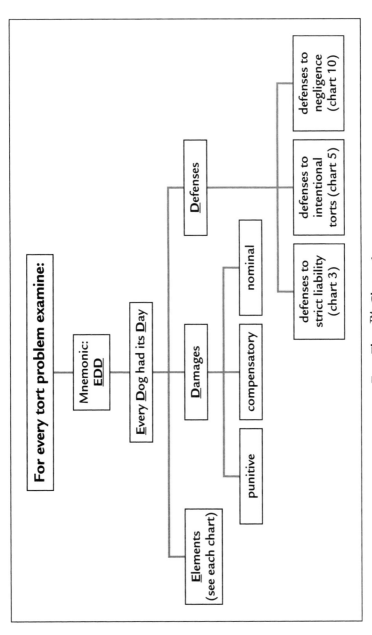

EasyFlow™ Chart 1

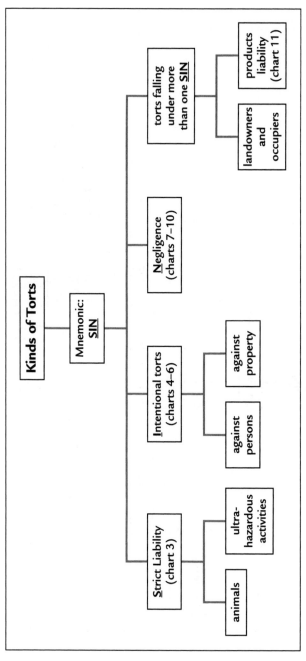

EasyFlow™ Chart 2

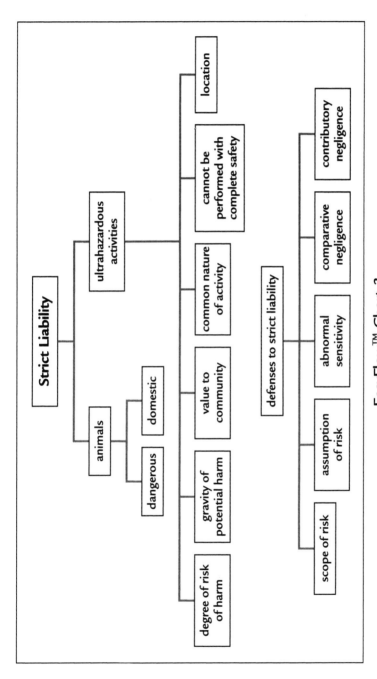

EasyFlow™ Chart 3

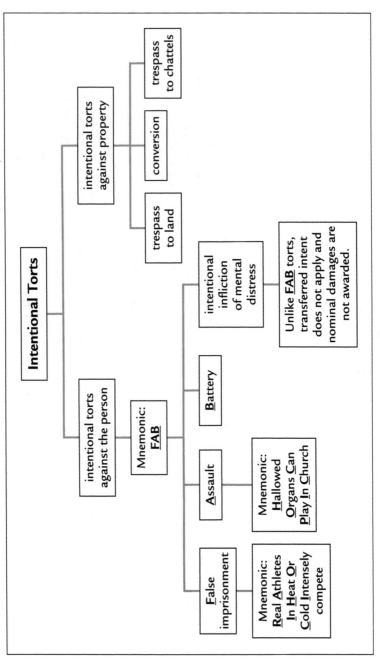

EasyFlow™ Chart 4

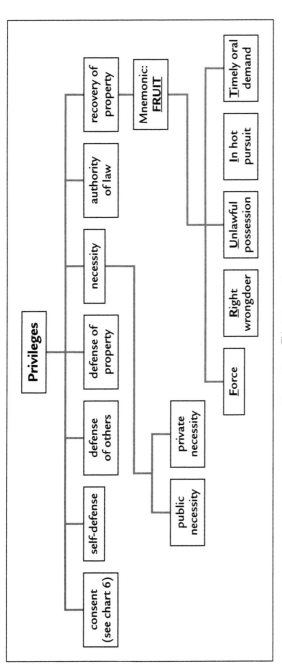

EasyFlow™ Chart 5

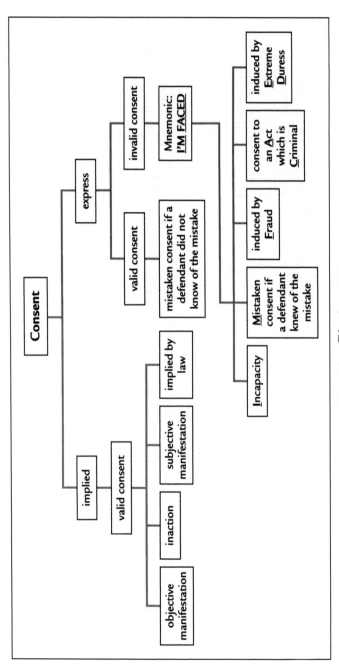

EasyFlow™ Chart 6

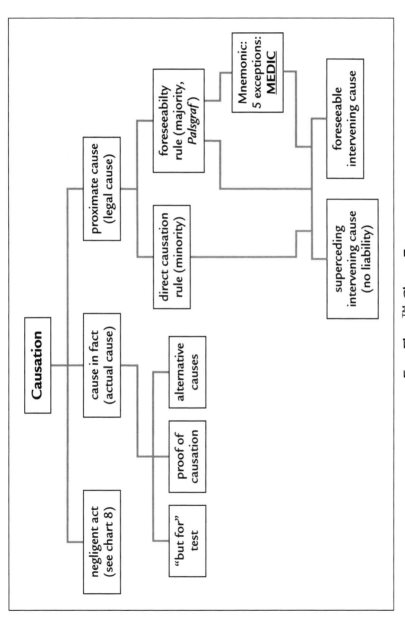

EasyFlow™ Chart 7

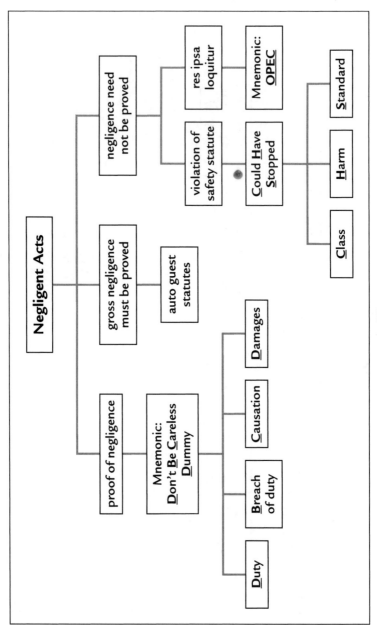

EasyFlow™ Chart 8

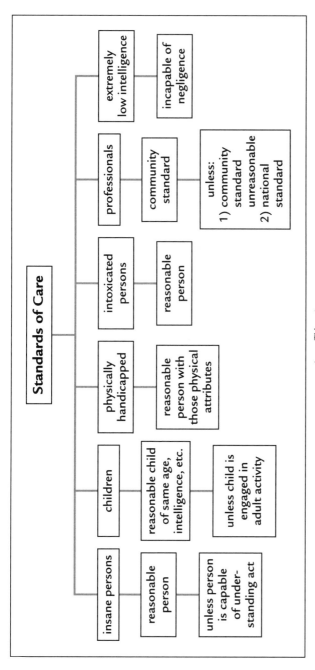

Standards of Care

insane persons — reasonable person — unless person is capable of understanding act

children — reasonable child of same age, intelligence, etc. — unless child is engaged in adult activity

physically handicapped — reasonable person with those physical attributes

intoxicated persons — reasonable person

professionals — community standard — unless: 1) community standard unreasonable 2) national standard

extremely low intelligence — incapable of negligence

EasyFlow™ Chart 9

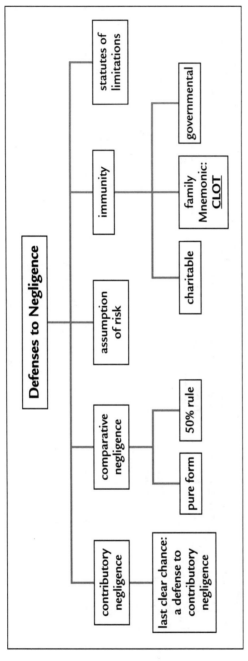

EasyFlow™ Chart 10

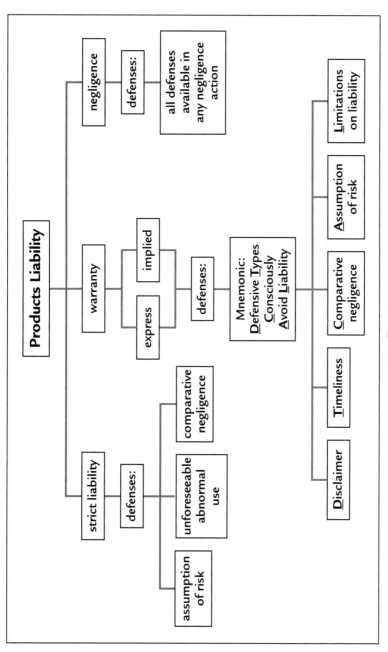

EasyFlow™ Chart 11

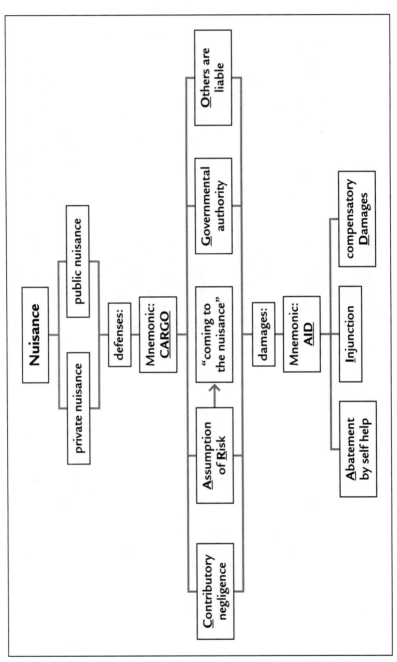

EasyFlow™ Chart 12

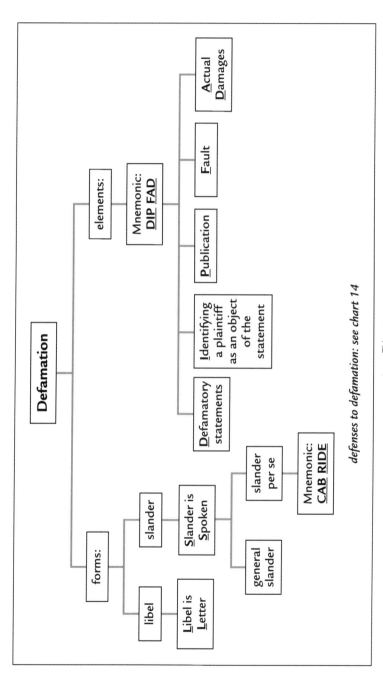

defenses to defamation: see chart 14

EasyFlow™ Chart 13

Defamation

elements:
Mnemonic: **DIP FAD**
- Defamatory statements
- Identifying a plaintiff as an object of the statement
- Publication
- Fault
- Actual Damages

forms:
- libel
  - Libel is Letter
- slander
  - Slander is Spoken
    - slander per se
      - Mnemonic: **CAB RIDE**
    - general slander

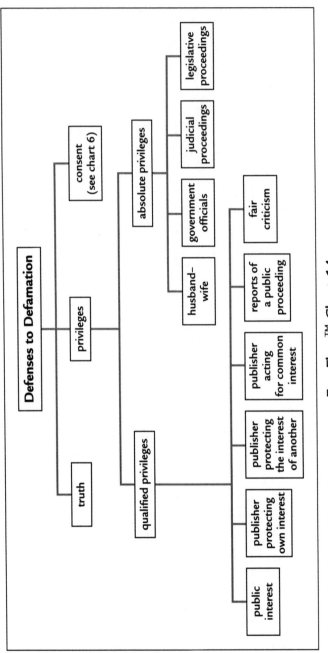

Defenses to Defamation

- truth
- privileges
  - consent (see chart 6)
  - absolute privileges
    - husband–wife
    - government officials
    - judicial proceedings
    - legislative proceedings
  - qualified privileges
    - public interest
    - publisher protecting own interest
    - publisher protecting the interest of another
    - publisher acting for common interest
    - reports of a public proceeding
    - fair criticism

EasyFlow™ Chart 14

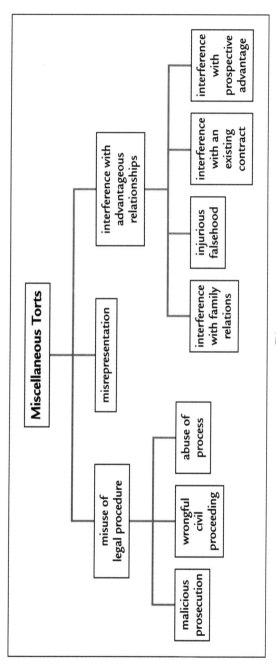

EasyFlow™ Chart 15

Development of Liability Based upon Fault

I. DEFINITION

A tort is a private wrong, independent of a contract, resulting from a breach of duty.

II. DEALING WITH TORT LAW

A. First

When discussing any tort, always consider the following:

Mnemonic: **E**very **D**og has its **D**ay

1. **E**lements of Torts Present?
   a. Act
   b. Intent
   c. Causation
2. Are There Any **D**efenses?
3. What Are the Possible **D**amages?

B. Second

Next consider the conduct of one who has committed a tort:

Mnemonic: **SIN**

1. **S**trict Liability
2. **I**ntentional
3. **N**egligent

CASE CLIPS

Anonymous (1466)

Facts: Not stated.
Issue: Are people liable for injuries they cause to others?
Rule: Actors are liable for the results of their tortious acts.

Weaver v. Ward (1616)

Facts: Ward's gun accidentally discharged during military maneuvers, injuring Weaver.
Issue: Is one excused for an injury caused without fault?
Rule: One can be excused from liability for injuries caused without fault.

Brown v. Kendall (1850)

Facts: The plaintiff's dog and the defendant's dog were fighting. The defendant repeatedly struck the dogs with a stick to separate them, but accidentally hit the plaintiff in the eye.
Issue: Is there liability for assault and battery for injuries that are inadvertent and unintentional?
Rule: One is liable for damages resulting from actions conducted in an unlawful, intentional, or negligent manner.

Cohen v. Petty (1933)

Facts: The plaintiff, a passenger in the defendant's car, was injured when the car crashed because the defendant had fainted while driving. The defendant had never fainted before.
Issue: Is one liable for damages resulting from an unforeseeable event?
Rule: One is not liable for injuries caused by completely unforeseeable events.

Spano v. Perini Corp. (1969)

Facts: Spano's garage was damaged by the blasting activities of the defendants.
Issue: Is one liable for damages resulting from dangerous activities without a showing of negligence?
Rule: A person engaged in activities that involve a substantial risk of harm no matter the degree of care exercised are strictly liable for damages caused, regardless of fault.

Exner v. Sherman Power Construction Co. (1931)

Facts: Exner was injured by an explosion of the defendant's dynamite. The defendant had taken all the necessary precautions in storing and using the dynamite.

Issue: Is a party liable for injuries resulting from an ultrahazardous activity even though the party exercised due care?

Rule: One is strictly liable, regardless of fault, for injuries caused by ultrahazardous activities.

Whetro v. Awkerman (1970)

Facts: Whetro was injured when a tornado destroyed his place of employment. His employers claimed no liability because the tornado was an "act of God," as opposed to a work-related hazard.

Issue: Are injuries resulting from "acts of God" during the course of employment compensable under the Worker's Compensation Act?

Rule: It is no longer necessary to establish a relationship of proximate causality between employment and an injury to establish compensability under the Worker's Compensation Act. It is not a defense that the injury was caused by an "act of God."

Hammontree v. Jenner (1971)

Facts: Jenner had a past history of epileptic seizures. After 14 years without a seizure, one occurred, causing him to have a car accident in which Hammontree was injured. Jenner had a valid driver's license and the authorities knew of his condition.

Issue: Is there strict liability for accidents occurring due to sudden forces beyond a defendant's control?

Rule: An accident caused by a force outside one's control will not lead to liability. However, if the person knew or should have known that the uncontrollable force was likely to come on suddenly, the person's conduct might be negligent.

CHAPTER 2

Intentional Interference with Person or Property

I. INTENT

A. Definition

Intent is generally defined as a purpose to bring about the invasion of another's protected interest by an act, or a failure to act, when there is a legal duty to do so.

1. An Act

An act is defined as a voluntary movement of the muscles.

2. The Invasion of Another's Protected Interest

The desire to invade another's protected interest is not necessarily the same as the desire to harm, or the desire to bring about specific consequences.

Example: Susan kicked Rob as a practical joke, honestly believing that Rob would not be harmed by the kick. Unfortunately, Rob's leg was particularly weak, and was fractured by the kick.

Result: Susan has the necessary intent to be liable for Rob's injuries. Even though she did not desire to harm Rob, or to specifically cause the leg to fracture, she intended to kick, which was an intentional invasion of Rob's interest in being free from harmful or offensive contact, an interest that is protected by the tort of battery.

B. Distinction Between Specific Intent and General Intent

1. Difference

a. Specific Intent

Tortfeasor's goal was to bring about consequences.

b. General Intent

Tortfeasor knew "with substantial certainty" that consequences would result.

2. Legal Significance

Either specific intent or general intent will satisfy the intent requirement for an intentional tort. If the "substantial certainty" test is not met, the tortfeasor may be liable for negligence, but not for an intentional tort.

C. Transferred Intent

1. Applicability

a. Transferred intent is only applied to the torts of: Mnemonic: **FAB**

i. **F**alse Imprisonment,

ii. **A**ssault, and

iii. **B**attery

b. Transferred intent is only applied if the harm resulting from the tort is direct and immediate, as opposed to consequential.

2. Ways of Transfer

a. If a party intends to commit a tort against one person but a second person is injured, the tortfeasor is held to have the intent necessary for liability to the second person.

Example: Rob shot at Susan, but missed. The bullet hit Brett, a bystander.

Result: Rob is liable for a battery to Brett, even though he only intended a battery upon Susan.

b. If an actor intends to commit one intentional tort but actually commits a different intentional tort, he is held to have the intent necessary for the second tort.

Example: Rob intended to scare Susan by throwing a baseball in her direction. Susan did not see the ball because her back was turned, but the baseball struck Brett.

Result: Rob is liable for a battery to Brett, even though he only intended to assault Susan.

D. Minors and Incompetents

The majority of jurisdictions hold that both minors and insane persons may have the competence to formulate the necessary intent to commit an intentional tort.

II. BATTERY

A. Definition

Battery is defined as the causing of harmful or offensive contact to the plaintiff's person with the intent to make contact.

Mnemonic: **H**allowed **O**rgans **C**an **P**lay **I**n **C**hurch

1. **H**armful or **O**ffensive **C**ontact

a. Harmful or offensive contact is determined by the reasonable person standard, i.e., whether a reasonable person would

consider such contact harmful or offensive to one's dignity or honor.
  b. A plaintiff does not have to be aware of the contact. For example, a valid battery occurs when someone is spit upon while sleeping.
  c. Harmful or offensive contact can be either direct or indirect. For example, if Rob punches Susan, this is direct contact. If Rob throws a baseball at Susan, this is indirect contact.

2. Plaintiff's Person
  A plaintiff's person includes not only the body, but also objects closely associated with the body, such as clothing, a cane, an object in hand, and dentures.

3. Intent to Make Contact
  One does not need to intend harm to another — rather an intent to cause contact is sufficient. Also, remember that transferred intent applies to battery. See Ch. 2, I, C.

B. Damages
  Actual damages are not necessary; a plaintiff may recover nominal damages. Punitive damages are available in cases of outrageous conduct. A plaintiff may recover for both mental and physical harm.

III. ASSAULT

A. Definition
  Assault is defined as the intentional act of causing a reasonable apprehension of immediate harmful or offensive contact. Assault focuses on mental well-being, whereas battery is concerned with physical well-being.
  Mnemonic: Real Athletes In Heat Or Cold Intensely compete

1. Reasonable Apprehension
  a. Reasonableness
     A reasonable person standard is used in determining the reasonableness of a plaintiff's apprehension. However, the minority view, as used in the Restatement, is that a defendant who has the requisite intent may commit an assault, regardless of whether the plaintiff's apprehension is reasonable.
  b. Awareness
     The plaintiff must have anticipated contact and known of the defendant's act to apprehend the contact.
     Example: Rob shoots at Susan and misses. Susan is unaware that Rob shot at her.

Result: Without awareness, there can be no apprehension and thus, no assault.

    c. Apprehension Is Not the Same as Fear

    A person who is aware that harmful or offensive contact will occur unless prevented may apprehend such contact, even if the person does not fear the contact.

  2. Immediacy of Harmful or Offensive Contact

  The harmful or offensive contact must appear imminent.

    a. Future Harm

    A threat of future harm, as opposed to imminent harm, may not constitute an assault.

    b. Apparent Ability

    A defendant must have the apparent ability to complete the act that the plaintiff apprehends.

    c. Mere Words

    Words alone are almost never sufficient to constitute an assault. Words must be accompanied by an overt act.

  3. Intent

    a. Two Types

    A defendant's intent must fit one of two types:

      i. Intent to cause apprehension, or

      ii. Intent to commit a battery. As in battery, the defendant need not intend harm.

    b. Transferred Intent

    The doctrine of transferred intent applies to assault. See Ch. 2, I, C.

B. Damages

Damages may be awarded for the mental and physical effects of an assault. Punitive and nominal damages may be awarded.

IV. FALSE IMPRISONMENT

A. Definition

False imprisonment is the intentional restraint of another to a confined area.

  1. Intent

  A defendant must have the intent to confine, or must act despite substantial certainty that confinement will result. Malice is not required and transferred intent applies.

  2. Restraint

    a. Physical Barriers, Force, or Threats

    Restraint can be accomplished by physical barriers, force, or threats against a person, property, or third parties. Threats of future harm are insufficient to constitute restraint, as are verbal commands unaccompanied by threats or force.

    b. The Assertion of Legal Authority

If a person submits to restraint because of a reasonable belief in another's asserted legal authority, there is a false arrest and false imprisonment if the detainment is without proper legal authority or cause.

  3. Confined Area

One must be restrained to a confined area. Mere obstruction of passage is not false imprisonment.

B. Awareness

The plaintiff must have either known of the confinement or suffered some harm from it.

C. Escape

There can be no recovery for false imprisonment if the plaintiff had knowledge of a reasonable means of escape.

D. Duty to Release

False imprisonment occurs when a lawful confinement is unlawfully extended.

E. Damages

In addition to compensatory damages, nominal and punitive damages may be awarded. Recovery for mental suffering is permitted.

V. INTENTIONAL INFLICTION OF MENTAL DISTRESS

A. Definition

The intentional infliction of mental distress occurs when one intentionally or recklessly causes severe emotional damage to another through extreme and outrageous conduct.

  1. Intent

A plaintiff must show that the defendant intended the infliction of distress, knew with substantial certainty that emotional distress would result, or acted with reckless disregard of a high probability that emotional distress would occur. Transferred intent does not generally apply, but see Ch. 8, I.

  2. Severe Emotional Damage

A plaintiff's emotional damage must be severe; annoyance or hurt feelings are insufficient. If a reasonable person would not have suffered shock or severe damage from the defendant's conduct, the defendant is not liable. If a defendant acted with knowledge of a plaintiff's extra sensitivity, the defendant will be liable without regard to the reasonableness of the plaintiff's damages.

3. Extreme and Outrageous Conduct
Extreme and outrageous conduct is intentional conduct that exceeds all reasonable bounds of decency in a civilized society.

B. Damages
A plaintiff must prove actual, but not necessarily physical, damages. Nominal damages are not awarded.

VI. TRESPASS TO LAND

A. Definition
A trespass to land is the intentional invasion of another's interest in the exclusive possession of land. A person in constructive or actual possession of the land can assert this action.

B. Physical Invasion
A physical invasion to another's land occurs if a defendant:
1. Enters upon the land,
2. Causes another person or an object to enter the land,
3. Fails to remove something from the land which the defendant is under a legal duty to remove, or
4. Wrongfully remains on the land, despite a legal entry.

C. Intent
1. Traditional Rule
Trespass was traditionally a strict liability offense under English common law.
2. Modern Rule
One must intend to commit or cause the physical invasion of the plaintiff's land. No intent to harm is necessary. A reasonable, but mistaken belief that the land was one's own, or that the actor had a privilege to enter the land, is not a defense to trespass. One needs only to intend to step on the land.

D. Damages
Nominal damages, as well as actual damages, may be recovered. A defendant is strictly liable for all consequential damages that naturally, directly, and proximately result from the trespass.

VII. TRESPASS TO CHATTELS

A. Definition
A trespass to chattel is the intentional interference with a chattel in someone else's possession. A person in constructive or actual possession of the chattel can assert this action.

B. Chattel
Chattels are personal property, as opposed to real property.

C. Act

One may commit trespass to chattel by either:

1. Damaging another's chattel, or
2. Dispossessing another of a chattel.

D. Intent

Intent to do the act that is a trespass suffices. One does not have to show intent to harm. A mistake as to ownership is not a defense to trespass to chattels.

E. Damages

Only actual damages, as opposed to nominal damages, may be recovered. Actual damages are presumed if possession is lost for any period of time. Because title never passes to the tortfeasor, the tortfeasor may return the chattel and pay reduced damages.

VIII. CONVERSION

A. Definition

Conversion is interference with another's property that is so substantial that the original possessor loses title to the property and is entitled to full compensation.

Examples of conversions:

1. Improper possession (e.g., theft, embezzlement, fraud),
2. Improper transfer of chattels (e.g., improper delivery, selling of stolen goods),
3. Improper retention of chattels (e.g., refusal to return to rightful owner),
4. Improper destruction or damaging of goods,
5. Improper use (e.g., use without permission).

B. Intent

One must only intend to do the act that is adverse to another's right to possess the chattel. One does not have to intend harm.

C. Property Subject to Conversion

All tangible personal property and any physical documents that represent intangible property are subject to conversion.

D. Factors Considered

1. Dominion

One's degree of control over the chattel.

2. Good Faith

An innocent mistake may prevent liability.

3. Harm

The amount of damage done to the chattel.

4. Inconvenience

The amount of inconvenience and expense caused the owner.

E. Damages

One whose property has been converted is entitled to the full value of the lost property.

Exception: Replevin – If the actor who converted the property acted in good faith and the property is undamaged, the actor may mitigate damages by returning the property. Damages for loss of possession and inconvenience would still be awarded.

CASE CLIPS

Garratt v. Dailey (1955)

Facts: Dailey, age 5, pulled a chair from under Garratt knowing she was about to sit down.
Issue: May one be liable for battery without an intent to harm?
Rule: The "intent" element of battery is fulfilled if one knew with "substantial certainty" that contact would occur.

Spivey v. Battaglia (1972)

Facts: Battaglia teased Spivey by hugging her and pulling her head toward him. The left side of Spivey's face was paralyzed as a result.
Issue: Has the element of intent been satisfied when one has knowledge and appreciation of a risk although harm is not substantially certain?
Rule: Courts have drawn a line between "foreseeable risk" and "substantial certainty," thereby separating negligence (intent not required) and assault (intent required). Conduct involving knowledge and appreciation of risk, but not substantial certainty of risk, will subject one to liability for negligence but not for an intentional tort.

Smith v. Stone (1648)

Facts: A third party threw Stone onto Smith's land.
Issue: Is one who involuntarily enters the land of another guilty of trespass?
Rule: When one party forces a second party onto another's land, only the first party is liable for trespass.

Ranson v. Kitner (1888)

Facts: Defendants were held liable for killing plaintiff's dog even though they believed in good faith that it was a wolf for which they were hunting.
Issue: Is one liable for damages caused when acting in good faith?
Rule: An intentional tort is committed even though one believes that one acted properly.

McGuire v. Almy (1937)

Facts: An insane person injured her caretaker-nurse.
Issue: May an insane person be held liable for an intentional tort?
Rule: An insane person who intentionally causes damage will be held liable. The insane person will not be excused even if a peculiar mental condition caused the person to entertain the intent.

Talmage v. Smith (1894)

Facts: Smith threw a stick at a boy. The stick missed the boy, striking and injuring Talmage.
Issue: When one intends to inflict unwarranted harm upon a person but unintentionally harms another, does one have the "intent" to injure the other person?
Rule: If one intends to commit a tort against a person but a different person is injured, one is held to have the "intent" necessary for liability to the other person.

Picard v. Barry Pontiac-Buick, Inc. (1995)

Facts: Picard was dissatisfied with the dealership's servicing of her car. She brought a camera to record her second visit to the service department, but a mechanic physically accosted her when she tried to take a picture.
Issue: Does a physical confrontation constitute an intrusion upon a person's dignitary interest?
Rule: For intentional tort liability, the plaintiff's perception of the character of the defendant's conduct is a significant factor in determining its legal quality. For an assault, there must be physical conduct or a verbal menace sufficient to place the victim in reasonable apprehension of bodily harm. For a battery, an unconsented-to or offensive touching must take place. Unpermitted touching of an object attached to a person's body (e.g., a camera) is sufficient to establish an intent to engage in offensive contact that constitutes a breach of dignitary interests.

Alcorn v. Mitchell (1872)

Facts: One person spit in the face of another.
Issue: Can there be a battery if there is no pecuniary loss?
Rule: Punitive damages may be awarded when there are circumstances of malice, willfulness, wantonness, outrage, and indignity attending the wrong.

Wishnatsky v. Huey (1998)

Facts: Attorney pushes door to a conference room shut to prevent paralegal from entering the room. Paralegal sues for battery.
Issue: Is indirect physical contact sufficient to constitute an offensive touching?
Rule: Offensiveness arises from conduct that is inapposite in the circumstances and causes the victim to have a reasonable sense of diminished personal dignity.

Vosburg v. Putney (1891)

Facts: One student lightly kicked the leg of another student during class intending no harm. The leg was sensitive from a previous injury and was severely damaged by the kick.
Issue: Is proof of intent to harm required to recover damages for assault and battery?
Rule: Intent to harm is not an element of battery. Only proof of unlawful intent or of fault is necessary. Intent to do an unlawful act is unlawful intent.

Leichtman v. WLW Jacor Communications, Inc. (1994)

Facts: Talk show host blew cigar smoke deliberately in P's face during an on-air interview. P was an antismoking activist. He sued the host for battery.
Issue: Is direct physical contact necessary for an action based on battery?
Rule: A battery can be established as long as the reasonable person would find the conduct or contact to be offensive to personal dignity.

Wallace v. Rosen (2002)

Facts: Mother visits high school to bring her daughter homework daughter forgot at home. While mother is in school and talking to daughter and her friends on a staircase, school initiates a fire drill, which mother and group seemingly ignore. Supervising teacher touches mother on the back to get her attention and have her comply with the exercise. Touching apparently causes mother to fall down the stairs.
Issue: Does an intentionally tortious touching require that it be accompanied by personal animosity or antisocial feelings?
Rule: A battery requires more than mere physical contact. In modern society, the tortious touching of another must involve some hostility or intent to cause harm to be legally actionable. Dignitary interests do not exist apart from practical social exigencies.

Fisher v. Carrousel Motor Hotel, Inc. (1967)

Facts: A plate was snatched from Fisher's hands by one of Carrousel Motor Hotel's employees while shouting "that no Negro could be served."
Issue: Is the intentional snatching of an object from a person's hands without touching or injuring his body a battery?
Rule: Knocking or snatching anything from a person's hand, or touching anything connected with his person in an offensive manner is an offense to his dignity and constitutes battery.

Western Union Telegraph Co. v. Hill (1933)

Facts: An employee of Western Union reached across the counter and tried to put his hands on Hill's wife.
Issue: Can assault occur even when contact is physically impossible?
Rule: Apparent ability to accomplish the threatened contact is required in an assault action.

Allen v. Hannaford (1926)

Facts: Hannaford threatened Allen with an unloaded gun.
Issue: Must one have the ability to carry out one's threats to be liable for assault?
Rule: Assault is an intentional act to create a reasonable apprehension of immediate harmful or offensive contact. One must appear to have the present ability to commit the act, but one need not in fact have the ability.

Big Town Nursing Home, Inc. v. Newman (1970)

Facts: Newman's admission papers to the nursing home stated that he "will not be forced to remain . . . against his will." Newman was placed in a wing with insane persons, punished for trying to escape, denied use of a telephone, and denied release.
Issue: May exemplary damages be awarded in a false imprisonment action?
Rule: False imprisonment is the direct restraint of a person's physical liberty without adequate legal justification. Exemplary damages may be awarded for an intentional false imprisonment in violation of one's rights.

Sindle v. New York City Transit Auth. (1973)

Facts: Sindle was a passenger on a school bus. The driver bypassed several stops and drove to a police station because the other students were damaging the bus. Sindle was injured when he jumped out of the bus.
Issue: May a person who is falsely imprisoned recover for injuries incurred while attempting to escape?
Rule: Even a person who is falsely imprisoned must exercise reasonable care when extricating himself from detention.

Parvi v. City of Kingston (1977)

Facts: The police picked up Parvi, who was severely drunk, and took him to an abandoned golf course. Parvi had no recollection of confinement.

Issue: Can one sue for false imprisonment if one does not remember the confinement?

Rule: Later recollection of confinement is distinguished from consciousness at the time of imprisonment. The latter, not the former, is required for a prima facie case of false imprisonment.

Hardy v. LaBelle's Distributing Co. (1983)

Facts: Hardy, a store clerk, was tricked into going to her manager's office because she was incorrectly suspected of stealing a watch. Hardy felt compelled to stay there although no force or threat of force was actually made to compel her to stay. Hardy said that she wanted to stay to clarify the situation and would have gone voluntarily if she knew the true purpose of the meeting.

Issue: Does causing one to feel compelled to remain constitute false imprisonment?

Rule: A person is not unlawfully restrained against one's will if the person's compulsion to remain is not caused by force or threat of force.

Enright v. Groves (1977)

Facts: While investigating a violation of the city's "dog leash" license ordinance, Groves, a police officer, arrested Enright for not producing her driver's license when he asked to see it.

Issue: Is an arrest by a police officer for conduct that does not constitute an offense a false arrest?

Rule: An officer may only arrest a person if he has a warrant or probable cause to believe an offense has been committed.

Whittaker v. Sandford (1912)

Facts: Whittaker voluntarily boarded Sandford's yacht and sailed from Syria to Maine. On arrival, Sandford refused to furnish Whittaker with a small boat to go ashore.

Issue: Can one commit false imprisonment without using physical force?

Rule: One need not exert physical force to be liable for false imprisonment; actual physical restraint is sufficient.

State Rubbish Collectors Association v. Siliznoff (1952)

Facts: The Association threatened to beat up Siliznoff, burn his truck, and destroy his business unless he joined the Association.

Issue: Can one be liable for inflicting severe emotional distress that is unaccompanied by physical injury?

Rule: One who, without privilege to do so, intentionally causes severe emotional distress to another is liable for such emotional distress, and for bodily harm resulting from it.

McDermott v. Reynolds (2000)

Facts: P sued D when the latter had an affair with P's wife.
Issue: Does an extramarital affair constitute an intentional infliction of emotional distress?
Rule: Claims for alienation of affection are barred by statute, which further negates the possibility of associated tort actions.

Wilkinson v. Downton (1897)

Facts: Downton, as a practical joke, told Wilkinson that her husband was severely injured in an accident and needed her to pick him up from the hospital. Wilkinson went into "nervous shock" with accompanying physical effects.
Issue: Can one recover for the intentional infliction of emotional distress as an independent tort?
Rule: Intentional, extreme, and malicious conduct causing mental and physical distress gives rise to a valid cause of action.

Slocum v. Food Fair Stores of Florida (1958)

Facts: An employee of the Food Fair Stores made rude remarks to Slocum, aggravating her heart disease and causing her emotional distress.
Issue: Does the use of insulting language give rise to a cause of action for intentional infliction of emotional distress?
Rule: Liability for intentional infliction of emotional distress exists only when conduct exceeds all socially tolerable bounds and is calculated to cause mental damage of a serious nature to a person of ordinary sensibilities in the absence of special knowledge or notice.

Harris v. Jones (1977)

Facts: Jones ridiculed Harris about his speech impediment with full awareness of Harris's sensitivity to the matter.
Issue: Is malicious and cruel conduct that causes another emotional distress sufficient to satisfy a claim for intentional infliction of emotional distress?
Rule: Liability for intentional infliction of emotional distress will lie only where conduct is so outrageous in character and severe in degree as to be

regarded as atrocious and utterly intolerable in a civilized community and where the emotional response to such conduct is severely disabling.

Taylor v. Vallelunga (1959)

Facts: Taylor watched Vallelunga beat her father.
Issue: Can an action for mental distress be brought against a person who unintentionally causes another severe emotional distress?
Rule: Liability for emotional distress only results when an act is done for the purpose of causing distress or with knowledge that severe emotional distress is substantially certain to result from one's conduct.

Dougherty v. Stepp (1835)

Facts: Stepp entered Dougherty's land without permission and surveyed it.
Issue: Has trespass to land occurred when one enters the land of another without damaging it?
Rule: Every unauthorized entry onto the land of another is a trespass. The law infers damages.

Bradley v. American Smelting and Refining Co. (1985)

Facts: A smelting factory emitted gases and chemicals on Bradley's property.
Issue: May an intangible intrusion be the subject of a trespass, as opposed to being a nuisance?
Rule: An action for trespass protects one's interest in exclusive possession of land regardless of whether the invasion is tangible. It is distinguished from a nuisance, which protects one's interest in the use and enjoyment of land. A nuisance may be a trespass if it is long-lived such that it constitutes an invasion of one's possessory rights and causes substantial damages.

City of Newark v. Eastern Airlines (1958)

Facts: Various cities and residents sought to enjoin several airlines from flying over their land.
Issue: To what extent is an invasion of air space a trespass?
Rule: An invasion of air space is a trespass if it is below the altitude at which the landowner can occupy or use the air space in connection with the enjoyment of the land. Air space above this altitude is part of the public domain.

Rogers v. Board of Road Comm'rs for Kent County (1948)

Facts: The Board of Road Commissioners failed to remove a snow fence upon expiration of a license to place it on Rogers's land.
Issue: Is it trespass to fail to remove a structure upon termination of consent or privilege?
Rule: Trespass is committed by the continued presence of a structure on another's land after consent or privilege has been terminated.

CompuServe, Inc. v. Cyber Productions, Inc. (1997)

Facts: Cyber Promotions sent unsolicited e-mails to Internet users. CompuServe, Inc. is an online computer service. It demanded that Cyber Promotions cease sending e-mails to CompuServe subscribers. When Cyber Promotions increased its e-mail transmissions to CompuServe subscribers in response to the demand, CompuServe filed for an injunction on the basis of trespass to chattels.
Issue: Does the theory of trespass to chattels permit damages for the interference with the possession of chattels?
Rule: "Intermeddling" with another's possession of its property may not constitute conversion, but recovery for the loss sustained is allowable. The interference is actionable when it diminishes the value of the property.

Glidden v. Szybiak (1949)

Facts: Szybiak's dog bit Glidden. Szybiak's defense was based on a local statute that stated that a dog owner is not liable for damages by the dog if the injured party was trespassing.
Issue: Can one claim trespass to chattel if the chattel is not injured?
Rule: Real damages must be proven to assert a successful action for trespass to chattel.

Intel Corp v. Hamidi (2003)

Facts: Former employer sent six e-mails to Intel's 35,000 employees using the company's computer system. Intel alleged that D's conduct amounted to a trespass to chattels.
Issue: Does the misuse of company electronic equipment that causes no damage or need for repair in the company's computer system constitute an intentional tort?
Rule: Even though the tort of trespass to chattels provides a remedy against interference with the possession of personal property, its scope of application does not reach the communication of harmless, albeit objectionable, e-mails.

Pearson v. Dodd (1969)

Facts: Pearson and Anderson published articles about Senator Dodd based on photocopies of documents obtained from third parties who had removed the documents from the Senator's office, copied them, and returned them to his files without authorization.
Issue: Is the taking and use of information or ideas a conversion?
Rule: Information is not subject to legal protection from conversion unless it had been held for sale or constituted literary property, scientific invention, or secret plans formulated for the conduct of commerce.

Zaslow v. Kroenert (1946)

Facts: Kroenert removed Zaslow's furniture from a house they owned in common and put it in storage.
Issue: Is it a conversion to intermeddle with one's property?
Rule: Conversion occurs when there is a substantial interference with the possession or right to property. Intermeddling with, use of, or damage to another's property is not conversion, although one may recover for impairment of the property or loss of its use in an action for trespass or case.

Russell-Vaughn Ford, Inc. v. Rouse (1968)

Facts: While discussing a possible trade-in, Rouse gave his car keys to an employee of Russell-Vaughn, who later refused to return the keys.
Issue: Must a person appropriate another's property to one's own use to commit conversion?
Rule: Conversion is not only the appropriation of property to one's own use, but is also the destruction of or exercise of dominion over another's property in exclusion or defiance of the owner's rights.

Ellis v. D'Angelo (1953)

Facts: Ellis was pushed by D'Angelo, age 4. She sued D'Angelo for battery and negligence and D'Angelo's parents for negligence because they knew of their child's propensity to attack others.
Issue 1: Can a minor formulate the intent needed for battery?
Rule 1: An infant tortfeasor is capable of having the intent to harm, and therefore can be liable as an adult.
Issue 2: Can a minor be negligent?
Rule 2: A minor may lack the mental capacity to be negligent.
Issue 3: Can a parent be found liable for failing to warn others of a child's violent propensities?

Rule 3: A parent is not vicariously liable for the torts of a child unless the parent's negligence made it possible for the child to cause the injury.

Beauchamp v. Dow Chemical Co. (1986)

Facts: Beauchamp brought an action against his employer alleging that the injury he suffered at his workplace was intentional.
Issue: Under what circumstances is a workplace injury considered to be an intentional tort by the employer?
Rule: Where an employer intended an act that injured an employee and knew that the injury was substantially certain to occur from the act, the employer has committed an intentional tort against the employee.

Jones v. Fisher (1969)

Facts: Fisher pulled out Jones's false teeth after Jones quit working for Fisher. Jones sued and recovered for emotional distress.
Issue: May a court modify a jury's award of damages?
Rule: A trial court can reduce the amount of compensatory or punitive damages.

Mink v. University of Chicago (1978)

Facts: Mink was treated with DES, an experimental drug, during her pregnancy. The treatment was without her knowledge.
Issue: Is it battery to administer treatment to a person who has not given consent?
Rule: Administering treatment without a patient's consent may be a battery. Hostile intent is not necessary.

Read v. Coker (1853)

Facts: The defendant and his employees threatened to break the plaintiff's neck if he did not leave the premises.
Issue: Can threatening words constitute an assault?
Rule: Words alone do not amount to an assault. An assault is an attempt, coupled with present ability, to do personal violence to another.

Eckenrode v. Life of America Ins. Co. (1972)

Facts: The defendants refused to pay the proceeds of Eckenrode's murdered husband's life insurance policy.
Issue: Under what circumstances does an intentional infliction of emotional distress occur?

Rule: The elements of intentional infliction of emotional distress are outrageous conduct, intent to cause or recklessly causing emotional distress, actual severe or extreme emotional distress, and proximate cause. The outrageous character of one's conduct is shown by an abuse of a position affecting the interest of another or knowledge of another's particular susceptibility.

Teel v. May Department Stores Co. (1941)

Facts: A department store detective confiscated goods that Teel had bought with a fraudulently obtained credit card, and detained her until she would sign a confession.
Issue: May a shopkeeper detain a person after illegally obtained goods are returned?
Rule: A suspected shoplifter may only be detained by a store owner until goods are recovered, innocence is determined, or police are notified.

Cleveland Park Club v. Perry (1960)

Facts: Perry, age 9, caused serious damage by placing a tennis ball under a drain cover of the plaintiff's pool.
Issue: Must a child have the intent necessary to perform an act that caused a trespass?
Rule: A minor is capable of forming the intent necessary to commit the intentional tort of trespass.

Monongahela Navigation Co. v. United States (S. Ct. 1893)

Facts: The federal government condemned a dam. The defendant had a right to collect tolls from those passing through the dam.
Issue: What compensation must the government provide to an owner of property when the government has condemned the property?
Rule: (Brewer, J.) Upon exercise of its right to condemn property, the federal government must provide "just compensation," which includes both the commercial value of the property as well as its intangible value.

Crescent Mining Co. v. Silver King Mining Co. (1898)

Facts: Silver King built a pipeline across Crescent's land without causing any damage. Crescent sought an injunction and damages.
Issue: Can one recover damages for a harmless intrusion on one's property?
Rule: A harmless intrusion on one's land is compensated by nominal damages.

Bird v. Jones (1845)

Facts: The defendant enclosed part of a public highway so spectators would have to pay him to watch a boat race. The plaintiff was prevented from advancing within the enclosed area.
Issue: Can partial obstruction constitute false imprisonment?
Rule: Partial obstruction does not constitute confinement for purposes of false imprisonment.

Coblyn v. Kennedy's Inc. (1971)

Facts: Coblyn was held on an erroneous suspicion of shoplifting.
Issue: Is it false imprisonment to detain someone inaccurately suspected of committing a crime?
Rule: Any general restraint or demonstration of physical power that can be avoided only by submission constitutes false imprisonment. However, shopkeepers may detain persons they reasonably suspect of shoplifting in a reasonable manner for a reasonable period of time.

Bouillon v. Laclede Gaslight Co. (1910)

Facts: The defendant engaged in a rude conversation with the plaintiff's nurse and blocked the doorway with his hand. The plaintiff was frightened and suffered a miscarriage.
Issue: Is one liable for injuries resulting directly and naturally from one's wrongful conduct?
Rule: Fright and mental anguish are competent elements of damage and if physical injury results from such fright, compensation is merited.

George v. Jordan Marsh Co. (1971)

Facts: Jordan Marsh repeatedly harassed the plaintiff to pay her son's debt.
Issue: May harassment create a compensable cause of action for emotional distress?
Rule: One who, without privilege, intentionally causes severe emotional distress by extreme and outrageous conduct is subject to liability if bodily harm results from such distress.

Lopez v. Winchell's Donut House (1984)

Facts: The Donut House suspected Lopez, an employee, of pocketing sales money. Lopez voluntarily came to the Donut House at the request of her employer, and remained in a room of the shop to clear her name. No force or threats were used to detain Lopez, and she left the room when she began to feel ill.

Issue: Does a false imprisonment occur if one is compelled to remain in a place to protect one's reputation?

Rule: Remaining in a place to clear one's name does not constitute false imprisonment. For a false imprisonment to occur, the plaintiff must have yielded to force, a threat of force (implied or express), economic duress, or the assertion of authority.

Womack v. Eldridge (1974)

Facts: Eldridge intentionally and recklessly obtained Womack's photograph for presentation at a criminal trial with which Womack had no real connection. After the presentation, the plaintiff had to appear in court numerous times, and was suspected of committing a crime. The ordeal caused the plaintiff serious emotional distress that was not accompanied by physical injury.

Issue: Is one who intentionally or recklessly causes severe emotional distress to another by extreme and outrageous conduct subject to liability for such emotional distress absent any bodily injury?

Rule: An action will lie for emotional distress unaccompanied by bodily injury if: (1) the wrongdoer's conduct was reckless or intentional, (2) the conduct was outrageous such that it went against accepted standards of decency and morality, (3) the conduct caused the plaintiff's emotional distress, and (4) the emotional distress was severe.

Atkinson v. Bernard, Inc. (1960)

Facts: Homeowners living near a small airport brought an action to enjoin planes from flying over their property. They argued that the airplanes trespassed on their air space, creating noise and vibrations that substantially interfered with the use and enjoyment of their property.

Issue: Is an action to enjoin airport operations properly brought under the theory of nuisance or trespass?

Rule: Suits to enjoin all or part of the operations of an airport should be brought under the theory of nuisance rather than trespass.

Davis v. Georgia-Pacific Corp. (1968)

Facts: Davis's home was made uninhabitable because of the odors, fumes, smoke, etc., that came from the defendant's pulp processing plant.

Issue: Can a jury weigh the social utility of the defendant's conduct against the harm caused in an action for trespass?

Rule: If a jury finds that an unprivileged trespass occurred, strict liability results. Weighing of social utility by a jury is permitted only in cases a court holds to constitute a nuisance, not a trespass.

Beach v. Hancock (1853)

Facts: The defendant allegedly pointed a gun in an angry and threatening way at Beach and pulled the trigger twice. The gun was not loaded, but the plaintiff was not aware of that fact.
Issue: Does a defendant commit an assault by threatening another with an unloaded gun if the victim is not aware that the gun is not loaded?
Rule: Apparent ability to commit harm will constitute assault even if the plaintiff is unaware that the defendant did not possess the actual ability to commit the harm.

Morgan v. Pistone (1970)

Facts: Morgan repeatedly called Dr. Pistone a "quack." Pistone gently touched Morgan as a warning.
Issue: Must a jury find that any kind of harmful or offensive contact without the plaintiff's permission amounts to battery?
Rule: When the touching is designed only to warn, not to wound, a jury may find that there is not the kind of *intentional* touching that amounts to technical battery.

Rougeau v. Firestone Tire & Rubber Co. (1973)

Facts: Rougeau was asked to wait in a guardhouse at work after he was suspected of stealing some lawnmowers. He was allowed to leave when he fell ill.
Issue: Is it false imprisonment if a plaintiff is asked to wait but is never totally restrained?
Rule: False imprisonment is the causing of an act that restrains another person to a confined area. A plaintiff may impliedly consent to stay by not revealing a desire to leave.

Meadows v. F. W. Woolworth Co. (1966)

Facts: A shopkeeper temporarily detained Meadows and searched her purse after he suspected her of shoplifting.
Issue: Can a shopkeeper detain a suspected shoplifter?
Rule: If a shopkeeper has reasonable cause to suspect a person of shoplifting, he may detain that person in a reasonable manner for a reasonable length of time.

Meyer v. Nottger (1976)

Facts: Nottger performed funeral services for Meyer's father in such a manner that Meyer claimed caused him to suffer a heart attack.

Issue: Is it necessary that a defendant acted with spite, hatred, or ill will in an action for intentional infliction of emotional distress?

Rule: An action for intentional infliction of emotional distress will lie when a defendant's outrageous conduct either intentionally or recklessly causes the plaintiff to suffer severe or extreme emotional distress. It is not necessary that the defendant's conduct be done with any ill will or wrongful intention.

Garland v. Herrin (1983)

Facts: Herrin, a disappointed suitor, bludgeoned the Garlands' daughter to death. The Garlands sought damages for infliction of emotional distress.

Issue: Can damages for recklessly inflicted emotional distress be awarded in a wrongful death action?

Rule: Damages may not be awarded for recklessly, as opposed to intentionally, inflicted emotional distress; nor to a plaintiff who is a "bystander" witnessing harm to another. Further, a wrongful death statute may preclude recovery for pecuniary damages resulting from severe emotional distress due to another's wrongful death.

Ford v. Revlon, Inc. (1987)

Facts: Ford suffered continual sexual harassment from her supervisor at Revlon. Despite repeated complaints by Ford to Revlon management, no action was taken for over a year.

Issue: Can an employer be liable for intentional infliction of emotional distress even if the agent whose acts gave rise to the complaint is not held liable?

Rule: When the independent acts of an employer complete a cause of action for intentional infliction of emotional distress, liability may be found apart from the agent. That is, an employer must intentionally or recklessly exhibit outrageous conduct that results in the severe emotional distress of the plaintiff.

Lugar v. Edmondson Oil Co. (1982)

Facts: Using a state prejudgment attachment statute, Edmondson attached property of Lugar's. The attachment was later dismissed for insufficient grounds for attachment, and Lugar brought a civil rights action against Edmondson alleging a due process violation.

Issue: Can a private misuse of a state statute give rise to a civil rights action under 42 U.S.C. §1983, which provides a remedy for deprivations of Constitutional rights that take place "under color of any statute . . . of any State or Territory"?

Rule: When a private party deprives another of a Constitutional right by the use of a procedural framework created by a state, that party is acting under color of state law, and so is subject to a civil rights action under 42 U.S.C. §1983.

Dissent: Merely invoking the procedural framework of a presumptively valid state statute does not transform the acts of a private party into the acts of the state.

CHAPTER 3

Privileges

I. CONSENT

Consent or permission relieves a defendant from liability. A plaintiff has the burden of proving that there was no consent. An exception to this is the tort of trespass to land.

A. Types of Consent

1. Express Consent

Express consent exists where a plaintiff directly states a willingness to accept a defendant's conduct.

2. Implied Consent

Implied consent exists where a plaintiff's behavior suggests consent to a defendant's actions. Consent may be implied in four major ways:

a. Objective Manifestation

Implied consent exists when a plaintiff's words or conduct are such that a reasonable person would interpret them to be consent; for example, entering a crowded bus suggests consent to being shoved, which would otherwise be battery.

b. Subjective Manifestation

Implied consent may be shown from a plaintiff's actions toward a third party. For example, Rob tells a third party that he will let Susan play on his lawn, but he does not tell this to Susan. If Susan plays on Rob's lawn, no trespass has been committed.

c. Implied by Law

Consent is implied by law when it is in the best interest of a party, such as in emergency situations where one cannot consent for oneself. See Ch. 3, I, D.

d. Inaction

A plaintiff's consent may be implied by inaction in certain situations.

B. Bars to Effective Consent

Even if consent is expressly given, it may be void under the following circumstances:

Mnemonic: **I'M FACED**

1. **I**ncapacity

   Infants, drunkards, and mentally incompetent persons are incapable of giving consent. However, a person who is responsible for such an incapacitated person can consent for that person.

2. **M**istake

   Consent mistakenly given by a plaintiff is generally valid. However, a mistake will negate consent if:

   a. The defendant knew of the plaintiff's mistake; or

   b. The defendant failed to warn the plaintiff of the inherent risks of the defendant's actions.

3. **F**raud

   Consent induced by fraud is invalid if the fraud concerns an essential matter.

4. **A**ct Is **C**riminal

   a. Majority View

      Consent to a criminal or illegal act is invalid.

   b. Minority and Restatement (2d) View

      Even consent to a criminal or illegal act can be valid.

   c. Generally

      When a law is passed with the purpose of protecting a class of persons against their own judgment, consent by a member of the protected class is ineffective (e.g., a minor cannot consent to sexual intercourse).

   d. **E**xtreme **D**uress

      Consent obtained under duress is invalid if the harm that was threatened was immediate; threat of a future harm will not negate consent.

C. Scope

A defendant cannot exceed the limits of the actual consent given without being exposed to liability. An exception is made in emergency situations.

D. Emergency Situations

A defendant can act without a plaintiff's consent if:

1. The plaintiff is unconscious or without the capacity to make a decision, and no one has been legally authorized to decide for the plaintiff;

2. Serious harm would result from a delay; or

3. A reasonable person would consent under the circumstances.

E. Note

Consent usually applies only to intentional tort cases and not negligence. The equivalent to consent in the area of negligence is assumption of risk.

II. SELF-DEFENSE

One is allowed to use reasonable force to defend against a threat of imminent harmful or offensive contact or the threat of confinement. The danger can be caused either intentionally or negligently.

A. Reasonable Belief

The belief upon which one bases the need for self-defense must satisfy the reasonable person standard.

B. Force

1. Reasonable Force

The minimum amount of force necessary to protect against a harm with which a person is faced.

2. Deadly Force

Can only be used when one is threatened with imminent death or serious bodily harm.

C. Retreat

The majority rule is that there is no obligation to retreat from danger before resorting to self-defense.

D. Third-Party Injuries

When one accidentally injures a third party while justifiably using force in self-defense, there is no liability if one did not act recklessly, negligently, or intentionally.

III. DEFENSE OF OTHERS

The majority view is that one acting upon a reasonable belief in the protection of another may use the same amount of force that the person being defended would be entitled to use.

IV. DEFENSE OF PROPERTY

A. Generally

One may use reasonable force to protect one's property after making a verbal demand that the invasion of the property be stopped.

B. Limitations

1. Reasonable Force

The minimum amount of force that would be necessary to protect the property. Only reasonable force can be used in the defense of property.

    a. Force may not be used to recapture property that has been permanently dispossessed.

    b. Deadly force may only be used to defend property under the following circumstances:

       i. When its use is necessary to prevent the burglary of a dwelling; or

       ii. When there is a threat to the safety of the defender.

2. Verbal Demand

A verbal demand is not required if harm or violence will occur immediately, or if verbal requests will be useless.

3. Mistake

A mistake may affect the validity of a use of force in defense of property.

    a. Mistake of Danger

    If an owner mistakenly but reasonably believes the use of force is necessary, the use is privileged.

    b. Mistake of Privilege

    If an owner mistakenly believes that an intruder is a trespasser, but the intruder really has a privilege to trespass, the use of force is not privileged.

4. Booby Traps

The use of booby traps is privileged only up to the amount of force an owner would be allowed to use had the owner been present.

Exception: Owners are never allowed to use a booby trap that causes death, even if they would have been allowed to use deadly force had they been present. The law prizes life over property.

V. RECOVERY OF PROPERTY

A. Generally

A property owner can recover a chattel if the following elements are met:

Mnemonic: **FRUIT**

1. Force

Any force used must be reasonable and not deadly or capable of causing serious injury.

2. Right Wrongdoer

Force may only be used against the person who actually has the chattel. There is no privilege allowed for making a "reasonable mistake."

3. Unlawful Possession

The chattel must have been unlawfully taken.

4. **I**n Hot Pursuit
An owner must be in hot pursuit of the taker. An owner cannot recover chattel by force after substantial time has elapsed.

5. **T**imely Oral Demand
There must be a timely oral demand to return the chattel before one may resort to force, unless such a demand would be futile or dangerous.

B. Location of Chattel

1. On a Wrongdoer's Land
When an owner's chattel is on a wrongdoer's land, the owner can enter upon the land in a reasonable manner to recover the chattel.

2. On a Third Party's Land

a. Another's Fault
When a chattel is on a third party's land due to the fault of someone other than the owner of the chattel, the owner can enter in a reasonable and peaceful manner, even if the third party refuses entry. Nonetheless, the owner is liable for any damages caused.

b. Chattel Owner's Fault
When a chattel is on the land of another by the fault of the chattel owner, the chattel owner has no privilege to enter the land without permission.

C. Shopkeepers
Shopkeepers have a privilege to temporarily detain persons who they reasonably believe have possession of "shoplifted" merchandise. Generally, this privilege is limited to the store's premises while the shoplifter is in the store. Some jurisdictions extend it to the area immediately outside the store.

VI. NECESSITY

A. Generally
A party is privileged to interfere with another's property to avoid an injury threatened by some force of nature or from some independent cause not connected to the property owner.

1. Reasonably Apparent
The privilege of necessity exists as long as the necessity is "reasonably apparent," regardless of whether it actually exists; a reasonable mistake is allowed.

2. Resistance
A property owner cannot resist a party who has the privilege to enter under necessity.

B. Types of Necessity
  1. Public Necessity
     If a danger affects an entire community, or so many people that the public interest is at stake, a defendant has an absolute privilege to avert the peril and is not liable for damages. The privilege of public necessity is often extended to cases involving the media and free speech.
  2. Private Necessity
     If a danger affects only a person's personal interests, the harm to another's property interest is weighed against the severity and likelihood of the danger to determine whether the person has a privilege. Even with a privilege, the person still has to pay the other for the damages caused.

VII. AUTHORITY OF LAW

Officers of the law and certain other people are privileged to make lawful arrests. They are not liable for any damage that results from the lawful arrest.

VIII. DISCIPLINE

Parents, teachers, and military superiors are privileged to use reasonable force in furtherance of their rightful duties.

IX. JUSTIFICATION IN GENERAL

Justification is a loosely defined "catch-all" privilege.

CASE CLIPS

O'Brien v. Cunard Steamship Co. (1891)

Facts: The defendant's doctor vaccinated O'Brien, who was holding out her arm and waiting in a line to be examined for immunization. O'Brien sued for assault, but Cunard claimed that she had consented.
Issue: Must consent be verbal?
Rule: Silence and inaction when considered in connection with the surrounding circumstances may constitute consent to what would otherwise be an assault.

Hackbart v. Cincinnati Bengals, Inc. (1979)

Facts: A member of the defendant's football team intentionally hit and injured Hackbart during a professional football game.
Issue: Does the violent nature of an activity preclude recovery in tort for an intentional blow?
Rule: If the general customs of an activity do not approve of intentional violence, an injury sustained from an intentional blow during that activity gives rise to an action in tort.

Mohr v. Williams (1905)

Facts: During surgery on the plaintiff's right ear, Williams, a doctor, discovered that the left ear was in worse condition and operated on it. The plaintiff had only consented to the right ear operation, and there was no emergency to perform the operation on the left ear.
Issue: Can a physician who discovers unexpected conditions during a consensual operation perform the necessary additional procedures?
Rule: A physician commits battery by performing a procedure that is different from the authorized procedure, unless the condition endangers the life or health of the patient.

De May v. Roberts (1881)

Facts: Roberts sued De May, her physician, for assault and invasion of privacy after De May led her to believe that the man who helped deliver her baby was a physician's assistant, which he was not.
Issue: Is consent obtained through misrepresentation valid?
Rule: Consent obtained through one's own misrepresentations voids its use as a defense.

Hart v. Geysel (1930)

Facts: The plaintiff died from the defendant's blow during a prize fight in a jurisdiction that outlawed such fights.
Issue: Is consent to an unlawful act a valid defense?
Rule: The defense of consent, even to an illegal act, can defeat an action in tort for wrongful death.

Hudson v. Craft (1949)

Facts: The plaintiff was injured by an opponent's blow in a boxing match at a carnival. The prize fight violated a state statute.
Issue: Can people forfeit their rights to sue under tort law by consenting to a violation of a statute written for their protection?
Rule: Members of a class cannot waive a right created by statute to protect their class.

Katko v. Briney (1971)

Facts: Briney booby-trapped his boarded-up farmhouse with a spring gun to protect against trespassers. Katko was severely wounded when he entered Briney's house to steal fruit jars.
Issue: May a person protect his property with deadly force?
Rule: A person may not take actions that would cause serious injury to another in defense of his property.

Bird v. Holbrook (1825)

Facts: The plaintiff was injured when he tripped a spring gun that the defendant had set to protect a flower garden.
Issue: May property be protected with devices that can cause serious injury?
Rule: Devices that cause serious injury may not be used to protect property unless sufficient warnings are posted.

Hodgeden v. Hubbard (1846)

Facts: The plaintiff purchased a stove on credit. Soon after the purchase, the defendants discovered the plaintiff had obtained the stove using fraudulent statements. They pursued and caught the plaintiff and took the stove by force.
Issue: Can an owner use force to recover property where possession was granted based on fraudulent statements?

Rule: An owner of property is privileged to use reasonable force, i.e., "no unnecessary violence," to retake possession of property that was obtained through fraudulent means.

Bonkowski v. Arlan's Department Store (1968)

Facts: The defendant stopped Bonkowski in a parking lot 30 yards from its store, having a reasonable suspicion that she was shoplifting.
Issue: Does a shopkeeper's privilege to detain suspected shoplifters extend outside the store?
Rule: A merchant's privilege to temporarily detain a person who is reasonably suspected of stealing property may be exercised in the merchant's store or its immediate vicinity.

Surocco v. Geary (1853)

Facts: Geary, a San Francisco Fire Warden, ordered the demolition of Surocco's private house in an unsuccessful attempt to stop an advancing fire. Geary's actions prevented Surocco from removing his belongings, which were consequently destroyed in the blast.
Issue: Is one who destroys another's property, in good faith and under apparent public necessity, personally liable to the owner of the destroyed property?
Rule: During an emergency, individual rights of property give way to public necessity.

Harrison v. Wisdom (1872)

Facts: The defendants destroyed all the liquor in their town, including the plaintiff's, to prevent an approaching Federal army from getting drunk and demolishing the town.
Issue: Is one personally liable for destroying the property of another if it is done for the good of the public?
Rule: There is no liability for the destruction of another's property if an impending and imminent peril makes it absolutely necessary. The destruction only needs to appear necessary at the time it is done.

Vincent v. Lake Erie Transportation Co. (1910)

Facts: The plaintiff's vessel was kept docked during a severe storm, causing damage to the dock.
Issue: Must a party who asserts private necessity as a defense to the invasion of another's property compensate the owner of the property for the resulting damage?

Rule: While private necessity permits the invasion of another's property, the invader remains liable for resulting damages.

Sindle v. New York City Transit Auth. (1973)

Facts: A school bus driver skipped his route and drove to a police station because students were vandalizing the bus. The driver was sued for false imprisonment.
Issue: When does the defense of justification make restraint lawful?
Rule: The defense of justification makes restraint or detention lawful when it is reasonable under the circumstances and it is imposed to prevent personal injuries or damage to property.

Markley v. Whitman (1893)

Facts: While walking home from school, the plaintiff was injured when the defendant was pushed into him by other students as part of a game. The plaintiff did not know about the game.
Issue: Are involuntary actions that occur during a possibly dangerous activity actionable if they cause an injury to a nonparticipant?
Rule: An actionable assault occurs when a nonparticipant is injured by persons engaged in a potentially dangerous activity. Participants in such an activity consent to the forms of the activity and thus are liable for even involuntary actions that are related to the activity.

Elkington v. Foust (1980)

Facts: Foust was accused of sexually abusing his minor daughter. He claimed her recovery of damages was barred because she consented.
Issue: Is consent by a minor a defense to a willful tort?
Rule: To constitute a defense to a willful tort, consent must be given by one with legal capacity to consent. Minors are incapable of legally consenting to acts of sexual abuse.

Kennedy v. Parrott (1956)

Facts: A surgeon discovered and removed a cyst on the plaintiff's ovary, which led to complications during an authorized appendectomy.
Issue: May a physician who finds an unexpected problem while doing an authorized procedure perform an unauthorized operation?
Rule: Physicians may lawfully perform necessary operations so long as they stay within the area of the original incision and the patient (or the patient's representative) is incapable of giving consent.

Fraguglia v. Sala (1936)

Facts: The plaintiff attacked the defendant with a pitchfork. In his defense, the defendant knocked the plaintiff down, causing injuries.
Issue: How much force may a person use in self-defense?
Rule: The amount of force allowed for self-defense is only that which is reasonably necessary to repel the attack. The question of what is reasonably necessary depends on the facts and circumstances of each case and how the circumstances appeared to the defendant. One is only liable for damages caused by excessive force.

Dupre v. Maryland Management Corp. (1954)

Facts: The defendant struck Dupre and fractured his jaw after Dupre had assaulted him and threatened further assaults.
Issue: Has excessive force been used when one's retaliatory blows result in a more serious injury than necessary to stall an attack?
Rule: To assert that excessive force was used by one who acted in self-defense a plaintiff must prove that the defendant intended to inflict unnecessary injury.

State v. Leidholm (1983)

Facts: Leidholm killed her sleeping husband after they had fought violently earlier in the evening. She claimed self-defense.
Issue: What standard of reasonableness is used to determine whether deadly force in self-defense was justified?
Rule: To use deadly force in defending oneself a person must have a sincere and reasonable belief that the use of force was necessary to protect oneself from an imminent and unlawful harm.

Commonwealth v. Drum (1868)

Facts: After the plaintiff struck the defendant with his fists, the defendant stabbed and killed the plaintiff.
Issue: May one use deadly force in response to an unarmed attack?
Rule: One may kill another in self-defense only if it is reasonable to believe that the assailant is about to take one's life or cause great bodily harm, and there is no opportunity to escape.

People v. Young (1962)

Facts: Young aided a person being arrested by an undercover police officer.

Issue: Is one criminally liable for the mistaken but reasonable belief that one is protecting another from an unlawful attack?

Rule: The right of a person to defend another is as great as that person's right to defend oneself.

Kirby v. Foster (1891)

Facts: Foster refused to give Kirby, his bookkeeper, a paycheck because Kirby could not account for missing funds. Kirby took money from the employees' payroll to reimburse himself. Foster used force to recover the money, injuring Kirby.

Issue: Can one use force to recover property?

Rule: The privilege of using force to recover one's personal property does not apply when the holder of the property lawfully obtained possession.

Ploof v. Putnam (1908)

Facts: While sailing with his family, the plaintiff was forced to moor his boat to the defendant's dock when a sudden storm developed. The defendant untied the boat, causing damage.

Issue: Can a property owner eject a trespasser who is using the property for refuge?

Rule: The privilege of private necessity, which allows one to use another's property to avoid serious injury, may not be defeated by the property owner.

Courvoisier v. Raymond (1896)

Facts: Courvoisier shot a police officer whom he erroneously thought was one of several persons attacking him.

Issue: May a defendant assert self-defense if the person who was injured did not attack the defendant?

Rule: Use of force may be justified as self-defense if the defendant reasonably believed there was a threat of a great harm and the actions taken were necessary to prevent such perceived harm.

McIlvoy v. Cockran (1820)

Facts: McIlvoy severely wounded Cockran because he was tearing McIlvoy's fence down.

Issue: May one use deadly force to protect one's property?

Rule: One may not inflict severe injury to protect property unless a trespasser is committing a violent felony or endangering human life.

Owen v. City of Independence (S. Ct. 1980)

Facts: Owen, a police chief, was fired without the benefit of a hearing. The defendant had acted in good faith in denying the hearing because the constitutional right to have a "name clearing" hearing was only recognized after the plaintiff was fired.

Issue: Can a municipality violate a person's civil rights in good faith without incurring liability?

Rule: (Brennan, J.) A municipality is liable for violations of civil rights even if the municipality acted in good faith.

Dissent: (Powell, J.) Municipalities should not be held strictly liable for violations of constitutional rights. If a municipality acted in good faith when denying the right, it should be immune from liability.

Barton v. Bee Line, Inc. (1933)

Facts: Plaintiff, 15 years old, claimed she was forcibly raped by defendant's chauffeur. The chauffeur claimed the plaintiff consented to sexual intercourse.

Issue: Can one recover for civil damages if one validly consents to an illegal act?

Rule: Consent to criminal or illegal actions can be valid and therefore preclude recovery.

Note: This is the minority view.

Bang v. Charles T. Miller Hospital (1958)

Facts: Bang went to the hospital for a prostate operation. As part of the operation, Bang's spermatic cords were severed. Bang claimed he never consented to such a procedure, and brought suit for an unauthorized operation.

Issue: Must a plaintiff knowingly consent to all operative procedures?

Rule: Under the doctrine of informed consent, a patient must be informed prior to the operation of relevant risks and procedures, except in emergency situations.

In Re Estate of Brooks (1965)

Facts: Brooks, a Jehovah's Witness, refused to have a blood transfusion because of her religious beliefs. Her doctor received a court order compelling transfusions despite Brooks's objections.

Issue: May a person be compelled to receive medical treatment if that treatment violates her religious beliefs?

Rule: A person may refuse necessary medical treatment when there is no public interest that outweighs that individual's First Amendment rights.

CHAPTER 4

Negligence

I. GENERALLY

Negligence is an unintentional tort, meaning that a defendant may be liable absent an intent to commit the tort. A plaintiff has to show that the defendant's behavior created an unreasonable risk of harm to others by departing from a reasonable standard of care, and that it was the proximate cause of the plaintiff's damages.

II. ELEMENTS OF CAUSE OF ACTION

Mnemonic: **D**on't **B**e **C**areless **D**ummy
A. **D**uty to Use Reasonable Care to Conform to a Standard of Conduct so as to Avoid Unreasonable Risks to Others
It is necessary to establish that the defendant had a duty to the specific plaintiff not to create an unreasonable risk. See Palsgraf v. Long Island R.R. Co.
B. **B**reach of the Duty
C. **C**ausation
The breach of the duty must be the proximate cause of the plaintiff's harm.
D. Actual **D**amages
Actual damages must be shown; one may not recover for nominal damages.

III. UNREASONABLE RISK OF HARM

In deciding whether a defendant caused an unreasonable risk of harm, the courts will look at several issues:
A. Foreseeability
Something is foreseeable if there is a significant likelihood of its occurring. No person is expected to guard against causing harm that is completely unforeseeable, or harm that is so unlikely as to be commonly disregarded.

B. Balancing Test

Using Judge Learned Hand's formula, liability will result when $B < L \times P$, where:

B = The defendant's Burden to avoid/prevent the risk.

L = Gravity of the injury or Loss.

P = Probability that an injury (loss) will occur.

Thus, one who is deciding whether to take a precaution so as to lower the risk of harm to others should weigh the cost of taking the precaution (B) against the probability (P) that an injury will occur if the precaution is not taken multiplied by the gravity of the loss (L).

C. Utility of Conduct

The court will look to the social utility of creating a risk when determining if the creation of the risk is unreasonable.

Example: Although the probability of grave injury from automobile accidents is high, we will not deem the mere use of an automobile negligent since the use of cars has an extremely high social utility.

IV. STANDARD OF CARE

A. Generally

A defendant's conduct is measured against a certain standard of care to determine if the defendant actually breached a duty, i.e., failed to meet the requirements of that standard.

B. Reasonable Person

The reasonable person standard is an objective standard. The relevant inquiry is how a reasonable person under the same circumstances as the defendant would have acted, as opposed to whether the defendant acted according to a personal notion regarding proper conduct.

1. Intoxication

Intoxication is not an excuse for unreasonable conduct.

2. Exceptions

a. Children

Children are held to the standard of a reasonable child of similar age, intelligence, and so on. However, the reasonable child standard is not used if the child is engaged in an adult activity.

b. Physical Attributes or Handicap

One is held to the standard of a reasonable person with one's physical attributes or handicaps.

c. Mental Capacity

     i. Slight Mental Deficiency
     One must act as a reasonable person of average mental
     ability. There is no excuse for a slight mental deficiency.

    ii. Extremely Low Intelligence
     For example, a moron or an imbecile. The majority view is
     that such a person is not capable of being negligent.

   iii. Insanity
     Insane persons are generally held to a reasonable person
     standard. The rationale is to encourage guardians to
     supervise their insane wards, to avoid false claims, and
     to make the party who actually caused the loss responsi-
     ble. However, a few courts have held that an insane
     person who is not capable of appreciating or avoiding
     danger is not negligent.

   iv. Sudden Illness or Unconsciousness
     For example, a seizure or delirium. One is not liable for
     the consequences of a sudden illness or unconsciousness
     if the sudden lapse was completely unforeseeable.

3. Knowledge
One is assumed to have the knowledge of a reasonable person of
ordinary experience.

  a. Strangers
    Strangers and newcomers to a community are assumed to
    know all the facts specific to that area that all the adults of
    that community know.

  b. Investigation
    In some instances one may have a duty to remedy one's
    ignorance by conducting a reasonable investigation, even if
    people of the community share the same ignorance.

C. Professionals
Professionals such as doctors, lawyers, and accountants are liable if
they do not meet the minimum standards of their professions.

1. Locality Rule
Generally, professionals are required to follow the standards of
their profession as practiced by other members in the same
locality. The more modern view is that a professional should
be judged according to a uniform national standard, especially
with regard to professions where there is nationwide uniformity
in certification.

2. Success Is Not Guaranteed
There is no requirement that a professional succeed for a
client, only that the professional act with the requisite amount
of skill.

3. Differing Schools of Thought

When opinions in a profession may reasonably differ, a professional can choose any reasonably accepted school of thought.

4. Specialists

Specialists are held to a higher standard than professionals without a specialty.

5. Novices

Newly licensed professionals are held to the same standard as experienced members of the profession.

6. Unreasonable Standard

If a court rules that a professional standard is inherently negligent, then professionals who follow the standard are also negligent.

7. Doctrine of Informed Consent

Physicians must inform patients of risks that are inherent in medical procedures, unless the treatment is given in an emergency situation and the patient is incapable of giving consent.

D. Custom and Usage

Custom and usage are the general practices of a particular community or industry within society, such as the medical profession or the mining industry.

1. Generally

In general, a defendant who has conformed with a custom may introduce such conformity as evidence of reasonable care. However, custom is not conclusive as to what is proper behavior.

2. Abandonment of Custom

Failure to adhere to a custom is irrelevant if one uses ordinary and reasonable care.

E. Aggravated Negligence

Some states have defined various degrees of negligence, such as gross negligence, recklessness, and willful and wanton conduct, in the context of automobile guest statutes.

1. Automobile Guest Statutes

Automobile guest statutes generally provide that a nonpaying passenger can only sue the car's driver if the driver was grossly negligent or acted with willful misconduct.

2. Rationale

The rationale behind automobile guest statutes is to prevent collusion between the driver and the passenger.

3. Constitutionality

Numerous state supreme courts have held automobile guest statutes as violative of state or federal constitutions. Few states still require aggravated negligence for liability to guests.

V. RULES OF LAW

Although negligence is generally a question for the jury, courts sometimes set out standards of behavior. These standards are usually, but not always, adopted by other courts.

VI. VIOLATION OF STATUTES

In some cases, the appropriate standard of conduct is determined by a statute (e.g., speed limits, drinking laws). An unexcused violation of a statute by a defendant resulting in injury to the plaintiff will invoke liability. In such cases, the usual negligence standards of the reasonable person are superseded by the more stringent standards set by the statute.

A. Applicability

A statute is applicable to prove liability if: Mnemonic: **C**ould **H**ave **S**topped

1. **C**lass

The plaintiff is part of the class of persons the statute is intended to protect.

2. **H**arm

The harm suffered by the plaintiff is the type that the statute is intended to prevent.

3. **S**tandard

The required standard of conduct is clearly defined in the statute.

B. Excuse

Violation of a statutory duty is excused if:

1. Compliance would be more dangerous than noncompliance,
2. Compliance is impossible, or
3. The defendant was faced with an emergency he did not create.

C. Criminal Liability

A statutory violation immediately invokes criminal liability.

D. Civil Liability

1. Majority View

A statutory violation is negligence per se.

2. Minority View

A statutory violation is only some evidence of negligence that may be outweighed by other evidence showing due care.

3. Statutory Reference

If the statute explicitly states that its violation gives rise to civil liability, then even the minority will impose liability.

E. Obsolete Statutes

A court will often ignore evidence of a statutory violation if the statute has not been enforced for a long time or if it is without foundation.

VII. PROOF OF NEGLIGENCE

A. Circumstantial Evidence

Circumstantial evidence is evidence of one fact from which another fact may be inferred. It can be used to show that a defendant breached the duty of care. Drawing inferences from circumstantial evidence, however, is highly prejudicial to a defendant who has the burden of rebutting the inference. Therefore, courts will carefully regulate its use.

B. Expert Testimony

A plaintiff in a malpractice suit must produce expert testimony unless the negligence is obvious to a lay person (e.g., doctor amputated wrong leg).

C. Res Ipsa Loquitur

Res ipsa loquitur means roughly that "the thing speaks for itself." This is the classic use of circumstantial evidence in torts. Under this doctrine, a plaintiff can create an inference or presumption of negligence against the defendant by the mere fact of the accident having occurred.

1. Elements

Mnemonic: **OPEC**

a. **O**rdinarily an accident of that nature would not have occurred unless someone was negligent.

b. **P**laintiff was free from fault.

c. **E**xclusive **C**ontrol

The defendant exercised exclusive control over the instrumentality that caused the injury.

Note: Recent cases indicate that courts require only a preponderance standard (51 percent probability) for each element.

2. Procedure

Once the plaintiff has asserted res ipsa loquitur, the defendant is allowed to rebut with evidence tending to show the use of due care.

a. Majority View

Res ipsa loquitur creates an inference of negligence from which a reasonable jury may conclude that the defendant was negligent. The plaintiff, however, cannot get a directed verdict even if the defendant does not introduce rebutting evidence.

b. Minority View

Res ipsa loquitur creates a presumption of negligence that entitles the plaintiff to a directed verdict if the defendant does not rebut.

3. Multiple Defendants

Res ipsa can be applied to two or more defendants even though only one was negligent if they were all involved with activities surrounding the injury and it is difficult to pinpoint the person who actually caused the injury.

CASE CLIPS

Blyth v. Birmingham Waterworks Co. (1856)

Facts: Blyth's house was damaged when a fire hydrant, installed by Birmingham, sprung a leak due to a severe and unusual frost. The hydrant had worked properly for 25 years prior to the incident.
Issue: Is it negligence to fail to plan for a rare and extraordinary situation?
Rule: Negligence involves the omission of an action that a reasonable person would perform, or acting in a way that a prudent and reasonable person would not.

Gulf Refining Co. v. Williams (1938)

Facts: Williams was severely burned when a gasoline drum distributed by Gulf Refining Co. exploded due to a spark produced by the poor condition of the cap.
Issue: Is a party liable for negligence when the injuries produced by its actions are the result of an unusual, extraordinary, and improbable occurrence?
Rule: Even if an injury-causing event is improbable, one may be negligent if there is some real and appreciable likelihood of damage in a particular situation and that person does not take action to avoid the damage when a reasonable and prudent person would have.

Hauser v. Chicago, R.I. & P. Railway (1928)

Facts: Hauser severely burned her face when she fainted and fell against an exposed steam pipe in the bathroom on a train.
Issue: Must a property owner anticipate and take precautions to prevent injuries to others who use the property in an unusual manner?
Rule: A party who takes reasonable precautions for the ordinary and safe use of its property is not liable for an injury that it could not have anticipated.

Harper v. Herman (1993)

Facts: P, a guest on D's boat, dove off the side of the boat while it was anchored in shallow water and was injured.
Issue: As a social host, does a boat owner owe his guests a duty to warn them of likely dangers?
Rule: The boat owner's duty of reasonable care does not extend to warning guests of reasonably foreseeable hazards when the guests are not particularly vulnerable and able to protect themselves.

Chicago, B. & Q. R. Co. v. Krayenbuhl (1902)

Facts: Krayenbuhl, age 4, had his leg severed while playing on a railroad turntable. The turntable was close to a path in common use by the general public and was often left unlocked.

Issue: Does a person's duty of care require one to take all possible precautions to eliminate injury to another?

Rule: The nature of precautions that must be taken depends on (1) the character and location of the premises; (2) the purposes for which they are used; (3) the probability of injury; (4) the precautions necessary to prevent injury; and (5) the relation of such precautions to the beneficial use of the premises.

Falzone v. Busch (1965)

Facts: D was negligent in bringing about an accident in which P's husband was injured. P, as a result of husband's injury, was alone and unsupported at the accident scene and became fearful for her personal safety. P sued D for the negligent infliction of emotional distress.

Issue: Is tort recovery allowable in the absence of a physical impact and injury?

Rule: The law no longer requires a physical impact to allow recovery for personal injury. The emotion of fear can entail physical problems that constitute actionable wrongs.

Metro-North Commuter RR Co. v. Buckley (1997)

Facts: During his employment with Metro-North, P was exposed to asbestos. After taking an asbestos awareness class, he became emotionally distressed. As a result, he sued his former employer for negligent infliction of emotional distress.

Issue: Can P recover for emotional distress when he has not developed any disease relating to his exposure to asbestos?

Rule: An action for emotional injury will lie only when there has been a physical impact or an immediate risk of physical impact. Fear of illness without disease or symptoms or physical impact or its immediate likelihood is not actionable.

United States v. Carroll Towing Co. (1947)

Facts: Plaintiff's barge broke away from a pier and sunk due to the defendant's negligence in shifting its mooring lines and the plaintiff's contributory negligence in not having an employee on board to prevent such an accident.

Issue: Has a party breached its duty of care when it could have avoided a tremendous risk with a relatively minimal amount of effort?

Rule: A party is liable for negligence when the burden (B) of adequate precautions is less than the probability (P) of the injury-causing event times the possible gravity of injury (L). (B < P × L)

Vaughan v. Menlove (1837)

Facts: Menlove stacked hay on the edge of his property near Vaughan's cottages in such a manner that the hay was likely to ignite. Menlove was warned by many people of the risk of fire but thought it best to "chance it."

Issue: Does the required standard of care involve acting to the "best of one's judgment" or with such reasonable caution as a prudent person under such circumstances?

Rule: Negligence is not determined by the subjective standard of one's own judgment but by the objective reasonable person standard.

Delair v. McAdoo (1936)

Facts: McAdoo's severely worn tire exploded, causing his car to collide with Delair's car. McAdoo claimed he did not know of the tire's condition.

Issue: May the owner or user of a dangerous instrumentality claim lack of knowledge of the risk involved as a defense to a negligence claim?

Rule: The law requires owners or users of dangerous instrumentalities to know, and will assume such knowledge of, the condition of those parts that are likely to become dangerous when the flaws or faults would be disclosed by reasonable inspection.

Trimarco v. Klein (1982)

Facts: Trimarco was injured when his bathtub's door enclosure shattered. He sued for negligence, asserting that the manufacturer should have made the door from the tempered safety glass used throughout the industry.

Issue: Is reasonableness determined by the custom and usage of one's trade?

Rule: The custom and usage of a profession or trade is one factor in deciding the reasonableness of conduct. The reasonableness of the custom itself need also be considered.

Mayhew v. Sullivan Mining Co. (1884)

Facts: Mayhew, a mine worker of Sullivan Mining, fell into an unlit and unguarded ladder hole in the mine. Sullivan tried to introduce evidence that it was an industry custom to cut such holes.

Issue: Is the standard of care determined by the custom of an industry?
Rule: Reasonableness, and not custom, determines the standard of care. A custom that, on its face, is inconsistent with ordinary care or a due regard for safety is properly excluded as evidence of due care.

Cordas v. Peerless Transportation Co. (1941)

Facts: A driver for Peerless Transportation Co. jumped out of his cab while it was moving to escape from an armed felon. The abandoned cab struck Cordas.
Issue: Is the duty to act as a reasonable person modified in an emergency situation?
Rule: When confronted with an emergency not of one's own making, one must only act as a reasonable person would during a similar emergency. There is no duty to be a hero.

Roberts v. State of Louisiana (1981)

Facts: A blind man collided with Roberts as he walked to the men's room without his cane.
Issue: Is a handicapped person held to the same standard of care as the ordinary reasonable person?
Rule: A handicapped person must take the precautions that reasonable people would take if they were so handicapped.

Smith v. Sneller (1942)

Facts: Smith, a man with very poor eyesight, fell into a trench dug by Sneller.
Issue: Is it contributorily negligent for a blind person to walk alone in a public area without a cane or other special precautions?
Rule: It is not negligence for a blind person to walk alone in public areas, but the blind person must conform to the standard of ordinary prudence (i.e., a reasonable blind person would have used a cane).

Fletcher v. City of Aberdeen (1959)

Facts: Barriers surrounding a ditch were negligently removed. Fletcher, a blind man walking with a cane, fell in the ditch and suffered injuries.
Issue: Does a keeper of public property have a duty to prevent injury to disabled people who might use the property?
Rule: The disabled have a right to use public property. Thus, keepers of public property must anticipate its use by disabled people and take necessary precautions to prevent them from being injured.

Robinson v. Pioche, Bayerque and Co. (1855)

Facts: Robinson, drunk, fell into a hole in a public street that Pioche, Bayerque and Co. left uncovered.
Issue: Does one owe a lesser duty of care to an intoxicated person?
Rule: Intoxication of a plaintiff cannot excuse a defendant's gross negligence.

Reynolds v. Hicks (1998)

Facts: Nephew consumed alcohol at a wedding party given by his aunt and uncle and later injured P in a car accident.
Issue: Does social host liability extend to the conduct of a minor relative who caused injury to a third party after consuming alcohol at the family social event?
Rule: The Washington statute in question does not allow the injured third party to sue social hosts in these circumstances. Social hosts have a more limited liability exposure than commercial vendors of alcohol and other dangerous products.

Nycal Corp. v. KPMG Peat Marwick LLP (1998)

Facts: An accounting firm did an audit report on a company that convinced P to enter into an agreement to purchase the stock of the company. When the company became insolvent, P filed suit against D to recover damages.
Issue: Does an accountant owe third parties a duty of care when it has no actual knowledge of them or their reliance?
Rule: Section 552(2) of the Restatement limits the liability of those who provide guidance for others to parties for whose benefit the guidance was intended to be supplied. Accountant liability, therefore, is limited to third parties whose reliance was known to the accountant.

Robinson v. Lindsay (1979)

Facts: Robinson, age 11, was injured in a snowmobile driven by Lindsay, age 13.
Issue: Should a minor participating in an inherently dangerous activity be held to the standard of a reasonably careful child of the same age, intelligence, maturity, and experience?
Rule: A child engaged in an inherently dangerous activity, as opposed to a traditional childhood activity, should be held to an adult standard of care.

Breunig v. American Family Ins. Co. (1970)

Facts: The defendant was overcome by a sudden mental delusion, causing her to crash into Breunig's oncoming truck.
Issue: Is insanity a defense to a negligence action?
Rule: Although insanity is generally not a defense to negligence, it is a valid defense where the actor, without forewarning, is overcome by a mentally disabling disorder. The defense for sudden mental incapacity is analogous to the defenses for sudden heart attack or epileptic seizure.

Wright v. Tate (1967)

Facts: Wright, an adult with low mental capacity, was killed while riding in a car driven by an intoxicated person. Tate charged that Wright was contributorily negligent for riding in the car when he knew the driver was intoxicated.
Issue: What standard of care should apply to determine the contributory negligence of a person of low intelligence?
Rule: One who has a mental deficiency that falls short of insanity is held to the same standard of reasonable care as a person of greater or normal intelligence.

Ortega v. Kmart Corp. (2001)

Facts: P slipped on a puddle of milk in a Kmart store and sustained serious injury to his knee. Although P was unable to prove how long the milk remained on the floor, he showed that Kmart personnel failed to inspect the premises for 15 to 30 minutes and perhaps longer. Arguably, the milk was on the floor long enough for reasonable employees to discover it. Kmart asserted that the lack of evidence failed to establish constructive notice of the condition.
Issue: Does a store owner's duty of care include the reasonably timely inspection of store premises that allows for the discovery of dangerous conditions?
Rule: Store owners have a duty to reasonably inspect their premises for potential hazards, especially when the store has high customer traffic.

Heath v. Swift Wings, Inc. (1979)

Facts: Relatives of two plane crash victims sued the pilot for negligence.
Issue: Should a professional be judged by a subjective standard (one's own training, abilities, etc., as factors) or by an objective standard (a minimum standard generally applicable to all members of a particular profession)?

Rule: Professionals are held to an objective standard of care that does not depend on their personal level of training or experience.

Andrews v. United Airlines, Inc. (1994)

Facts: A passenger on a United flight was injured when a briefcase fell out of a overhead bin and hit her on the head.

Issue: Is a common carrier liable for an incident when the circumstances indicate that the risk of serious injury was small but the risk could have been eliminated in the course of normal business operations?

Rule: United was liable for the consequences of the hazard because it could have easily warned the passenger of the possible danger.

Bethel v. New York City Transit Authority (1998)

Facts: P was injured when a wheelchair-accessible bus seat collapsed under him. He brought suit against the Transit Authority.

Issue: Does the Transit Authority, as a common carrier, owe its passengers the highest degree of care or some measure of?

Rule: A single standard of reasonable care applies. The special duty imposed on common carriers is no longer viable in modern society.

Hodges v. Carter (1954)

Facts: Hodges sued his attorneys, whose invalid method of serving process barred him from bringing a further suit. Such method of serving process had been commonly used without problem for decades.

Issue: Is it negligent for an attorney to make an honest and reasonable mistake?

Rule: Attorneys who honestly believe that their actions are correct and in their client's best interest are not liable because of a mere error of judgment or a mistake on a point of law that has not been settled by the highest court in the state and on which there is reasonable doubt by well-informed lawyers.

Emerson v. Magendantz (1997)

Facts: After undergoing a tubal ligation, wife became pregnant and gave birth to a child with congenital problems. Husband and wife sued the physician who performed the sterilization procedure.

Issue: Can a tort suit be brought for a failed sterilization procedure and what damages can be recovered?

Rule: Tort damages can be recovered for a negligently done sterilization procedure, but the allowable damages do not include emotional distress (for the birth of an essentially healthy child).

Boyce v. Brown (1938)

Facts: Boyce sued her physician, Brown, because he failed to take an X-ray of her broken bone after resetting it. Boyce did not offer an expert witness to testify that failure to take an X-ray was negligent under the circumstances.

Issue: Must the plaintiff in a malpractice suit produce an expert witness to establish the physician's departure from the proper medical standard?

Rule: In a medical malpractice suit, the plaintiff must produce an expert to establish the proper medical standard by which the physician is to be evaluated unless the negligence was so obvious that even an ordinary person knows it was a departure from the proper standard.

Helling v. Carey (1974)

Facts: Helling's eye was permanently damaged because Carey failed to diagnose her glaucoma. Experts for both parties agreed that standards of the specialty did not require an exam for glaucoma for patients below the age of 40. Helling was under 40.

Issue: Does compliance with the professional standards of a specialty satisfy the appropriate duty of care?

Rule: Professionals whose actions conform to the standards of their given specialty may, nevertheless, commit malpractice if such conduct is not reasonably prudent.

Morrison v. MacNamara (1979)

Facts: Morrison sued for medical malpractice after suffering an adverse reaction to a medical test administered by MacNamara. The test was performed in a manner that conformed with the medical standards of the local community, but did not meet nationally accepted medical standards.

Issue: Is a laboratory, hospital, physician, or health care provider required to follow local community standards or nationally accepted standards?

Rule: Physicians certified by national boards, hospitals, medical laboratories, and other health care providers are held to the national standard of care.

Scott v. Bradford (1979)

Facts: Complications occurred after Bradford, a physician, performed surgery on Scott. Scott claimed that had Bradford advised her of the possible complications she would not have opted for the surgery.

Issue 1: Does a doctor have a duty to inform patients of their medical options and the risks associated with each to enable patients to make informed decisions regarding appropriate treatment?

Rule 1: Patients asserting medical malpractice actions under the theory of informed consent must allege and prove that (1) the physician failed to provide information on a material risk before securing consent to the treatment; (2) the patient would not have consented to the treatment if the proper information had been provided; and (3) the adverse consequences that the physician did not warn of actually occurred.

Issue 2: Does a physician ever have a privilege to withhold material information from a patient?

Rule 2: A physician has a privilege to withhold information if (1) the patient already knew or should have known of the risks; (2) full disclosure would be detrimental to the patient's best interests (e.g., emotional well-being); or (3) an emergency exists requiring prompt treatment and the patient is in no condition to make such a decision.

Matthies v. Mastromonaco (1999)

Facts: Physician failed to discuss treatment alternatives with patient. He simply chose on his own to have the patient avoid hip surgery. As a result, the elderly patient was eventually confined to a nursing home because she could no longer walk.

Issue: Does a treating physician have a duty to inform a patient and discuss with her both invasive and noninvasive treatment alternatives and their possible consequences?

Rule: To secure effective informed consent to treatment, a physician must explain and discuss the available medical options with the patient.

Burgess v. Superior Court (1992)

Facts: P's baby sustained brain and nervous system damage when it was deprived of oxygen during a cesarean procedure.

Issue: Did the attending obstetrician owe a duty to both the mother and the fetus?

Rule: In light of the realities of pregnancy and childbirth, the mother is not restricted to recovery as a bystander, but rather is owed a duty by the physician for the treatment given to the fetus. The mother's action or status is not derivative.

Moore v. The Regents of the University of California (1990)

Facts: Dr. Golde removed plaintiff's spleen and other bodily tissues after learning that the cells were unusually useful to his genetic research. A cell wall was then developed by Golde and his colleagues that was licensed for commercial development.

Issue: Does an individual have the right to informed consent as to the taking of his cells for genetic research?

Rule: A physician who is seeking a patient's consent for a medical procedure must disclose personal interests unrelated to the patient's health, whether research or economic, that may affect his medical judgment.

Pokora v. Wabash Railway Co. (S. Ct. 1934)

Facts: Pokora was hit by a train after he failed to get out of his car at a railroad track crossing to look for oncoming trains, as was required under B. & O. Ry. Co. v. Goodman. It was unclear whether a prudent person under the circumstances would have adhered to the Goodman standard.
Issue: Is noncompliance with a given standard of care determinative of negligence?
Rule: (Cardozo, J.) Extraordinary situations may not wisely or fairly be subjected to tests or regulations that are fitting for the commonplace or normal. If a person determines that adherence to a given standard is unwise, one is not negligent by law for such deviation, but rather is subject to the judgment of a jury.

Posecai v. Wal-Mart Stores, Inc. (1999)

Facts: P was robbed in the store parking lot after shopping at a Wal-Mart store.
Issue: Do commercial establishments owe their customers a duty to provide reasonable security while they are on store grounds?
Rule: When third-party criminal acts are reasonably foreseeable, store owners owe their patrons a duty to engage in reasonable measures of protection.

Osborne v. McMasters (1889)

Facts: McMasters sold an unlabeled bottle of deadly poison to the plaintiff, in violation of a labeling statute. The plaintiff accidentally drank the poison and died.
Issue: Does a statutorily defined duty of care supersede the common law standard?
Rule: When a duty of care is established by statute, the common law duty to act with reasonable care is superseded so that violation of the statute constitutes conclusive evidence of negligence.

Stachniewicz v. Mar-Cam Corp. (1971)

Facts: Stachniewicz, injured in a barroom brawl, sued the tavern owner for violating a local statute that prohibited tavern owners from serving liquor to a visibly intoxicated person. The statute also required them to prohibit "loud, noisy, disorderly, or boisterous conduct."

Issue: Is violation of a statute negligence per se?
Rule: A violation of a statute or regulation constitutes negligence as a matter of law when the violation results in injury to a member of the class of persons intended to be protected by the legislation and when the harm is of the kind that the statute was enacted to prevent. The statute must also be appropriate to act as a standard of care (e.g., not vague or overbroad).

Sheeley v. Mem. Hosp. (1998)

Facts: P underwent an injurious episiotomy and sued the hospital and the family practice resident for malpractice.
Issue: Does the locality rule dictate the applicable standard of care in medical injury cases?
Rule: The locality rule has been superseded by a national standard that requires physicians to use the degree of care and skill expected of the reasonably competent physician in the same field of medical practice.

Ney v. Yellow Cab Co. (1954)

Facts: An employee of Yellow Cab Co. left his taxi unattended on a public street with the engine running and the key in the ignition, contrary to a state statute. A thief stole the taxi and crashed into Ney.
Issue: Does the court or the jury determine if the violation of a statute is negligence per se?
Rule: In determining whether the violation of a statute is negligence per se, the court determines the legislative purpose of the statute and the jury determines ordinary questions of fact such as negligence, due care, and proximate cause.

States v. Lourdes Hosp. (2003)

Facts: P had successful surgery at the hospital, but awoke with pain in her right arm and shoulder. She claimed the injury occurred during the surgery, but D argued that the cause of the injury was unknown.
Issue: Can P introduce expert testimony to establish the res ipsa element that the event complained of does not usually occur without negligence?
Rule: Expert testimony can be used to establish the likelihood of the negligence element of res ipsa.

Brown v. Shyne (1926)

Facts: Brown was paralyzed by Shyne's chiropractic treatment. Shyne practiced medicine without a license, in violation of a state statute.
Issue: Is violation of a statute negligence per se if the statute was not intended to protect the public from the party in violation?

Rule: If a statute is not intended to protect against certain proscribed conduct, but rather against such conduct by a certain class of people, a violation of the statute by one who is not part of the regulated class is not negligence per se. Such a violation is not the proximate cause of an injury against which protection is afforded.

Martin v. Herzog (1920)

Facts: Martin was killed when his buggy was struck by Herzog's car. Herzog alleged that Martin was contributorily negligent by driving without lights, contrary to a safety statute.
Issue: Is violation of a safety statute evidence of contributory negligence?
Rule: Unexcused omission of a statutory requirement is more than evidence of negligence; it is negligence per se, which cannot be nullified by a jury. However, it must be shown that such omission contributed to the damages to be contributory negligence.

Zeni v. Anderson (1976)

Facts: Because of a heavy snowfall, Zeni traveled a well-used pedestrian snow path in the street. With her back to oncoming traffic, she was struck by Anderson's car. A penal statute required pedestrians to use provided sidewalks and to proceed facing traffic.
Issue: Is a violation of a penal statute contributory negligence per se?
Rule: In a civil action for damages, violation of a penal statute that has been found to apply to a particular set of facts establishes only a prima facie case of negligence, a presumption that may be rebutted by an adequate excuse under the facts and circumstances of the case.

Goddard v. Boston & Maine R.R. Co. (1901)

Facts: Goddard slipped on a banana peel lying upon the crowded platform of a train station.
Issue: When should circumstantial evidence be submitted to the jury?
Rule: Negligence may be established by circumstantial evidence only if the evidence would positively establish negligence in the eyes of a reasonable jury. If negligence is only one of several possible explanations, such evidence will not be submitted.

Joye v. Great Atlantic and Pacific Tea Co. (1968)

Facts: Joye slipped on a banana in a supermarket.
Issue: When may circumstantial evidence be used to prove negligence?
Rule: One may be liable for negligence based on circumstantial evidence only if one had constructive notice of a dangerous condition.

Jasko v. F.W. Woolworth Co. (1972)

Facts: Jasko was injured when she slipped on a piece of pizza near the pizza counter in a Woolworth store. The store customarily sold the pizza on waxed paper to people who would eat it while standing.

Issue: Is it necessary to show that a proprietor had constructive notice of danger if it created a situation in which danger is continuous and easily foreseeable?

Rule: When a proprietor's operating methods are such that dangerous conditions are continuous or easily foreseeable, the proprietor is negligent even without actual notice of the particular dangerous condition.

H.E. Butt Groc. Co. v. Resendez (1999)

Facts: Customer had a slip and fall in a grocery store near a grape display that permitted customer sampling. The table with the bowl of samples was surrounded by a rail and rubber mats. The floor was a nonskid floor. There were warning cones placed near the display.

Issue: Does having a produce display permitting customer sampling constitute an unreasonable risk of harm?

Rule: Merely stating that a commercial display could result in the causation of injury is not sufficient to establish negligence. The P needs to prove that aspects of the display were likely to lead to injury and could have been readily corrected.

Byrne v. Boadle (1863)

Facts: As he walked on a public street, Byrne was struck by a barrel of flour that fell out of a window of Boadle's shop.

Issue: Can the mere occurrence of an accident provide a presumption of negligence even though no other evidence of negligence is offered?

Rule: The doctrine of res ipsa loquitur provides that the mere fact of an accident having occurred is evidence of a defendant's negligence. A plaintiff is not bound to show the accident could not happen without negligence. If there are any facts inconsistent with negligence, it is for the defendant to prove them.

Cox v. Northwest Airlines, Inc. (1967)

Facts: Cox was killed when a Northwest Airlines plane crashed for no apparent reason.

Issue: Is the doctrine of res ipsa loquitur applicable when there is no evidence of the cause of an accident, and when evidence of due care prior to an accident is provided?

Rule: The doctrine of res ipsa loquitur applies when the instrumentality that caused damages was under the exclusive control and management of a defendant, the occurrence in question does not usually occur in the absence of negligence, and when there is no possibility of contributory negligence. General evidence of due care is insufficient to preclude the application of res ipsa loquitur if the specific cause of the accident is unknown.

McDougald v. Perry (1998)

Facts: D's spare tire struck P's windshield when the chain holding the tire underneath the truck apparently broke.
Issue: Does res ipsa loquitur provide P with an inference of negligence when direct proof is unavailable?
Rule: Although injury alone does not establish negligence, if P establishes D's exclusive control over the source of injury and that the occurrence would generally not take place without negligence, an inference of negligence is warranted.

Holmes v. Gamble (1982)

Facts: Holmes asserted the doctrine of res ipsa loquitur to prove the negligence of a physician and an anesthetist after he experienced permanent paralysis in his fingers following a knee operation.
Issue: Must a plaintiff establish the elements of res ipsa loquitur by a preponderance of the evidence?
Rule: A directed verdict may not be granted if a reasonable jury could find that the elements of res ipsa loquitur were established by a preponderance of the evidence. The court, viewing the evidence in the light most favorable to the plaintiff, determines the sufficiency of the evidence, and the jury weighs the evidence and determines if the preponderance of the evidence standard has actually been met.

Larson v. St. Francis Hotel (1948)

Facts: Larson was struck by a heavy chair that fell from a window of the St. Francis Hotel.
Issue: May the doctrine of res ipsa loquitur be applied when the unexplained event may have been caused by a party other than the defendant?
Rule: The doctrine of res ipsa loquitur applies only where the instrumentality of the injury is shown to be under the exclusive control and management of the defendant.

Ybarra v. Spangard (1944)

Facts: Asserting res ipsa loquitur, Ybarra sued his surgeon and other hospital staff after suffering paralysis of his shoulder and arm following an operation to remove his appendix.

Issue: May the doctrine of res ipsa loquitur be applied against several defendants when there is no showing of who specifically caused the injury and when no particular defendant ever had exclusive control over the plaintiff?

Rule: The doctrine of res ipsa loquitur will apply to all those defendants who had any control over the plaintiff's body or the instrumentalities that might have caused the injuries to the plaintiff. It is up to each defendant to rebut the presumption of negligence.

Note: This case illustrates the "smoking out of the evidence" policy used when members of the same profession will not testify against each other.

Sullivan v. Crabtree (1953)

Facts: Crabtree's truck ran off the road, killing his passenger Sullivan. The cause of the accident was unclear.

Issue: Must a jury rule in favor of a plaintiff just because the doctrine of res ipsa loquitur is applicable to the circumstances?

Rule: Res ipsa loquitur allows, but does not require, a jury to find negligence. The jury is free to choose another inference from the evidence presented.

The Nitro-Glycerine Case (S. Ct. 1872)

Facts: The defendant, a common carrier, transported an unmarked box containing a new experimental chemical. The defendant did not make inquiries as to its contents. When the box leaked, the defendant attempted to open it, causing an explosion that destroyed the plaintiff's nearby building.

Issue: What degree of care must a person exercise to avoid liability for negligence?

Rule: (Field, J.) A person must take the precautions that a reasonable person, guided by considerations that ordinarily regulate the conduct of human affairs, would take. One who exercises reasonable care will not be liable for unintentional injuries.

Losee v. Buchanan (1873)

Facts: The defendant's boiler exploded, damaging the plaintiff's property. The plaintiff did not allege that the defendant was negligent in any way.

Issue: Is one who nonnegligently causes damage liable?

Rule: One who is free of fault, intent, or negligence is not liable for damages.

J.S. and M.S. v. R.T.H. (1998)

Facts: Neighbor sexually abused two young girls. Parents brought suit against both husband and wife. Wife argued that she owed no duty of care to any of the affected parties.
Issue: Does the spouse of an abuser who might have either actual knowledge or reason to know of the abuse owe a duty to warn of or prevent the abuse and does a breach of that duty act as a proximate cause of the abuse?
Rule: Given the seriousness of the harm to innocent victims, spouses who have actual knowledge or reason to know of the abuse to a particular person(s) have a duty to warn of or prevent the abuse.

Van Skike v. Zussman (1974)

Facts: Van Skike, a minor, obtained a toy cigarette lighter as a prize from a gumball machine in Zussman's store. He immediately purchased lighter fluid from Zussman and accidentally set himself on fire.
Issue: Is a defendant negligent for allowing a minor to come into possession of a remotely dangerous article?
Rule: A defendant who supplies a minor with a remotely dangerous article will only be negligent if the harm or danger caused by the article is reasonably foreseeable, as opposed to merely possible.

Davis v. Consolidated Rail Corp. (1986)

Facts: One of Davis's legs and part of his foot were severed from his body when a train he was inspecting was moved without warning.
Issue: Will the absence of safety precautions invariably result in the imposition of liability?
Rule: A defendant who fails to take a safety precaution is liable for negligence only if the burden (B) of taking the precaution is less than the magnitude of the potential loss (L) multiplied by the probability (P) of the accident occurring (i.e., $B < P \times L$).

Beatty v. Central Iowa Railway (1882)

Facts: The defendant placed a railroad track in close proximity to a public highway. Beatty was killed when the approach of a train caused his horse to become unmanageable and run into the train.
Issue: Is a party who could have avoided the occurrence of an accident negligent?

Rule: A party is negligent only if it did not use reasonable care and diligence, in light of the existing circumstances, to guard against danger.

La Marra v. Adam (1949)

Facts: A police car carrying a premature baby to a hospital drove through a red light at 45 miles per hour without using a siren. The plaintiff collided with the police car.
Issue: Does conduct involving a high probability of hurting someone constitute recklessness or negligence?
Rule: Recklessness implies conscious appreciation of the probable extent of danger or risk incident to a contemplated action, whereas negligence in the legal sense implies knowledge only of a probable source of danger in the act.
Note: This is the minority rule (distinguishing between recklessness and negligence). Most states would likely hold the officer negligent based on the theory that a reasonable person would exercise extra caution in more dangerous situations.

Whicher v. Phinney (1942)

Facts: The defendant drove behind another car that struck a wagon, causing the plaintiff to be ejected from the wagon. When the defendant became aware of the dangerous situation ahead he only had time to act instinctively, and ran over the plaintiff.
Issue: Is it possible for one who is acting according to instinct to be negligent?
Rule: An act committed when there is only a short time to act is called an instinctive action. A party who has not negligently caused an emergency situation and who has acted instinctively is not negligent, unless the party was unfit to act in an emergency.

Public Service of New Hampshire v. Elliott (1941)

Facts: Elliott, an electrical construction student, was electrocuted because he came too close to a high-tension wire when he pointed to a piece of machinery in the defendant's electrical substation.
Issue: Is a spontaneous and natural gesture that results in injury a contributorily negligent action if the person making the gesture has special knowledge of the danger?
Rule: A reasonable person may make a spontaneous movement without analyzing all of the ramifications. In such a case, the standard to be used is that of a reasonable person in like circumstances, for example, what a reasonable student of electricity would do.

Williamson v. Garland (1966)

Facts: An 11-year-old was injured when his bicycle was struck by an automobile.
Issue: Is a minor capable of negligence?
Rule: A minor who does not exercise the degree of care reasonably expected from a child of like age and experience may be negligent.

Titus v. Bradford, B. & K. R.R. (1890)

Facts: The Bradford, B. & K. Railroad followed a common industry practice of removing broad gauge boxcars from their wheel assemblies and setting them on narrow gauge assemblies. In the process, a boxcar tipped off its wheel assembly and killed Titus.
Issue: Does following the custom and usage of a trade or business satisfy the requirement of exercising a reasonable standard of care?
Rule: The test for negligence is whether a defendant's methods, machinery, and appliances comport with the ordinary usage of the business or trade.

The T.J. Hooper (1932)

Facts: The defendant's tugboats and the barges they towed sunk during a storm. The tugs did not have radios capable of transmitting warning of the storm. It was not common to equip tugboats with radios at the time.
Issue: Does following a common custom and usage satisfy the obligation to exercise the proper duty of care?
Rule: The common practice of a profession is relevant but not conclusive in determining one's use of due care. The practice itself may be unreasonable and negligent according to common knowledge and the judgment of a prudent and reasonable person.

Rossell v. Volkswagen of America (1985)

Facts: Rossell's Volkswagen rolled over in an accident. The battery, which was inside the passenger compartment, fractured and leaked sulfuric acid, disfiguring Rossell.
Issue: In negligent design cases, are product manufacturers held to an expert's standard of care?
Rule: In determining what is reasonable care for manufacturers, a plaintiff need only prove that the defendant's conduct presented an unreasonable risk of harm. As in all other negligence cases, the jury is permitted to decide what is reasonable according to common experience.

Bly v. Rhoads (1976)

Facts: The plaintiff sued her doctor after adverse complications arose from a hysterectomy, claiming that her physician did not comply with the informed consent doctrine. The plaintiff introduced an expert who was unfamiliar with local community medical standards.

Issue 1: May lay testimony as to a "patient's need" for information be used to determine what information a physician must disclose?

Rule 1: A plaintiff must produce an expert to establish the prevailing medical practice with respect to the disclosure of information to patients, that the information was material to an informed decision, and that disclosure would not have posed an unreasonable threat to the patient's well-being.

Issue 2: Is familiarity with the local community medical standards required of an expert giving testimony in a malpractice suit?

Rule 2: An expert must have knowledge of a same or similar community standard to testify in a malpractice action.

Tedla v. Ellman (1939)

Facts: The plaintiffs were struck by the defendant's negligently driven automobile. The defendant claimed that the plaintiffs were contributorily negligent for failing to obey a statute requiring pedestrians to walk facing oncoming traffic.

Issue: Is violation of a safety statute negligence per se?

Rule: Violation of a safety statute may be excused if a greater risk of harm would have resulted from complying with the statute.

Bauman v. Crawford (1985)

Facts: While riding his bicycle after dark, the plaintiff, age 14, was injured in a collision with the defendant's car. Contrary to a statute, the plaintiff's bicycle lacked a headlight.

Issue: Is the negligence per se doctrine applicable to minors?

Rule: A minor's statutory violation is not negligence per se, but may be introduced as evidence of a minor's negligence. The minor is negligent only if the jury finds that a reasonable child of the same age, intelligence, maturity, and experience would not have acted in violation of the statute under the circumstances.

Zerby v. Warren (1973)

Facts: The plaintiff, age 14, died after sniffing glue that his friend, also a minor, purchased from Warren. Warren asserted the defenses of contributory negligence and assumption of the risk. A statute prohibited the sale of glue to minors.

Issue: Does violating a child protection statute create absolute liability on the part of a retailer for the wrongful death of a minor that resulted from an intentional act?

Rule: Liability for the violation of a statute designed to protect a child is absolute. Therefore, defenses such as contributory negligence and assumption of the risk are inapplicable.

Thompson v. Frankus (1955)

Facts: The plaintiff was injured when she fell down the defendant's poorly maintained and unlit stairway. The plaintiff was not sure of the cause of her fall.

Issue: Can a plaintiff who is unaware of the specific cause of injury sue for negligence?

Rule: A plaintiff who is unable to recount or explain an accident may nevertheless recover if the deficiency is met by other direct or circumstantial evidence.

Newing v. Cheatham (1975)

Facts: The plaintiff was killed when the defendant's plane crashed. The cause of the crash could not be determined.

Issue: What must be established to assert a negligence action based on res ipsa loquitur?

Rule: The doctrine of res ipsa loquitur may be invoked when (1) the accident is of a kind that ordinarily does not occur in the absence of negligence; (2) the accident is caused by an instrumentality within the exclusive control of the defendant; and (3) the plaintiff is free from fault.

Sutor v. Rogotzke (1972)

Facts: A hunter accidentally fired his gun, killing the plaintiff.

Issue: Does the doctrine of res ipsa loquitur apply to accidental injuries caused by dangerous instrumentalities?

Rule: In cases involving dangerous instrumentalities, res ipsa loquitur is applicable.

Note: This case represents the majority view.

Scott v. Shepherd (1773)

Facts: Shepherd threw a lit explosive into a marketplace. Several persons threw the device away from themselves to avoid injury. Scott lost an eye when he was struck by the explosive.

Issue: Is an originator of mischief relieved of liability due to the presence of intervening parties?

Rule: One is liable for injuries that result from unlawful, deliberate, indiscriminate, and wanton mischief despite the intervening conduct of other parties acting under a compulsive necessity for their own safety and self-preservation.

Powell v. Fall (1880)

Facts: Fall's tractor, operating in a lawful manner and without mechanical defect, emitted a spark that caused Powell's hay to catch fire.
Issue: Is a party liable for damages caused by its potentially dangerous activity without any negligence or fault?
Rule: A party who conducts a dangerous activity is liable for damages caused regardless of fault or negligence.

Louisville Railway Co. v. Sweeney (1914)

Facts: Defendant's trolley car jumped from its tracks and hit a telephone pole. The telephone pole hit a gate, which struck Sweeney, who was standing in her front yard.
Issue: Is negligence required to effect a trespass?
Rule: A defendant's action need not be negligent to be a trespass. One who trespasses upon another or sets a force in motion that causes trespass upon another is liable unless the trespass is caused by an act of God or forces beyond the defendant's control.

Stone v. Bolton (1950); Bolton v. Stone (1951)

Facts: As Stone passed outside some cricket grounds she was struck by a cricket ball that Bolton hit. The cricket grounds were quite large and were surrounded by a fence. Only six to ten balls had ever been hit outside the grounds in 30 years.
Issue: Is one liable for failing to protect against an extremely unlikely, but foreseeable risk?
Rule: There is no liability for a foreseeable injury that is not caused by negligence or an intentional action if the known risk of the injury is extremely minimal.
Note: Some courts will find liability if precautions were easily available and inexpensive.

Roberts v. Ring (1919)

Facts: The plaintiff, a 7-year-old boy, was struck by the defendant's automobile while crossing the street. The defendant was a 77-year-old man with defective sight and hearing.

Issue: Is it proper to consider one's age, maturity, or infirmities when determining negligence or contributory negligence?
Rule: Negligence is judged by the standard of care usually exercised by the ordinarily prudent normal person, whereas contributory negligence is judged by the standard of care commonly exercised by an ordinary person in the actor's position, taking into account factors such as age and maturity.

Daniels v. Evans (1966)

Facts: Daniels, age 19, was killed when his motorcycle struck Evans's automobile. The trial court instructed the jury that because Daniels was a minor he should have exercised the care of the average child of his age and experience and should not be held to the same standard as an adult.
Issue: Is a minor engaged in an adult activity held to the same standard of care as an adult?
Rule: When a minor undertakes an adult activity that can result in grave danger to others and to the minor, the minor should be held to the standard of a reasonable adult.

Smith v. Lampe (1933)

Facts: Smith, hearing a boat coming to shore at the wrong place on a foggy night, drove his car to the shore and blew his horn to warn the captain. Lampe mistook Smith's horn for a prearranged safe passage signal, and crashed his boat on the rocks.
Issue: Is one liable for innocent actions that result in unforeseeable injury?
Rule: One is not liable for unforeseeable injuries resulting from nonnegligent conduct.

Eckert v. Long Island R.R. (1871)

Facts: Eckert was struck by the defendant's negligently operated train when he saved a child who was sitting on the tracks.
Issue: Is it negligent to place one's life in danger to save the life of another?
Rule: Risking one's life for the purpose of saving another is not wrongful, and therefore, not negligent, unless it was either rash or reckless.

Osborne v. Montgomery (1931)

Facts: The plaintiff was injured when his bicycle crashed into the partly opened door of the defendant's double-parked car.
Issue: Is all conduct that creates risk to others considered below the required standard of ordinary care?

Rule: Social value should be balanced against the degree of risk to determine the question of negligence. A reasonable amount of risk that naturally flows from socially acceptable and desirable conduct has to be tolerated.

Brune v. Belinkoff (1968)

Facts: Brune fell down 11 hours after Belinkoff injected her with a spinal anesthetic. In response to an allegation that the dosage was excessive, Belinkoff claimed the dosage was customary in New Bedford, Massachusetts, even though lower dosages were used in Boston and New York.
Issue: Should a local or national standard be used to determine a physician's duty of care?
Rule: The locality rule is abandoned; physicians are to be held to one national standard.

Canterbury v. Spence (1972)

Facts: Canterbury sued Spence, a physician, for failing to provide adequate information and warning concerning a medical procedure after complications from a spinal operation resulted in partial paralysis.
Issue: Is a doctor required to explain the risks inherent in a medical procedure when the custom of the profession is not to do so?
Rule: A physician must disclose the likelihood and possibility of complications to a patient before performing a procedure.

Vesely v. Sager (1971)

Facts: Sager, in violation of a state statute, served a large quantity of alcoholic beverages to a customer who he knew was excessively intoxicated. As a result of intoxication, the customer negligently injured Vesely in a car accident. At the time the beverages were served, Sager also knew that the customer would be driving after consumption of the beverages.
Issue: Can negligent conduct be the proximate cause of an injury if there is intervening action by a third person between the negligent conduct and the injury caused?
Rule: If negligent conduct is a substantial factor in bringing about an injury, and the intervening causes of the injury are reasonably foreseeable or normal incidents of the risk created, the negligent conduct may be deemed the proximate cause of the injury.

Baltimore and Ohio R.R. v. Goodman (S. Ct. 1927)

Facts: Goodman drove across the defendant's railroad tracks without stopping. He did not see the approaching train because it was obscured by a house. Goodman died in the collision.

Issue: May a judge establish a standard of appropriate conduct?
Rule: (Holmes, J.) Although the question of due care is generally left to the jury, if the court is dealing with a standard of conduct and the standard is clear, it should be laid down by the court.

McGonigal v. Gearhart Industries, Inc. (1986)

Facts: McGonigal was seriously injured when he threw a defective hand grenade that was assembled and inspected by the defendant.
Issue: Must a plaintiff foreclose all possible nonnegligent causes of an accident to employ res ipsa loquitur?
Rule: A plaintiff is not required to eliminate with certainty all possible nonnegligent causes of the accident, but rather need only show that on the whole it is more likely than not that the asserted negligence was the cause of the accident.

Colmenares Vivas v. Sun Alliance Insurance Co. (1986)

Facts: The plaintiffs were injured when the handrail of a moving escalator stopped moving. Although the Puerto Rico Ports Authority owned the escalator and controlled the public area in which it was found, it contracted with another party to inspect, maintain, and repair the escalator.
Issue: Is it necessary for a party to have exclusive physical control over an instrumentality that causes an accident to apply res ipsa loquitur against the party?
Rule: If a defendant has a nondelegable duty to maintain an instrumentality in a safe condition, it is ultimately responsible for the instrumentality and effectively has exclusive control over it. Unless the duty is delegable, the res ipsa loquitur inference is not defeated if the defendant shifts physical control to an agent or contracts with another to carry out its responsibilities.

Dillon v. Legg (1968)

Facts: Dillon suffered great emotional injury when she saw her daughter killed by Legg's negligent driving. Her safety was at no time endangered.
Issue: Can one recover for emotional trauma caused by witnessing the death of a close relative if one does not fear for his own safety?
Rule: In an action for emotional distress, factors such as proximity to the "zone of danger" and the relationship to the physically injured party may be considered in allowing for recovery.

Molien v. Kaiser Foundation Hospitals (1980)

Facts: The defendant erroneously diagnosed Molien as having syphilis. As a result, his wife divorced him.

Issue: Can one recover damages for the negligent infliction of emotional distress?
Rule: Even without physical harm, damages may be awarded for negligent infliction of emotional distress if the trier of fact is convinced of the genuineness of the claim in light of the circumstances.

Adams v. Bullock (1919)

Facts: The plaintiff was electrocuted when the eight-foot-long wire he was carrying struck the overhead wire for the defendant's trolley.
Issue: Must a party take every possible precaution to protect the welfare of others?
Rule: A duty exists to adopt all reasonable precautions to minimize possible perils. A party is not negligent for not providing protection against an unforeseeable, extraordinary injury that would be extremely difficult to prevent.

Negri v. Stop and Shop, Inc. (1985)

Facts: Negri slipped and fell in the defendant's store. The floor was covered with broken jars and spilled food. The evidence showed that the food was dirty, one witness had not heard any jars break within the 20 minutes prior to the accident, and the floor had been cleaned between 50 minutes and two hours before the accident.
Issue: Is circumstantial evidence that a party should have known a dangerous condition existed on its property enough to establish a prima facie case of negligence?
Rule: A prima facie case of negligence may be established by circumstantial evidence that a party did not act to remedy a potentially hazardous condition of which the party had constructive notice.

Gordon v. American Museum of Natural History (1986)

Facts: Gordon fell down a museum's steps after slipping on a piece of waxy paper that came from the museum's concession stand.
Issue: What constitutes constructive notice of a dangerous situation for the purpose of establishing negligence on the basis of circumstantial evidence?
Rule: To be liable for negligence under the theory of constructive notice, a defect must be visible and apparent, and it must exist for a sufficient length of time to permit the defendant to discover and remedy it.

Henning v. Thomas (1988)

Facts: The defendants, Henning and Pruner, questioned on appeal the qualification of the plaintiff's expert to testify about the standard of care in Virginia, and the trial court's limitation on testimony concerning the expert's salary and relationship with the plaintiff.

Issue 1: May the determination of an expert's qualification to testify be overturned on appeal?

Rule 1: The question of whether an expert is qualified to testify rests largely within the sound discretion of the trial court. The decision to allow an expert to testify will not be reversed unless it clearly appears that the witness was unqualified.

Issue 2: Is testimony as to an expert's salary and relationship to the controversy admissible to establish bias and prejudice?

Rule 2: A court must permit a party to explore an expert's relationship to the plaintiff to allow the party to establish bias and prejudice.

Pauscher v. Iowa Methodist Medical Center (1987)

Facts: Pauscher died after the defendants performed a medical procedure without informing her of the risks involved.

Issue: If a physician withholds information from a patient to obtain the patient's consent to a medical procedure, must the patient suing for malpractice produce expert testimony establishing that the physician's nondisclosure was a deviation from professional standards?

Rule: Because the physician's duty to disclose is governed by each patient's need for particular information as opposed to professional standards, a patient is not required to prove that a physician's withholding of information was a deviation from professional standards. Rather, a physician who withholds information must assert a defense justifying the nondisclosure.

Ellis v. Louisville & Nashville R.R. (1952)

Facts: Ellis contracted silicosis after working for the defendant, who did not supply Ellis with protective equipment.

Issue: Where an injury results from a common industrial practice, what is the required standard of care?

Rule: The standard of care for industrial practices is determined by the ordinary custom and usage of the industry, as long as there is a reasonably safe work place and ordinary care is exercised.

Note: Applying custom and usage as the *sole criterion* for standard of care is the minority view.

Pittsburgh, S. & N. R.R. v. Lamphere (1905)

Facts: Lamphere, a brakeman for the railroad, was struck and injured by a low trestle. Lamphere claimed damage for negligence due to the railroad's failure to provide any warnings of the trestle.

Issue: Should a court allow evidence concerning ordinary custom and usage of an industry to show negligence?

Rule: Where the question of negligence concerns a common industrial practice, evidence of ordinary custom and usage should be introduced to avoid uninformed or capricious judgments by juries.

Marigold Coal, Inc. v. Thames (1962)

Facts: Thames's house was damaged by blasting done by Marigold. Thames introduced an expert witness to show that the amount of explosive used was excessive.

Issue: When may an expert witness give an opinion as evidence?

Rule: Where the subject matter is not one of common knowledge, an expert witness is qualified to give his opinion.

Shutka v. Pennsylvania R.R. (1962)

Facts: Shutka's son was killed in a railroad grade crossing accident. Shutka claimed the railroad negligently maintained the crossing, and introduced expert testimony as evidence.

Issue 1: May expert testimony be introduced when the subject matter is one of common knowledge?

Rule 1: Expert testimony may be used if it aids a jury in reaching a verdict, even if the subject is common knowledge.

Issue 2: May expert testimony be introduced when it directly relates to the ultimate issue for the jury to decide?

Rule 2: Expert testimony may be admitted even if it embraces the ultimate issue. A jury is never bound by an expert's opinion.

Shutt v. Kaufman's, Inc. (1968)

Facts: Shutt was struck by a metal shoe stand that fell when she bumped into a table.

Issue: May res ipsa be applied if the plaintiff can otherwise establish the defendant's negligence?

Rule: If the plaintiff has the means of establishing the defendant's negligence, the doctrine of res ipsa should not be applied.

Note: This is the minority view. Generally, res ipsa is precluded only if the plaintiff offers a complete explanation of the defendant's negligence.

City of Louisville v. Humphrey (1970)

Facts: Humphrey died from head wounds after being arrested and locked up in the drunk tank. His widow brought a wrongful death suit, asserting the doctrine of res ipsa loquitur.

Issue: Does the doctrine of res ipsa apply when the injury may have been caused by a third party?

Rule: If an injury may have been caused by a third party not under the control of the defendant, res ipsa does not apply. If the third party was under the control or in the custody of the defendant, res ipsa may apply only if the defendant knew of the third party's violent tendencies.

Brown v. Merlo (1973)

Facts: Brown was injured while riding as a guest in Merlo's car. Brown challenged the state's automobile guest statute that denied recovery except when the guest was injured through the host's willful misconduct or intoxication.

Issue: Is an automobile guest statute violative of equal protection rights?

Rule: Automobile guest statutes violate equal protection guarantees because they unfairly deny one class of persons (i.e., automobile guests) the same rights granted to other citizens.

Tubbs v. Argus (1967)

Facts: Following a car accident, Argus, the driver, abandoned the car without assisting Tubbs, her passenger, whose injuries were aggravated on being abandoned by Argus.

Issue: What is the duty of one whose conduct places another in peril?

Rule: When a person's tortious or innocent conduct has injured another, that person is under a duty to use reasonable care to prevent further injuries.

Johnson v. State (1975)

Facts: Johnson was mistakenly informed by the hospital that her mother had died. Johnson learned of the mistake only after paying funeral expenses and viewing the wrong body.

Issue: When may one recover for emotional distress absent physical injury?

Rule: One exception to the general rule of not allowing for infliction of emotional distress absent physical injury involves the mishandling of corpses.

Wehrling v. Sandy (1985)

Facts: Wehrling brought suit for wrongful death of a stillborn fetus that was negligently injured while in the womb.
Issue: When may beneficiaries of an unborn fetus recover damages for the fetus's death?
Rule: One may recover for a fetus's death occurring prior to birth as long as the fetus was still viable when the injuries were sustained.

Turpin v. Sortini (1982)

Facts: The Turpins brought a negligence suit against their physician and hospital for failing to inform them that their baby was likely to be totally deaf. The daughter, who was born deaf, sought damages for being deprived of being born whole, and for specialized training.
Issue: Can one recover for medical expenses and the pain of having been born handicapped when otherwise the child would not have been born at all?
Rule: Because life is preferred to nonexistence, the plaintiff in a wrongful life suit cannot recover for normal medical expenses or for the pain of being handicapped. The plaintiff may recover for extra medical and professional expenses.

Barber Lines A/S v. M/V Donau Mara (1985)

Facts: The defendant negligently spilled oil in a docking area, causing the plaintiff to dock at a different port and incur added transportation costs.
Issue: Are damages for negligently caused financial harm recoverable absent any physical injury?
Rule: Damages for negligently caused financial harm are recoverable only where there has been accompanying physical harm or loss.

J'Aire Corp. v. Gregory (1979)

Facts: J'Aire filed a complaint for negligence when Gregory, a contractor, failed to complete construction within a reasonable time.
Issue: When will a cause of action arise for loss of expected economic advantage due to a delay in the completion of a contract's performance?
Rule: A cause of action will arise if a loss of expected economic advantage is due to one's failure to use reasonable care to avoid foreseeable damages caused by delay in completion, even in a contractual situation.

CHAPTER 5

Causation in Fact

I. SINE QUA NON ("BUT FOR" CAUSATION)

The basic test to determine if there was causation in fact is to ask whether "but for" a defendant's negligence a plaintiff's injuries would have resulted.

This test is too broad, however, because it does not bar liability for the remote results of one's conduct.

The test is also underinclusive because it does not allow recovery in cases of joint causation as, "but for" one cause the other cause would have hurt the plaintiff anyway.

II. PROOF OF CAUSATION

One does not have to prove that "but for" a defendant's negligence the injury would not have occurred. It is sufficient to prove by a preponderance of the evidence that the defendant's negligence increased the risk that the accident would occur.

III. CONCURRENT CAUSES

If one's injury is caused by the combined negligence of multiple tortfeasors, liability will be determined according to one of several tests.

A. Substantial Factor Test

In cases where the negligent actions of each tortfeasor alone would have caused the entire injury by itself and the harm is indivisible such that damages cannot be apportioned among the tortfeasors, each is liable for causing the entire harm. To be liable, a defendant's negligence must have played a substantial part in causing the harm.

B. Multiple Negligence

In cases where the negligent actions of each defendant would not have caused the injury alone, each is liable for the damage each defendant actually caused.

C. Alternative Causes

If it cannot be determined which of the two negligent actors caused the injury, both are liable unless one can prove his innocence.

D. Enterprise Liability Theory

Each member of an enterprise is liable for damages caused by the enterprise as a whole when there has been close cooperation among the different members and damages cannot be apportioned.

CASE CLIPS

Perkins v. Texas and New Orleans Railway Co. (1962)

Facts: Perkins was killed when the car he was riding in attempted to cross railroad tracks against the warning signals and was struck by defendant's train, which was negligently exceeding the speed limit.
Issue: Is the negligence of a defendant actionable where it is not the cause in fact of an accident?
Rule: When a harm would have resulted regardless of a defendant's negligence, the negligence is not a substantial factor in causing the harm and the defendant is not liable.

Doe v. Manheimer (1989)

Facts: Meter reader was raped on D's property. Rapist forced her onto the property from the sidewalk and raped her in overgrown vegetation. She sued landowner because the condition of the land shielded the incident from public view.
Issue: Can a landowner's responsibility for the land and its condition extend to heinous criminal acts done by a third party?
Rule: The causal relationship between the condition of the land and the commission of the crime was haphazard and, as a matter of policy, was not a substantial factor in causing P's harm.

Haft v. Lone Palm Hotel (1970)

Facts: Plaintiffs were found drowned in defendant's pool, which did not have a lifeguard or a warning that no lifeguard was present, as required by statute. It was unknown how the deaths occurred.
Issue: Must a plaintiff prove cause in fact when because of the defendant's negligence there was no witness to the accident?
Rule: The plaintiff's burden of proving cause in fact of an injury may be shifted to the defendant when defendant's negligence detracted from plaintiff's ability to prove causation.

Pafford v. Secretary of HHS (2006)

Facts: P claims to have developed Still's disease (juvenile rheumatoid arthritis) as a result of vaccinations. His evidence did not link receiving the shots and contraction of the disease in terms of time or exclude other possible explanations.
Issue: Is the mere allegation that vaccinations led to P's contracting of the disease as a side effect sufficient to state a cause of action?

Rule: P failed to establish to a preponderance of the evidence the necessary casual link between the onset of the disease and the vaccines in terms of timing. He also failed to discredit other possible causes for his illness.

Reynolds v. Texas & Pacific Railway Co. (1885)

Facts: Reynolds fell down the defendant's unlit stairway at a railroad.
Issue: Will one's negligence be a cause in fact of an injury if there is a chance the injury may have occurred without the negligence?
Rule: When a defendant's negligence greatly multiplies the chances of an accident, the mere possibility that it may have happened without the negligence is not sufficient to relieve liability.

Kramer Service, Inc. v. Wilkins (1939)

Facts: Wilkins was injured due to defendant's negligence. Two years later cancer developed in the location of the injury.
Issue: May one recover for the negligence of another if there is only a slight chance the injury was caused by the defendant's negligence?
Rule: Recovery is barred when there is only a small possibility that "but for" the defendant's negligence the injury would not have resulted.

Zuchowicz v. United States (1998)

Facts: P took a prescription drug at a negligently prescribed dose. She developed a variety of symptoms thereafter and eventually contracted primary pulmonary hypertension. While she was waiting for a lung transplant, she became pregnant and gave birth to a son. She died 30 days later.
Issue: Is there a sufficient causal connection between the negligently prescribed dosage and P's illness and eventual death?
Rule: When a negligent act increases the likelihood of an injury that P actually suffers, the trier of fact may conclude that there is a sufficient causal linkage between the two events to establish liability.

Wilder v. Eberhart (1992)

Facts: The trial court allowed the plaintiff's expert witness to testify that the sole cause of injury to her esophagus was its movement during surgery performed by Dr. Eberhart. Defendant's experts, who were planning to testify that there were other possible causes of the injury, however, were excluded.
Issue: Does the fact that experts could not express their opinions with "probability" rather than "mere possibility" preclude admission of their testimony?

Rule: The preclusion of expert testimony that is based on the possibility of a cause of injury, rather than certainty or probability, is admissible. A defendant need only produce enough evidence to convince the trier of fact that the alleged negligence was not the legal cause of the injury.

Herskovits v. Group Health Cooperative of Puget Sound (1983)

Facts: The defendant failed to diagnose Herskovits's lung cancer, thereby reducing his chances for survival. The defendant argued Herskovits would have died anyway so they were not the cause in fact of his death.
Issue: Are defendants liable when, by their negligence, they increase the risk of harm to one who might have suffered the harm anyway?
Rule: If a defendant's acts or omissions increase a preexisting risk of harm to another the defendant is only liable for a proportionate share of the harm caused.

Alberts v. Schultz (1999)

Facts: D failed to perform tests when P saw him for leg pain. P saw a specialist two weeks later, who concluded that the leg needed to be amputated. P sued D for malpractice.
Issue: Can a patient recover damages when he or she loses a chance or opportunity for medical treatment due to a physician error or omission?
Rule: Recovery for "lost chance" medical malpractice is possible as long as P establishes to a preponderance that the medical condition was made worse by the loss of the treatment opportunity.

Daubert v. Merrell Dow Pharmaceuticals, Inc. (S. Ct. 1993)

Facts: Plaintiffs alleged that the birth defects of their children were caused by the mothers' ingestion of a prescription drug sold by Merrell Dow. Respondents answered with an affidavit from a well-credentialed expert. The expert reviewed all the literature and concluded that maternal use of the drug during the first trimester of pregnancy had not been shown to be a risk factor for human birth defects. Plaintiffs then answered with eight of their own experts, who analyzed animal-cell studies, live animal studies, and chemical structural analyses. Plaintiffs' experts concluded that the drug can cause birth defects.
Issue: In a federal trial, may expert scientific testimony be admissible if the foundation on which the testimony is based is not "generally accepted" as reliable in the relevant scientific community?
Rule: The Frye test, which held that expert testimony is inadmissible unless the foundation on which it is based is "generally accepted," has

been superseded by the Federal Rules of Evidence. Under the Rules, the trial judge must ensure that the scientific testimony or evidence that is admitted is relevant and has a reliable foundation. A study's publication and the prior case law should not be the predominant gauge of admissibility.

Hill v. Edmonds (1966)

Facts: Plaintiff was a passenger in a negligently driven car that hit defendant's unlit truck, which was parked in the middle of a road.
Issue: Is one completely liable for an injury when one's negligence, by itself, would not have caused the accident?
Rule: When separate acts of negligence combine to produce a single injury, each tortfeasor is responsible for the entire result, even though the tortfeasor's act, by itself, would not have caused the injury.

Benn v. Thomas (1994)

Facts: P died soon after D negligently rear-ended the vehicle in which he was a passenger. P had coronary disease and his medical expert testified the accident was "the straw that broke the camel's back."
Issue: Is a tortfeasor liable for the totality of the harm suffered by P when there is a latent condition or susceptibility and the likelihood of concurrent causation?
Rule: The "eggshell" victim rule applies in these circumstances. The combined impact of the tortious conduct and an existing condition can result in a determination by the fact-finder that the tortfeasor is liable for the totality of the harm suffered by P.

Anderson v. Minneapolis, St. P. & S.St. M. R.R. Co. (1920)

Facts: A fire caused by the defendant's negligence combined with a second fire of uncertain origin and destroyed Anderson's property.
Issue: May a plaintiff recover complete damages from one party for injuries caused by the combined negligence of two parties?
Rule: Under the concurrent liability rule, if one's negligence could have caused an injury by itself, the negligent actor will not be relieved from liability because another party was also negligent.

Summers v. Tice (1948)

Facts: A bullet struck Summers when the two defendants negligently fired their rifles. It was unknown which gun fired the bullet.
Issue: Can two negligent actors be held jointly liable for an injury that only one of them could have caused?

Rule: Two negligent parties who act in concert are jointly liable for an injury only one of them could have committed, unless they are able to prove which one of them committed the act that caused the injury.

Sindell v. Abbott Laboratories (1980)

Facts: Sindell alleged that she suffered injuries from a drug manufactured by the defendants and approximately 195 other companies.

Issue: When several manufacturers distribute the same product, how should liability for damages caused by the product be apportioned?

Rule: When several manufacturers produce identical products that injure a plaintiff, and it is impossible to know which manufacturer produced the specific product that caused the injury, the liability of the defendants is proportionate to their share of the overall market.

To avoid such liability, a manufacturer would have to prove its product did not cause plaintiff's injuries.

Barnes v. Bovenmyer (1963)

Facts: The plaintiff lost his eye because the defendant, his doctor, failed to find a piece of steel that was in the eye upon examination.

Issue: Is an actor liable for a negligent act when it is less than likely that the resulting injury was caused by it?

Rule: A party may not recover for the negligence of another unless "but for" the negligence, the injury would not have resulted.

Waffen v. United States Dept. of Health & Human Services (1986)

Facts: Waffen's cancer was negligently diagnosed. Consequently, a delay in treatment ensued, during which the cancer became terminal.

Issue: What burden of proof must plaintiffs satisfy to successfully claim that a defendant's negligence deprived them of a substantial possibility of survival?

Rule: Plaintiffs must prove by a "preponderance of the evidence" that a defendant's negligence actually deprived them of a substantial possibility of survival.

Allen v. United States (1984)

Facts: The plaintiffs sued the United States, claiming that their illnesses were caused by the government's testing of the atom bomb.

Issue: Must a plaintiff show the precise connection between a defendant's act and the plaintiff's injury to establish cause-in-fact?

Rule: When a defendant negligently creates a hazard that puts an iden-
tifiable population group at increased risk, a member of that group that
develops a condition that is consistent with the hazard need only show
that the defendant's conduct was more likely than not a substantial factor
contributing to the plaintiff's injury.

Stimpson v. Wellington Service Corp. (1969)

Facts: The plaintiff claimed that the pipes in his basement became
uncoupled because the defendants drove their 137-ton rig in violation
of a statutory weight limitation.
Issue: Must a plaintiff exclude other possible causes to establish that a
defendant's negligence was the cause in fact of the damages?
Rule: A plaintiff is not required to exclude other possible causes. It is
sufficient for the plaintiff to show that the defendant's negligent act
was the probable cause in fact of the damages.

Gentry v. Douglas Hereford Ranch, Inc. (1998)

Facts: P's wife was accidently shot and killed by a family friend. The friend
tripped on deck steps and his rifle discharged. He was on his way to hunt
deer. P sued the ranch and a part-owner cattle company for failing to
maintain the steps in reasonable condition. Testimony on the actual
condition of the steps was contradictory and inconclusive.
Issue: Should summary judgment be granted against P when P fails to
establish to a preponderance that D's conduct was a necessary factor in the
causation of harm to the victim?
Rule: The plaintiff bears the burden of establishing by a preponderance of
the evidence that "but for" D's conduct the victim would not have suffered
injury.

Richardson v. Richardson-Merrell (1986)

Facts: Richardson alleged that her child's severe limb deformities were
caused by a drug she took during pregnancy, which was manufactured
by Richardson-Merrell.
Issue: Is circumstantial evidence sufficient to show that a drug is the cause
in fact of an injury?
Rule: A plaintiff has the burden of proving, by a preponderance of the
evidence, that a drug in question can cause injury and that the drug was the
cause of the plaintiff's injury. Evidence must be given on which a reasonable jury could conclude that the injury was more likely than not caused by
the drug.

City of Piqua v. Morris (1918)

Facts: The City of Piqua maintained a series of overflow ducts to its ponds that were negligently allowed to clog up. During a severe storm, water overflowed from the ducts and flooded the plaintiff's property. The flooding would have occurred regardless of the negligence.
Issue: Is a negligent party responsible for damages not caused by the party's negligence?
Rule: A party is not liable when "but for" the negligent act, the damages would have occurred anyway.

Stubbs v. City of Rochester (1919)

Facts: The plaintiff became infected with typhoid after drinking water supplied by the defendants. Evidence indicated that drinking water and firefighting water had been negligently mixed.
Issue: Must a plaintiff prove that no possible cause other than the defendant's negligence caused the plaintiff's injury?
Rule: The mere possibility that the cause in fact of a plaintiff's injury was not the defendant's negligence does not obligate the plaintiff to disprove the applicability of all possible causes.

Falcon v. Memorial Hospital (1990)

Facts: Falcon suffered from a respiratory and cardiac collapse and died after giving birth. Had her physicians inserted an intravenous line, she would have had a 37.5 percent greater chance of surviving.
Issue: May a person recover for a lost opportunity of avoiding physical harm that is less than 50 percent?
Rule: A person may recover for any *substantial* loss of opportunity of avoiding physical harm. However, one may only recover an amount equal to the percent chance lost times the value of the total harm incurred.
Note: A 37.5 percent greater chance of survival was considered substantial.

Mauro v. Raymark Industries, Inc. (1989)

Facts: Mauro was exposed to asbestos and sued for the enhanced risk of developing cancer. The experts he presented at trial could not quantify the risk he faced of developing the disease.
Issue: May one recover from a private entity for an unquantified enhanced risk of disease resulting from exposure to toxic chemicals?
Rule: One may not recover from a private entity for an unquantified enhanced risk of disease resulting from the exposure to toxic chemicals,

unless its occurrence is established as a matter of reasonable medical probability.

Hoyt v. Jeffers (1874)

Facts: Plaintiff claimed that a sawmill owned by the defendant emitted sparks that set fire to the plaintiff's hotel.
Issue: Can circumstantial evidence be used to prove causation?
Rule: Circumstantial evidence is admissible in an action for negligence; it is for the jury to decide what weight to give the evidence.

Smith v. Rapid Transit, Inc. (1945)

Facts: Smith's car was forced off the road by a bus, which she claimed was operated by the defendant. The defendant had the sole franchise for operating a bus line on that road.
Issue: Can mathematical probabilities be used to prove causation?
Rule: Absent other convincing evidence, mathematical probabilities cannot be used to prove causation.

CHAPTER 6

Proximate or Legal Cause

I. INTRODUCTION

The issue of proximate cause only arises after the plaintiff has proven that the defendant's negligence was the cause in fact of the plaintiff's injury. The doctrine limits liability for the effects of the defendant's negligence based on a policy determination that the defendant should not automatically be held liable for all the improbable and far-reaching consequences of an act.

II. UNFORESEEABLE CONSEQUENCES

A. Foreseeability
  1. Generally
     The majority of jurisdictions will hold a defendant liable for the results of negligent conduct only if the results were reasonably foreseeable. Both the type of damage and the specific plaintiff must be reasonably foreseeable. See Chief Judge Cardozo's opinion in Palsgraf v. Long Island R.R. Co.
  2. Exceptions to Foreseeability Rule
     Mnemonic: **MEDIC**
     a. Unforeseeable **M**anner
        One is liable for foreseeable harm that occurs in an unforeseeable manner.
        Example: An asbestos cement cover is dropped into a boiling vat of chemicals, placing others at risk of injury from the splash of the chemicals, but no one is actually hurt. A short time later the cover explodes (completely unforeseeable) and a plaintiff is hurt by the resulting splash (foreseeable injury caused in an unforeseeable manner).

b. Extent of Damages
One is liable for the unforeseeable extent of damages if they result from a foreseeable type of injury.

c. Improbability
Injury that is only remotely likely is considered foreseeable for purposes of liability.

d. Plaintiff Class
Even if injury to a particular plaintiff is not foreseeable, liability may be imposed if the plaintiff is a member of a class that could foreseeably be injured.
Example: Two boats crash into a bridge and the debris clogs the river. As a result, the backed-up water floods the plaintiff's land. The landowners are held to be a foreseeable class. See Petition of Kinsman Transit Co. (Kinsman No. 1).

B. Direct Causation
The minority of jurisdictions will hold a defendant liable for all the direct consequences of negligent conduct, regardless of whether the consequences are foreseeable.

III. INTERVENING CAUSES

A. Generally
An intervening cause is an action by a different party or entity that occurs after a defendant's negligent action and contributes to the plaintiff's injury. The main issue is whether the intervening cause breaks the chain of causation such that the original defendant is no longer liable.

B. Foreseeable Intervening Cause
Where the acts of the intervening party are foreseeable, or the kind of harm suffered by the plaintiff is foreseeable, the defendant is not relieved of liability.
Examples of foreseeable intervening causes:

1. Responses to Danger
Responses to a dangerous situation created by the defendant are generally considered foreseeable intervening causes. For example, a defendant who created a dangerous situation would be liable for injuries incurred during:
   a. a reasonable escape attempt,
   b. rescue effort, or
   c. an attempt to provide medical treatment.

2. Negligence of Intervening Party
The negligence of a third party is generally a foreseeable intervening cause. Such is the case when it is the risk of negligence by the third party that makes the original party's conduct

negligent. For example, one who sells liquor to an intoxicated person, knowing that the person will subsequently drive a car, will be liable for the consequences of the intoxicated person's negligent driving. Note that this usually applies to tavern keepers and not to social hosts.

3. Subsequent Disease or Accident

If one's negligent act causes another to be more susceptible to disease or further accident, the negligent actor is liable for the consequences of the subsequent intervening disease or accident.

C. Superseding Intervening Cause

If the intervening act is not foreseeable, it is a superseding cause such that the original negligent defendant may be relieved of liability for the damages caused by the intervening party.

Examples of superseding intervening causes:

1. Malicious Acts

Intentional, malicious, or criminal conduct by a third party is sufficiently unforeseeable to relieve a defendant of liability.

2. Gross or Extraordinary Negligence

Whereas ordinary negligence by a third party is considered foreseeable, extraordinary negligence is not and may relieve a defendant of liability.

3. Acts of Nature

Acts of nature, also known as acts of God, are unforeseeable, and will relieve a defendant of liability if the damage caused is different than that which was threatened by the defendant.

4. Suicide

Suicide is a superseding intervening cause if the person who committed suicide was not driven by an irresistible impulse.

IV. SHIFTING RESPONSIBILITY

Sometimes a negligent actor will be relieved of liability if responsibility for the dangerous situation passes to a third party. Although there is no general rule stating when responsibility will pass from one party to another, the courts will generally consider whether:

A. the actor's negligence was a substantial cause of the plaintiff's injury,

B. the actor's negligence was of a continuing nature,

C. the injury incurred was of the same type expected to result from the actor's negligence, and

D. the actor should reasonably have foreseen the negligence of the third party.

CASE CLIPS

Atlantic Coast Line R. Co. v. Daniels (1911)

Facts: Not presented.
Issue: Can an injured party recover for any injury when "but for" defendant's action, the injury would not have occurred?
Rule: When the "but for" test has established cause in fact, the courts must determine if the wrongful act was also the proximate cause before allowing recovery.

Enright v. Eli Lilly and Co. (1991)

Facts: Plaintiff alleged that the disabilities suffered by her daughter were attributable to the ingestion of DES by the plaintiff's mother during pregnancy.
Issue: Does a cause of action lie in favor of a child for injuries to its mother suffered as a result of exposure to a prescription drug?
Rule: Multigenerational causes of action are not valid. An injury to a mother that results in a later-conceived child does not establish a cause of action in favor of the child against the original tortfeasor. Liability is limited to those who ingested the drug or were exposed to it in utero.

Ryan v. New York Central R.R. Co. (1866)

Facts: The Railroad Company carelessly burned its own woodshed. The fire spread and burned Ryan's house.
Issue: What factors distinguish proximate damages of an accident (recoverable) from remote damages of an accident (not recoverable)?
Rule: Proximate damages are the anticipated, ordinary, natural, and necessary consequence of an accident. Remote damages do not necessarily follow from the occurrence of an accident, but rather result from accidental and varying circumstances.

Bartolone v. Jeckovich (1984)

Facts: Bartolone was in a car accident from which he received minor physical injuries that caused him to have an acute psychotic breakdown.
Issue: Is a defendant who negligently inflicts physical harm on another liable for unforeseeable damages caused by that harm?
Rule: A defendant is liable for all damages proximately caused by one's negligent conduct, even if the specific extent or type of injury was unforeseeable. The defendant must take the plaintiff as he finds him.

Steinhauser v. Hertz Corp. (1970)

Facts: Steinhauser's schizophrenic tendencies were severely aggravated by a car accident that resulted from the defendant's negligence.
Issue: Is a negligent actor liable for aggravating an underlying illness?
Rule: An actor who negligently aggravates a preexisting illness is liable, but damages should be lower than if the actor had caused the illness originally.

In Re Arbitration Between Polemis and Furness, Withy and Co., Ltd. (1921)

Facts: The defendant chartered a vessel from the plaintiff to transport chemicals. The defendant's negligent handling of a plank on the ship created a spark. The resulting explosion destroyed the plaintiff's ship.
Issue: Is a person liable for those consequences of a negligent act that are not reasonably foreseeable?
Rule: One is liable for all direct results of one's negligence regardless of whether the type of injury could have been anticipated.
Note: This case was later overruled by Wagon Mound No. 1.

Overseas Tankship (U.K.) Ltd. v. Morts Dock & Engineering Co., Ltd. (1961) "Wagon Mound No. 1"

Facts: A vessel owned by Overseas Tankship negligently discharged oil, which caused minor damage to a wharf owned by Morts Dock. Further, the oil ignited, causing severe damage to the wharf.
Issue: Is a party liable for damages that arise directly from its negligent act if they are not reasonably foreseeable?
Rule: One is not liable for unlikely and unforeseeable results of a negligent act, even if they are direct.
Note: This case expressly rejects the rule set forth in In re Polemis.

Overseas Tankship (U.K.) Ltd. v. Miller Steamship Co. (1966) "Wagon Mound No. 2"

Facts: Same as previous case, but the plaintiffs were the owners of two ships docked at the wharf.
Issue: Are damages that result from a remote risk considered reasonably foreseeable?
Rule: Damages that result from a remote risk are reasonably foreseeable such that one who knows of a remote risk, and can reasonably limit that risk, is liable for damages resulting from the failure to take precautions against it.

Palsgraf v. Long Island R.R. Co. (1928)

Facts: A railroad employee pushed a man from behind, hoping to help him board a moving train. The man dropped his package, causing the fireworks contained within to explode. The explosion caused scales at the other end of the platform to fall, injuring Palsgraf.

Issue: Is one liable for damages to an unforeseeable third party resulting from one's negligent acts toward a second party?

Rule: An actor owes no duty of care to unforeseeable plaintiffs, and thus is not liable to an unforeseeable plaintiff for damages resulting from a negligent act toward another.

Dissent: An actor has a duty to the public at large. An actor who commits a wrongful act is liable not only to those who would likely be injured by the act, but to all whose injuries are in fact proximately caused by the act.

Note: Chief Judge Cardozo, addressing the question as an issue of duty, never reaches the question of proximate cause as does Judge Andrews in the dissent.

Petition of Kinsman Transit Co. (1964) "Kinsman No. 1"

Facts: Employees of Kinsman Transit negligently moored a boat. The boat broke loose due to pressure from floating ice and floated downstream. The ship hit another ship and both crashed into a city-owned drawbridge, clogging up the river and causing a flood on plaintiffs' property.

Issue: Is a negligent party liable for completely unforeseeable damages?

Rule: Unforeseeability of the exact developments and of the extent of loss will not limit liability if the damages are the consequence of the same risk that made the original act negligent and are of the same general sort that was expected.

Derdiarian v. Felix Contracting Corp. (1981)

Facts: Derdiarian was hit by a negligently driven car while at work. Derdiarian alleged that the accident was cause by his employer's failure to erect a barrier or to install warning signs around the construction site.

Issue: Is the negligence of a third party always a superseding act that will relieve a negligent defendant of liability?

Rule: An intervening act may not serve as a superseding cause to relieve an actor of responsibility where the risk of the intervening act occurring is the very same risk that renders the actor negligent. The negligence of the intervening actor is irrelevant because the risk created by the intervening actor was foreseeable.

Weirum v. RKO General, Inc. (1975)

Facts: A radio station sponsored a contest giving prizes to the first person to find its disc jockey at different locations in the city. The plaintiff was killed by a driver who was speeding to reach the disc jockey's location.
Issue: If one's conduct encourages a negligent response by another, is the party liable for the other's negligence?
Rule: If it is foreseeable that a party's conduct will cause others to behave in a negligent and dangerous manner, that party will not be relieved of liability by the intervening negligence of another.

Watson v. Kentucky & Indiana Bridge & R.R. Co. (1910)

Facts: A derailed railroad car spewed gasoline onto the street. Watson sued the railroad company for injuries suffered when a third party ignited the gasoline by throwing a match.
Issue: Is an unexpected and extraordinary act by a third party an intervening cause that relieves a negligent defendant from liability?
Rule: Whether an intervening act supersedes a defendant's liability depends on whether the act is negligent or intentional. Because an intervening negligent act by a third party is foreseeable, it does not relieve a negligent defendant from liability. However, an intervening act that is intentional, malicious, or criminal is less likely to be foreseeable and may relieve a defendant from liability.

Kelly v. Gwinnell (1984)

Facts: Defendant, Zak, served a number of drinks to Gwinnell, a guest in his home, and escorted him to his car. Kelly was injured in a head-on collision with Gwinnell, who was intoxicated.
Issue: Is a host liable for the negligence of an adult social guest who has become intoxicated at the host's home?
Rule: A host who serves liquor to an adult social guest, knowing that the guest is intoxicated and will thereafter be operating a motor vehicle, is liable for injuries to a third party that result from the guest's negligent driving when such negligence is caused by the intoxication.
Note: Holding a social host liable for the actions of an intoxicated guest is the minority rule.

Wagner v. International Railway Co. (1921)

Facts: Wagner's cousin was thrown from a door left open on the defendant's train after the train suddenly swayed. Wagner was killed while attempting to rescue his cousin.

Issue: Is a party whose negligence placed another in peril liable for injuries suffered by rescuers?
Rule: Because it is foreseeable that rescuers will attempt to assist a person in peril, the party that placed the person in peril is liable for injuries sustained by the rescuers.

Tuttle v. Atlantic City R.R. (1901)

Facts: Tuttle fell while running from a derailed railroad car that was heading toward her. Had she stayed in her original place she would not have been injured.
Issue: Can a person who is injured while escaping from what is perceived as a danger recover from a negligent defendant who caused the situation?
Rule: If a negligent defendant puts a plaintiff under a reasonable apprehension of personal physical injury and the plaintiff is injured in a reasonable effort to escape, a right of action arises to recover for the injury.

Fuller v. Preis (1974)

Facts: Dr. Lewis suffered traumatic damage to his brain after a car accident with the defendant. Seven months later, Lewis committed suicide after suffering three seizures in one day. The plaintiff asserted that the defendant proximately caused decedent's suicide.
Issue: Is suicide a superseding cause precluding liability?
Rule: Suicide is not a superseding cause precluding liability if the suicide is the result of an irresistible impulse (e.g., mental derangement).

Larrimore v. American National Insurance Co. (1939)

Facts: The plaintiff was injured by an exploding can of rat poison placed near a stove by his employer. A state statute prohibited storage of rat poison in an unsafe place.
Issue: Is one liable for neglecting a duty imposed by statute?
Rule: One is liable for neglecting a duty imposed by statute only when the injury is of the kind that the statute is designed to protect against.

Carter v. Kinney (1995)

Facts: P went to Ds' home to attend a Bible study class. He slipped and fell on a patch of ice in the driveway and broke his leg. D had shoveled the driveway the night before but was unaware that ice had formed.
Issue: Does the homeowner's duty of care extend to all hazards on the property that might be reasonably foreseeable or discoverable?

Rule: The social host owes licensees a duty of reasonable warning and protection against known dangers, but not those that could have been discovered only by reasonable inspection.

Dellwo v. Pearson (1961)

Facts: The defendant, age 12, drove a motorboat over the plaintiff's fishing line, shattering the plaintiff's reel. A piece of the reel struck the plaintiff's glasses, causing an eye injury.

Issue: Is one's negligence the proximate cause of an injury when the injury is an unforeseeable result of the negligent act?

Rule: Negligence is judged by foresight, whereas proximate cause is judged by hindsight. Proximate cause exists whether or not the actor could have foreseen the outcome of the negligent act. There is no foreseeability requirement for proximate cause.

Herrera v. Quality Pontiac (2003)

Facts: D failed to lock or remove keys from a customer's car left for servicing. The car was stolen and later involved in a high-speed chase. The stolen car collided with a parked car, killing one person and injuring another. The latter sued D for their personal injuries.

Issue: Are the plaintiffs' injuries beyond the car dealership's scope of duty in tort?

Rule: The car dealership's initial negligence set in motion a series of events that (arguably) reasonably foreseeably reached the plaintiffs in question despite the intervening criminal conduct of the thief.

Watson v. Rheinderknecht (1901)

Facts: The plaintiff was injured by the defendant's assault and battery. The plaintiff was especially sensitive because of prior injuries suffered while serving in the army.

Issue: May a party recover for an injury that was especially severe because of prior trauma?

Rule: A party is liable for the direct and immediate consequences of its negligent acts, including the aggravation of an existing injury.

Heins v. Webster Cty. (1996)

Facts: P visited his daughter at her place of work in the hospital. At the hospital entrance, he fell on snow and ice and brought suit against the hospital for his injuries.

Issue: What standard of care applies to the owner of land (or occupiers of premises) in regard to persons who come onto the land?
Rule: The common-law classification of invitee and licensee is no longer applicable; rather, a standard of reasonable care applies to all who are on the land but for trespassers.

McLaughlin v. Mine Safety Appliance Co. (1962)

Facts: McLaughlin was burned when a firefighter tried to warm her with heating blocks. The blocks' manufacturer had posted a warning on the wrapping, but not on the item itself, and had demonstrated proper use of the blocks, which the firefighter ignored.
Issue: Is a negligent manufacturer liable for injuries despite the negligence of the person using the products?
Rule: Gross negligence in the use of a product is a superseding intervening cause relieving a manufacturer of liability for its negligence.

Stahlecker v. Ford Motor Co. (2003)

Facts: Owner of a Ford Explorer was stranded in a remote area when a defective tire on her vehicle failed. She then was assaulted and killed. Her parents sued Ford and the tire manufacturer for negligently enabling a murder.
Issue: What scope of duty applies to commercial vendors who make and sell products to the public at large?
Rule: The commercial vendors of tires that turn out to be defective do not assume responsibility for the criminal conduct of others when their so-called negligence itself does not produce injury. The murder of the victim was a "superseding intervening cause" that broke the causal linking.

Godesky v. Provo City (1984)

Facts: Godesky was electrocuted when, at his boss's instruction, he grabbed an uninsulated wire owned by the defendant.
Issue: Does an intervening negligent act automatically become a superseding cause, relieving the original actor of liability?
Rule: A foreseeable intervening negligent act does not become a superseding cause that relieves the original actor of liability. The foreseeable intervening negligence is a concurrent cause.

Virden v. Betts & Beer Constr. Co. (2003)

Facts: Maintenance worker fell from a ladder when he attempted to reinstall an iron bar in the weight room. D built the weight room, but was not consulted on how to reattach the iron bar. Although the positioning of the ladder was hindered by weight equipment, P did not seek assistance in placing the ladder.

Issue: Did the construction company's alleged negligence play a significant role in bringing about P's injury?

Rule: If the D's would-be negligence is not a substantial factor in bringing about P's harm, it cannot serve as a proximate cause of the injury.

Newlin v. The New England Telephone & Telegraph Co. (1944)

Facts: The New England Telephone and Telegraph Company's negligently maintained telephone pole fell on a power line, cutting off Newlin's cooling system and killing his mushrooms.

Issue: Is a party liable for all the results of its negligent acts?

Rule: A party is liable for all damages that are the proximate result of its negligence. Proximate cause does not involve foresight.

Union Oil Co. v. Oppen (1974)

Facts: Union Oil Company's oil drilling operations caused an oil spill that killed a large number of fish, causing economic losses to the plaintiff, a commercial fisher.

Issue: Does a cause of action lie for loss of prospective income caused by a defendant's negligence?

Rule: Foreseeable economic losses may be recovered in a negligence action.

Gorris v. Scott (1874)

Facts: The plaintiff's sheep were washed overboard from the defendant's ship. Had the defendant complied with health statutes, the sheep would not have been lost.

Issue: Is a statutory violation alone sufficient evidence to prove a defendant's negligence?

Rule: To invoke a violation of a statute as evidence of negligence, the plaintiff must show that the injury sustained was of the type the statute was intended to prevent.

Berry v. The Borough of Sugar Notch (1899)

Facts: Berry, a train engineer, was injured when a tree fell on him as the train he operated passed underneath the tree at a rate in excess of a local speeding ordinance. The borough of Sugar Notch had been negligent in maintaining the tree.

Issue: Does a plaintiff's statutory violation at the time of a defendant's negligence bar the plaintiff from recovery of damages?
Rule: A plaintiff's statutory violation will not bar a plaintiff from recovering if the violation was not the cause of the accident, and did not contribute to it.

Brower v. New York Central & H.R.R. (1918)

Facts: The defendant's negligence in its operation of a train crossing caused Brower's horse and wagon to be destroyed in a train collision. The driver of the wagon was stunned and unable to stop thieves from stealing merchandise that was in the wagon.
Issue: If a defendant's negligence causes an accident, is it also the proximate cause of the theft of property that occurs after the accident?
Rule: When negligence leaves a person unable to protect one's property, it is foreseeable that the property will be stolen. Thus, the party's negligence is the proximate cause of the property loss.

McCoy v. Am. Suzuki Motor Corp. (1998)

Facts: P sued American Suzuki for the injuries he sustained after assisting in an accident involving a Suzuki Samurai. P rendered assistance to a badly injured driver who swerved off the road and rolled in front of him. Upon returning to his vehicle, P was struck by a hit-and-run driver. He sued the car manufacturer and others, claiming that the car's defective condition was the proximate cause of his injuries.
Issue: Can a party injured by the act of another party allege that a manufacturing defect in yet another party's vehicle created the danger that led to his injury?
Rule: The rescue doctrine allows an injured rescuer to claim that a defective product created the danger that required the rescue and engendered its attendant consequences.

Marshall v. Nugent (1955)

Facts: A defendant forced Marshall's car off the road, offered to help get the car back on the road, and suggested that the driver of the car warn oncoming traffic. As the driver of the car tried to give warning, Nugent lost control of his oncoming car and hit him.
Issue: If a person is rendered vulnerable to further injury by a party's negligence, is the negligent party liable for the further injuries that result?
Rule: An injury that is a foreseeable result of a negligent act is not a superseding intervening cause. The defendant is liable to the plaintiff for such an injury.

Ford v. Trident Fisheries Co. (1919)

Facts: Ford fell overboard from the defendant's trawler and immediately disappeared. The rescue attempt was slowed by the improper installation of a lifeboat, and Ford drowned.

Issue: When is an act or omission regarded as a proximate cause?

Rule: An act is not regarded as a proximate cause if the particular event would have occurred without it.

Hill v. Lundin & Associates, Inc. (1972)

Facts: Lundin left a ladder leaning against a house at a job site. A third party later placed the ladder on the ground, where Hill subsequently tripped over it and injured herself.

Issue: When is a person liable for a harm that would not have occurred but for their actions?

Rule: For a person to be liable, that person must be a proximate cause of the accident creating the risk of harm that subsequently injures the plaintiff.

Herbert v. Enos (2004)

Facts: P suffered an electrical shock allegedly when he touched an outdoor faucet. He claimed that D's faulty repair of a toilet caused flooding in the home that he further contended damaged the home electrical system, causing it to electrify the faucet.

Issue: Does the plaintiff need to establish a credible link between his injury and D's conduct and that his injury was a reasonably foreseeable consequence of D's alleged negligence?

Rule: The connection between toilet flooding and an electrified external faucet is too "extraordinary" and tenuous to establish reasonably foreseeable causality between D's would-be negligence and P's injury.

Yun v. Ford Motor Co. (1994)

Facts: P's father ran across two lanes of traffic to retrieve a spare tire assembly unit that dislodged from the van while it was being driven. The bracket holding the tire apparently failed. During the attempted retrieval, P's father was struck by a vehicle and killed.

Issue: Did the decedent's conduct constitute an intervening superseding event that defeated a claim based on strict product liability and defectiveness?

Rule: Victim's conduct constituted an intervening superseding event that warranted dismissal of the action because his behavior was highly extraordinary and did not comply with normal standards and expectations. Victim causation was further substantiated by the victim's decision not to repair the bracket mechanism 30 days before.

CHAPTER 7

Joint Tortfeasors

I. LIABILITY AND JOINDER OF DEFENDANTS

A. Plaintiff Recovers Once

A plaintiff can only recover once for an injury; that is, the entire amount paid by all the joint tortfeasors has to equal the value of the plaintiff's damages.

B. Indivisible Harm

If more than one tortfeasor was a proximate cause of an injury and the harm to a plaintiff is indivisible, then each tortfeasor is liable for the entire harm (i.e., jointly and severally liable). If one party does not pay its share of the damages, the other parties will have to pay for that share.

1. Burden of Proof

The defendants have the burden of proving apportionment of the harm among themselves. Harm that occurs from successive accidents is sometimes considered indivisible.

2. Those to Whom Joint and Several Liability Applies

a. Concurrent Tortfeasors

Each defendant acts independently of the others, but they all combine to cause a single indivisible injury.

b. Joint Tortfeasors

All the defendants have acted together to harm the plaintiff.

c. Divisible Harm

If the harm is divisible, then each tortfeasor is only liable for that part of the harm that each proximately caused, unless the two tortfeasors acted in concert. If one party does not pay its share, the other parties are still only liable for their own shares.

II. SATISFACTION AND RELEASE

A. Satisfaction

Once a party has recovered the entire value of its injury from the defendant(s), the party may no longer collect against the other defendant(s).

B. Release

If a party settles its case with one of the defendants, this may release the other defendants from liability unless the party manifests an intent to still hold the other defendants liable.

III. CONTRIBUTION

This is an action by one party against the other jointly and severally liable parties to recover the amount the party had to pay in excess of its share of the damages.

A. Not Applicable To:

1. Intentional Tortfeasors
2. Worker's Compensation Cases
3. Individual Defense

   For example, a party who has some defense that makes it not liable to the original plaintiff, even though it acted in concert with the other parties.

B. Settlement

If one party settles with a plaintiff, it is entitled to contribution from its cotortfeasors if the settlement amount was reasonable. The settling party may nevertheless have to pay contribution to other parties who go to court and lose their cases. Some courts, in the latter case, reduce the plaintiff's total claim by the amount of the first party's pro rata share, so that the other parties cannot get contribution.

IV. INDEMNITY

Indemnity is the shifting of the entire loss to the tortfeasor with a disproportionate share of the culpability. Unlike contribution, the court makes a 100 percent shift in payment.

Examples:

A. Passive Negligence

A passively negligent defendant can recover from one who is actively negligent.

B. Reliance

A retailer who relies on the quality control of a manufacturer may recover from the manufacturer if a defective product causes damage.

C. Degree

In situations where there are vast differences in the degrees of fault of each defendant, one defendant may have to take the responsibility for all the damages.

D. Vicariously Liable

One defendant may be vicariously liable for another's negligence due to a legal relationship (i.e., employer-employee).

CASE CLIPS

Bierczynski v. Rogers (1968)

Facts: Two defendants were drag racing when one of them struck Rogers's car, injuring the plaintiffs.
Issue: Are multiple tortfeasors each liable where only one of them actually caused the injuries to a third party?
Rule: When tortfeasors act in concert, each participant is liable for harm to third persons arising from the tortious conduct of the other.

Coney v. J.L.G. Indus., Inc. (1983)

Facts: Coney died while operating a machine manufactured by J.L.G. J.L.G. argued that Coney's employer was guilty of comparative negligence, and thus joint and several liability did not apply.
Issue: Does the doctrine of comparative negligence eliminate joint and several liability?
Rule: Where damages are apportioned according to each party's fault, under the doctrine of comparative negligence, joint and several liability is still used to protect the interests of plaintiffs.

Bartlett v. New Mexico Welding Supply, Inc. (1982)

Facts: Bartlett slammed her brakes to avoid a negligently driven car. The defendant, unable to stop, crashed into Bartlett's car from behind.
Issue: Does the doctrine of "pure" comparative negligence eliminate joint and several liability?
Rule: Pure comparative negligence eliminates joint and several liability; a concurrent tortfeasor is not liable.
Note: Jurisdictions are divided on this issue.

Bundt v. Embro (1965)

Facts: Several plaintiffs and defendants were involved in an accident between two cars. Some defendants asserted the defense of discharge and satisfaction because the plaintiffs had recovered against the state.
Issue: Can a party sue one joint tortfeasor for damages if the party has already recovered full damages from the other joint tortfeasor?
Rule: One who is injured by joint tortfeasors can recover damages against each or all, but the total damages recovered cannot exceed the single damage award (i.e., there can be only one satisfaction).

Cox v. Pearl Investment Co. (1969)

Facts: Cox signed a document with one joint tortfeasor settling Cox's case, but expressly reserved the right to sue other joint tortfeasors.

Issue: When signing a release of one joint tortfeasor, is a clause that retains the right to sue other joint tortfeasors valid?

Rule: A contract releasing one joint tortfeasor but expressly reserving the right to sue other tortfeasors is valid in its entirety.

Elbaor v. Smith (1992)

Facts: Smith settled all medical malpractice claims against one group of defendants and entered into a "Mary Carter" settlement agreement with all but one doctor in the second group. That doctor, Elbaor, requested that the agreements be voided. A Mary Carter agreement exists when a plaintiff enters into a settlement with one defendant and goes to trial against the other defendant(s).

Issue: Should Mary Carter agreements, in which a plaintiff enters into an agreement with one defendant and goes to trial against the other defendant(s), thereby discouraging compromise and skewing the trial process, be voided as violative of public policy?

Rule: Mary Carter agreements, which exist when a plaintiff enters into a settlement with one defendant and goes to trial against the other defendant(s), violate notions of strong public policy. They inflict damage on the adversarial system through their advancement of partial settlements, which promote rather than discourage further litigation.

Note: This is the minority view. The majority of jurisdictions allow the agreements so long as procedural safeguards are implemented and enforced.

Knell v. Feltman (1949)

Facts: Feltman and Knell were involved in a car accident in which Knell's passenger was injured. Both were negligently responsible, but the passenger only sued Feltman, who brought a third-party complaint against Knell to have the court force Knell to share in the damages.

Issue: Is contribution between two concurrently negligent tortfeasors allowed when only one was named in a plaintiff's action?

Rule: The right to seek contribution belongs to tortfeasors who must pay damages and it permits the inclusion of concurrently negligent tortfeasors, even if there was not a joint judgment against them.

Yellow Cab Co. of D.C., Inc. v. Dreslin (1950)

Facts: Defendants and Dreslin were involved in a car accident in which Dreslin's passenger, his wife, was injured and both parties were negligently responsible. Defendants sued Dreslin for contribution.

Issue: May a defendant sue for contribution against a joint tortfeasor who could not be held liable to the plaintiff?

Rule: Because the right of contribution arises out of the joint liability of both defendants, there is no contribution against a tortfeasor who is not liable to a plaintiff.

Note: Interspousal tort immunity and parent-child tort immunity are some examples where neither party is liable in tort to the other.

Tolbert v. Gerber Indus., Inc. (1977)

Facts: Defendants, a manufacturer and an installer of defective equipment, were found jointly and severally liable. The trial court ordered 100 percent indemnity for the installer from the manufacturer.

Issue: May a joint tortfeasor, who was "passively" or "secondarily" negligent, seek full indemnification from the other tortfeasor, who was "actively" or "primarily" negligent, or should the joint tortfeasors be liable according to their degrees of culpability?

Rule: Each joint tortfeasor should pay their proportional share of the negligence because indemnity is not available to one joint tortfeasor who was passively negligent in discovering the other's negligence.

Bruckman v. Pena (1971)

Facts: Pena was injured in a car accident with Bruckman. The injuries were aggravated in another accident almost a year later, at which point Pena sued Bruckman for the entire injury.

Issue: Is a defendant liable for the entire injury when the original injury caused by the defendant is later aggravated?

Rule: Defendants are not liable for a subsequent injury that aggravates an injury they originally caused, even if damages cannot be apportioned.

Michie v. Great Lakes Steel Division, Nat'l Steel Corp. (1974)

Facts: Plaintiffs were injured by the negligent actions of three individual corporations, who acted independently of each other.

Issue: Can individual tortfeasors be jointly and severally liable even if they operate independently of each other?

Rule: Where the combined negligence of independent parties causes a single and indivisible injury, the parties are held jointly and severally liable. The defendants then have the burden of proving the scope of their individual contributions.

Dillon v. Twin State Gas & Electric Co. (1932)

Facts: Dillon slipped while playing on a bridge and was electrocuted when he grabbed a wire in an effort to save himself.
Issue: Should a damages award for wrongful death be reduced when a plaintiff would have died regardless of a defendant's negligence?
Rule: The court can restrict a damages award for wrongful death by considering the alternative outcomes and awarding only the difference between one of those possibilities and what actually happened.

Johnson v. Chapman (1897)

Facts: The defendants were negligent in maintaining a wall common to both their warehouses. The wall collapsed, injuring the plaintiff.
Issue: Can two defendants be held jointly liable when their separate negligent acts caused an injury?
Rule: Two persons separately and independently contributing to an injury may be held jointly and severally liable for the entire injury. A court will hold each proportionally liable.

Hillman v. Wallin (1974)

Facts: Hillman was hit in the eye with a plastic hose that several boys were playing with while riding in a school bus. Wallin, the bus driver, was aware that the boys were playing with the hose, but he did not stop them.
Issue: Can a defendant who is passively negligent seek indemnity from defendants who are actively negligent?
Rule: A party who is passively negligent in failing to supervise actively negligent persons is only secondarily liable and can recover indemnification from the actively negligent defendants.

Hymowitz v. Eli Lilly & Co. (1989)

Facts: The plaintiffs alleged that they were injured by prenatal exposure to the drug DES. There were approximately 300 manufacturers who at one time produced DES, and there were numerous DES cases pending. DES had a single chemical composition and was marketed generically.

Issue: May a plaintiff recover against the manufacturer of a generically marketed drug when identification of the producer of the specific drug that caused the plaintiff's injury is impossible?

Rule: When there are numerous plaintiffs and numerous defendant manufacturers, and neither the plaintiffs nor the defendants can identify who caused each plaintiff's injuries, plaintiffs may recover from each defendant an amount of damages that corresponds to the defendant's share of the national market.

Note: Defendants who can prove that their drug did not injure a particular plaintiff are not relieved of liability because liability is no longer based on the causal link between a particular defendant and a particular plaintiff, but rather is based on each defendant's overall liability.

CHAPTER 8

Limited Duty

I. GENERALLY

As part of the cause of action for negligence, the plaintiff must show that the defendant actually had a duty not to expose the plaintiff to an unreasonable risk.

One of the issues that requires further examination is how far the duty extends. This explores whether one has a duty to avoid causing mental disturbance to another, whether one has an affirmative duty to act, whether there is a duty to unborn children, and whether parties to a contract have a duty to parties not in privity.

II. MENTAL DISTURBANCE AND RESULTING INJURY

It is difficult for plaintiffs to recover damages for mental suffering that is unaccompanied by physical injury. The reluctance to grant recovery is due to the difficulty in proving emotional damage in the absence of physical proof, the fear of excessive and fraudulent claims, and an absence of precedent.

A. Physical Impact Rule

If a plaintiff was actually hit and injured by a defendant, the courts will allow recovery for mental suffering that naturally follows from the impact as a "parasitic" damage.

B. Emotional Injury Without Physical Impact

1. Majority View

In the absence of a physical impact, the majority of jurisdictions will only allow recovery for mental distress if it is accompanied by physical symptoms.

Exception: Recovery for pure emotional distress that is unaccompanied by physical symptoms is allowed in extreme cases such as the mishandling of a corpse or the misdiagnosis of a serious illness.

2. Minority View
A minority of courts allow recovery for the negligent infliction of emotional distress in the absence of physical impact or physical symptoms where the facts are such that a reasonable jury could believe that the emotional distress was genuine.

C. Physical Injury Without Physical Impact
The majority view is that a plaintiff can recover for physical injuries that result from emotional distress even if there was no physical impact.

D. Fear for the Safety of Others
1. "Zone of Danger" Rule
Some jurisdictions will not allow recovery for emotional distress caused by the fear for another's safety, unless the plaintiff's safety was imperiled as well. That is, the plaintiff must have been within the "zone of danger" to recover, even if the emotional distress was accompanied by physical symptoms.

2. Other View
Some states have abandoned the "zone of danger" rule and will allow recovery depending on:
a. How near the plaintiff was to the place of the accident,
b. Whether the plaintiff directly witnessed the accident, and
c. Whether the plaintiff was closely related to the injured party.

III. FAILURE TO ACT

A. Generally
There is generally no duty to act for the benefit of another if one has not created the risk.

B. Exceptions
There are certain situations where one has an affirmative duty to act such that liability will be imposed for failing to act.
Mnemonic: **SAP**

1. **S**pecial Relationship
a. Between Defendant and Plaintiff
If the defendant has a special relationship with the plaintiff such as parent-child, husband-wife, or hospital-patient, there is an affirmative duty to act on the plaintiff's behalf. This category also covers innkeepers, common carriers, and other business relationships.

b. Between Defendant and Third Party
In certain cases the defendant may have a special relationship with a third party that places a duty on the defendant

to control that party or prevent that party from harming others.

Example: The relationship between a psychiatrist and a patient imparts a duty on the psychiatrist to warn a party to whom the patient poses an immediate threat of serious harm. See Tarasoff v. Regents of Univ. of California.

2. Assumption of Duty

One who is not under a duty to act but does so anyway must proceed with reasonable care, and cannot leave the party if doing so would leave the injured party in worse condition than when assistance began.

Note: A physician who helps on the scene is only liable for "gross negligence."

3. Peril Caused by Defendant

If the defendant either negligently or innocently puts the plaintiff in danger, the defendant has a duty to help.

IV. UNBORN CHILDREN

A. At Common Law

At common law, one did not owe a duty to an unborn child. For example, a child born with defects that were caused while still in the womb could not sue the responsible party for damages.

B. Recently

Over the past 40 years, some courts have modified the common law view by allowing recovery for damages caused while one was still in the womb in one of two situations:

1. Viable Fetus

Some courts require that there be a viable fetus at the time that the injury occurred. Some courts have considered a fetus that was a few weeks old to be viable.

2. Born Alive

Some courts require that the child be born alive.

C. Wrongful Life

A suit was brought by a plaintiff against those people responsible for the plaintiff's birth. Courts have generally rejected such suits on the theory that one cannot argue that he was better off not being born. These suits are most likely to be allowed for congenital defects that, if properly diagnosed during a mother's pregnancy, would have led her to abort. Usually plaintiffs recover for medical expenses and sometimes for mental and emotional suffering.

V. PRIVITY OF CONTRACT

A. Nonfeasance

Nonfeasance is the failure to perform a contractual promise.

1. Parties to the Contract

One party to a contract may sue another party to the contract for nonfeasance under contract law, but not under tort law.

Exception: Common carriers and public utilities are liable in tort even when a contract exists.

2. Third Parties

One who is not a party to a contract may not sue a party to the contract for nonfeasance under contract law or tort law.

Exception: A third-party beneficiary of a contract may sue a party to a contract for nonfeasance under contract law.

B. Misfeasance

Misfeasance of a contract is the improper performance of a duty under the contract.

1. Parties to the Contract

A party to a contract may recover for another party's misfeasance under either contract law or tort law.

2. Third Parties

Modern courts have not usually required a party to be in privity to a contract to recover in tort. For example, a third party may recover in tort from a manufacturer of a defective good even if the good was purchased from a dealer.

Exception: A party who has not contracted with an attorney may not sue the attorney for misfeasance unless the party is an intended beneficiary of the contract.

CASE CLIPS

Daley v. LaCroix (1970)

Facts: LaCroix's negligent driving caused a chain of events that led to an explosion in Daley's house. Daley did not suffer any physical injury from the explosion, but sued for physical injuries caused by her emotional distress.

Issue: May one recover for physical injuries that result from the negligent infliction of emotional distress?

Rule: When a physical illness or injury arises naturally from emotional distress that was proximately caused by a defendant's negligent conduct, a plaintiff may recover for such physical injury even in the absence of physical impact at the time of the accident.

Thing v. La Chusa (1989)

Facts: Thing neither saw nor heard the accident in which her son was injured, yet she alleged that she suffered great emotional distress, proximately caused by the defendant's negligence.

Issue: Can a mother who did not witness an accident in which her child was struck by an automobile recover damages for the emotional distress she suffered upon her arrival on the scene?

Rule: Recovery of damages for emotional distress is limited to persons closely related by blood or marriage. A relative claiming emotional distress must have been present at the scene of the accident at the time it occurred and must have been aware that an injury occurred.

St. Elizabeth Hospital v. Garrard (1987)

Facts: Garrard sued the hospital for mental anguish arising from its negligent disposal of her stillborn child in an unmarked, common grave.

Issue: May one assert an action for negligent infliction of mental anguish without physical manifestation of the anguish?

Rule: Physical injury resulting from mental anguish is not a necessary element in an action for negligent infliction of mental anguish.

Hegel v. Langsam (1971)

Facts: Plaintiff's child associated with criminals, started using drugs, and was regularly absent from her dormitory while she attended the defendant's university.

Issue: Does a university have a special relationship with its students that would create an affirmative obligation to act on the students' behalf?

Rule: A university and its employees are not required to regulate the private lives of their students, to control their comings and goings, or to supervise their associations.

Yania v. Bigan (1959)

Facts: Bigan taunted Yania into jumping in a water-filled ditch on his property. Yania drowned after Bigan failed to rescue him.
Issue: Does a defendant have a duty to rescue an actor who has placed himself in peril on the defendant's property?
Rule: A party is not under a duty to rescue another in peril when it is not legally responsible for causing that peril.

Farwell v. Keaton (1976)

Facts: Farwell and Seigrist, two friends, were attacked. Seigrist attempted to treat Farwell, but after two hours left him in a car in his grandparents' driveway. Farwell died three days later.
Issue: When does a party have a duty to rescue another?
Rule: One who voluntarily comes to the aid of another in peril, or has a special relationship with another in peril, has a duty to rescue the party in peril if the rescue can be accomplished without risking personal danger.

Riss v. City of New York (1968)

Facts: Riss was blinded and maimed by a party who had repeatedly threatened her. Her repeated requests for police protection had been denied.
Issue: Is a municipality liable for the negligent failure to protect a citizen from crime?
Rule: Local governments, through their police departments, may not be held liable in the absence of legislation for failure to protect members of the public from external hazards and the activities of criminal wrongdoers.

Hurley v. Eddingfield (1901)

Facts: The defendant, a physician, refused to respond when a messenger told him that the plaintiff was violently ill and that no other doctor was available.
Issue: Must a physician assist any person requiring treatment?
Rule: A physician is not required to treat every patient who has requested medical services.

L.S. Ayres & Co. v. Hicks (1942)

Facts: Hicks fell and caught his fingers in the defendant's escalator. The injury was aggravated by the defendant's slow reaction to the emergency.
Issue: Is there a duty to rescue a person in peril?
Rule: An actor has an affirmative legal duty to rescue a person in peril when the actor is an invitor, or when the injury resulted from an instrumentality under the actor's control.

Soldano v. O'Daniels (1983)

Facts: Soldano was murdered in a bar. A patron seeking to avert the murder tried to call the police at another public establishment, but was refused permission to use the telephone.
Issue: Is there a duty to come to the aid of another?
Rule: Although citizens are not generally required to aid a person in danger, an owner of a public establishment may not impede a person who has chosen to summon aid within that establishment.

Montgomery v. National Convoy & Trucking Co. (1937)

Facts: Montgomery's car hit the defendant's truck that, through no fault of the defendant, was stalled in the middle of the road. The defendant knew the truck was in a blind spot but did not sufficiently warn oncoming traffic.
Issue: Does a party have a duty to warn highway travelers of a peril it caused without negligence?
Rule: A party who creates a dangerous situation on a highway, even absent negligence, has a duty to other highway users to take precautions reasonably calculated to prevent injury.

Union Pacific Railway v. Cappier (1903)

Facts: Although the railroad had operated its train with due care, it struck and killed Cappier's trespassing son. The train operator did not stop the train to give immediate medical attention to Cappier's son, but summoned an ambulance that arrived 30 minutes later.
Issue: Does a party who nonnegligently injured another party have a duty to rescue the injured party?
Rule: There is no obligation to rescue a stranger from life-threatening peril where the defendant has not caused the peril.

Coffee v. McDonnell-Douglas Corp. (1972)

Facts: McDonnell-Douglas required Coffee to undergo a preemployment physical. Although the defendant's doctors took a blood sample from Coffee, they failed to examine the results. Had they done so, they would have discovered that Coffee had a serious illness.

Issue: Does a party who voluntarily assumes a duty have an obligation to perform the duty with due care?

Rule: If a party voluntarily assumes a duty toward another, it is liable if it performs the duty negligently.

Note: An employer does not have a duty to ascertain the fitness of prospective employees unless the employer voluntarily assumes the duty.

Erie R.R. v. Stewart (1930)

Facts: Stewart was injured when his truck was hit by an Erie Railroad train. Erie usually maintained a watchman at the crossing, although it was not obligated to do so. Stewart relied on the presence of the watchman and interpreted the absence of warning from the watchman as an assurance of safety in crossing the tracks.

Issue: May one who voluntarily assumes a greater standard of care than that required by law discontinue the use of such care at any time?

Rule: If a party acts in accordance with a greater standard of care than that required by law, and another party relies on the provision of extra care, it may be negligent to discontinue the use of extra care without adequately warning of the discontinuance.

Crowley v. Spivey (1985)

Facts: Crowley refused to allow his mentally disturbed ex-wife to visit their children when he learned that she had a gun. The Spiveys promised to ensure the children's safety if Crowley allowed his ex-wife to visit the children at their home. Crowley agreed and his wife killed the children.

Issue: Does a party that has no duty of care to another have to act reasonably if it assumes such a duty?

Rule: One who assumes a duty toward another must perform it in a reasonable and prudent manner and is liable if the negligent performance of the duty is the proximate cause of injury.

Marsalis v. LaSalle (1957)

Facts: Marsalis was scratched by LaSalle's cat. LaSalle agreed to quarantine the cat to see if it had rabies, even though he was not obligated to do so. Marsalis had to undergo painful treatments because LaSalle negligently allowed the cat to escape five days after the incident.

Issue: Is a party who promises to perform an act it is not legally obligated to perform liable for the results of improper performance?

Rule: Failure to reasonably perform an act that was not legally required, but was promised, gives rise to liability.

Linder v. Bidner (1966)

Facts: The Bidners' 18-year-old son, unsupervised at a children's playground, assaulted Linder's son. The Binders knew that their son habitually assaulted and mistreated children.

Issue: Must parents take measures to protect third parties from their children?

Rule: Parents who know or should know of the dangerous propensities of their child, and who have the ability to control the child, have an affirmative duty to protect others from the child's specific harmful conduct.

Tarasoff v. Regents of University of California (1976)

Facts: Doctors at the defendant's university hospital knew that a mental patient they were releasing intended to kill Tatiana Tarasoff. The defendants did not warn Tarasoff of the danger, and she was murdered.

Issue: Does a psychologist have a duty to warn a third party of a danger posed by one of the psychologist's patients?

Rule: Because of a psychologist's special relationship with a patient, the psychologist has a duty to warn third persons of the patient's violent intentions, even if the psychologist has no special relationship with the foreseeable victim.

Endresz v. Friedberg (1969)

Facts: Endresz, a pregnant woman, was injured in a car accident. Two days later she delivered stillborn twins.

Issue: Can a wrongful death action be brought for the stillbirth of an unborn child caused by a defendant's negligence?

Rule: One may not assert a wrongful death action for the birth of a stillborn child. Whereas a child injured in utero could receive compensation for those injuries, one deprived of life while yet unborn is not entitled to compensation. The parents may recover personal damages using other theories of recovery.

Procanik By Procanik v. Cillo (1984)

Facts: Dr. Cillo failed to diagnose a disease that Procanik's mother contracted during the first trimester of her pregnancy. As a result, Procanik was born with severe birth defects.

Issue: Can a wrongful birth action be brought on the theory that but for a defendant's negligence, the pregnancy that resulted in the plaintiff's birth would have been terminated?

Rule: In a suit for wrongful birth, a plaintiff may recover special damages but not general damages. Special damages include extraordinary medical expenses, whereas general damages involve the difference in value between an impaired life and no life at all.

Winterbottom v. Wright (1842)

Facts: Wright had a contract to supply and maintain mail coaches for the Postmaster General. Winterbottom's employer had a contract to supply the Postmaster with horses and drivers. Winterbottom, a driver, was injured when a coach broke.

Issue: Is one who contracts with a party liable to a third party injured by a breach of the contract?

Rule: One is not liable to third parties for negligently performing a private contract.

MacPherson v. Buick Motor Co. (1916)

Facts: MacPherson was injured when his car's defective wheel broke. MacPherson had bought the car from a dealer who had bought it from Buick Motors, the manufacturer of the car. A reasonable safety inspection would have revealed the defect in the wheel.

Issue: Is a manufacturer liable to one who is not a direct purchaser?

Rule: Manufacturers of products that are "reasonably certain to place life and limb in peril when negligently made" owe a duty of reasonable care to all foreseeable users.

H.R. Moch Co. v. Rensselaer Water Co. (1928)

Facts: Rensselaer Water Co. contracted to supply water to the city. A warehouse of H.R. Moch Co. burned down because a sufficient quantity of water was not available to firefighters.

Issue: May a third-party beneficiary of a contract bring an action in tort for nonfeasance?

Rule: An actor who is not a party to a contract but benefits from its performance may not recover in tort for a contracting party's nonfeasance.

Clagett v. Dacy (1980)

Facts: Clagett's purchase of property at a foreclosure sale was invalidated when Dacy, the attorney, committed procedural errors.

Issue: Can an attorney owe a duty to a third party absent an agreement between them?

Rule: The duties inherent in an attorney-client relationship will not be presumed to flow to a third party and will not be implied when such a duty to a third party would conflict with the attorney's duty to a client.

State of Louisiana ex rel. Guste v. M/V Testbank (1985)

Facts: A suit was brought by commercial fishermen who were forced to stop fishing after toxic chemicals spilled from the defendant's container ships.

Issue: Under maritime tort law, are claims for economic loss recoverable if they are not accompanied by physical damage?

Rule: Damages for economic loss may not be recovered under maritime tort law if the economic loss is not accompanied by physical damage to a proprietary interest.

Rex v. Smith (1826)

Facts: The defendants kept their mentally retarded brother in a cold and dirty room without a window.

Issue: Is there a duty to act on behalf of a sibling unable to care for one's own welfare?

Rule: Siblings living in their parents' home do not owe each other a duty of care.

Szabo v. Pennsylvania Railroad (1945)

Facts: The defendant failed to assist Szabo, its employee, when he was overcome by heat.

Issue: Does an employer have a duty to assist a sick employee?

Rule: If an employee engaged in the work of his employer receives injuries, the employer must render assistance regardless of whether the injuries are a result of the employer's negligence.

Thomas v. Winchester (1852)

Facts: The defendant, a druggist, bought falsely labeled poison from the manufacturer and sold it to the plaintiff, who suffered injuries.

Issue: Is a manufacturer liable in negligence to an ultimate user who did not purchase directly from the manufacturer?

Rule: A manufacturer does not owe a duty to an ultimate user. A party is liable only to the person with whom the party contracted.

Ward v. Morehead City Sea Food Co. (1916)

Facts: The defendant sold spoiled fish to a grocer, who sold it to the plaintiff. The plaintiff died from eating the fish.
Issue: Is one selling infected food liable to an ultimate consumer who purchased the food from an intermediary?
Rule: One who sells food owes a duty of care to the ultimate consumer of the food.

Coggs v. Bernard (1703)

Facts: The defendant negligently broke some bottles of brandy while he was moving them for Coggs. Although Coggs had a contract with the defendant, it was invalid because there was no consideration.
Issue: Is one liable for negligent performance of an unenforceable contract?
Rule: One who undertakes the performance of a service contract is liable for negligence in performing such service even if the contract is found to be invalid.

Vince v. Wilson (1989)

Facts: Vince was seriously injured in a car accident with Wilson's grand-nephew. The plaintiff sued Wilson, who bought the car for her grand-nephew, for the tort of negligent entrustment.
Issue: May a person who knowingly purchases a car for an incompetent driver be liable for the tort of negligent entrustment?
Rule: A person who knowingly purchases a car for an incompetent driver may be liable for negligent entrustment (i.e., liability from the combined negligence of both the negligence in trusting the incompetent driver with the car and the negligent operation of the car).

Battalia v. State of New York (1961)

Facts: The plaintiff suffered severe emotional and neurological distress after the defendant failed to lock a ski lift belt on him.
Issue: Can one recover for injuries caused by the negligent infliction of emotional harm?
Rule: An action may be asserted for the negligent infliction of emotional harm.

Gammon v. Osteopathic Hospital of Maine, Inc. (1987)

Facts: After Gammon's father died he received a bag from the Osteopathic Hospital of Maine that supposedly contained his father's personal belongings, but in fact contained a severed leg. Gammon suffered severe emotional stress, but showed no physical symptoms and sought no medical treatment.

Issue: Must a plaintiff show physical impact, objective manifestation, accompanying tort, or special circumstances to recover a claim for severe emotional distress without physical injury?

Rule: A plaintiff's claim for compensation for severe emotional distress without physical injury may not be barred solely because the plaintiff has failed to show some physical manifestation of the injury.

Portee v. Jaffee (1980)

Facts: The plaintiff sued for emotional distress after her son was killed when he became trapped between an elevator door and a shaft wall in Jaffee's building. The son was contributorily negligent.

Issue: May damages for emotional harm be reduced when the party whose injury caused the emotional harm was contributorily negligent?

Rule: Damages for emotional harm resulting from death or serious injury to another may be reduced if that person was contributorily negligent in causing the injury.

Johnson v. Jamaica Hospital (1984)

Facts: The Johnsons claimed they suffered emotional harm when their child was kidnapped from the nursery of Jamaica Hospital due to the hospital's negligence.

Issue: May parents recover damages for emotional harm from a hospital whose negligence caused injury to their children?

Rule: Parents may not recover damages from a hospital for any emotional duress suffered as a result of an injury inflicted upon their child by the hospital because the hospital does not owe a duty of care directly to the parents (only to the hospitalized children themselves).

Burke v. Rivo (1990)

Facts: Rivo negligently performed a sterilization operation on Burke. Burke originally chose to be sterilized for economic reasons and sued for the costs of raising the child that was conceived after the unsuccessful operation.

Issue: May the parents of a child conceived as a result of a physician's negligent performance of a sterilization procedure recover for the costs of rearing the child?

Rule: The costs of raising a child after an unsuccessful and negligently performed sterilization are reasonably foreseeable and are a natural and probable consequence of the physician's negligence. As there are no social policy concerns that require that damages be limited, the costs of raising the child are recoverable if the parents chose sterilization for economic purposes.

Viccaro v. Milunsky (1990)

Facts: A geneticist wrongly determined that the Viccaros could conceive children who would be free from a genetic defect that was common in the Viccaro family. A son was born to the Viccaros with the defect.

Issue 1: May a child born with a genetic defect sue a party whose negligence contributed to its birth?

Rule 1: A defendant whose negligence is a reason for a child's existence is not liable for the unfortunate consequences associated with the child's birth.

Issue 2: May the parents of a child born with a genetic defect recover damages from a negligent party whose negligence contributed to the child being born?

Rule 2: The parents of a child with a genetic birth defect may recover from the party whose negligence contributed to the child's birth, the extraordinary medical, educational, and other expenses associated with the child's disorder. They may also recover for emotional distress and any physical results thereof. However, they may not recover for the loss of companionship of a normal child, and the total damages may be offset by any benefits the parents derive from the child's existence.

Wilbur v. Kerr (1982)

Facts: Wilbur fathered a child after undergoing a vasectomy that was performed by Kerr.

Issue: May parents recover for the expenses of raising a child that was born because of a doctor's negligence in performing a sterilization operation?

Rule: Parents may not recover for the expense of a child born after a negligently performed sterilization.

CHAPTER 9

Owners and Occupiers of Land

At common law, an owner or occupier of land had a much lower duty of care to avoid causing an unreasonable risk of harm to others from the use of the land.

I. OUTSIDE THE PREMISES

    A. Natural Hazards Located on the Property
    Landowners do not have a duty to protect persons outside their land from natural hazards on their land.
    Exception: Persons in densely populated areas must protect a public road from trees on their property.
    B. Artificial Hazards Located on the Property
    Landowners have a duty to protect persons outside their land from an unreasonably dangerous risk of harm.

II. ON THE PREMISES

There are three types of persons who come onto a landowner's property: trespassers, licensees, and invitees. The owner's duty of care to each type of visitor is different. Some states (led by California and New York) have rejected the various categories of visitors in favor of requiring a landowner to exercise a standard of reasonable care to all of them.
    A. Invitees
      1. Two Types
        a. Business Visitors
        Business visitors are persons invited by the owner onto the property to conduct business with the owner.
        b. Public Invitees
        Public invitees are persons who enter property that is open to the public for their own use.

2. Duty of an Owner

An owner has a duty to exercise ordinary care in keeping the property safe. The owner has a duty to inspect the property for unknown dangers.

3. Exceptions

Persons who exceed the scope of an invitation onto the property will void their status as invitees.

B. Licensees

1. Definition

Licensees are persons who enter an owner's property with the owner's consent (e.g., social guests). Firefighters and police officers are usually considered to be licensees.

2. Duty of an Owner

An owner does not have a duty to inspect the property for unknown dangers, but does have a duty to warn a licensee of any dangerous conditions of which the owner is aware.

3. Exceptions

Owners have a duty to exercise reasonable care when they are involved in "active operations of their land."

C. Trespassers

1. Undiscovered Trespassers

a. Definition

Persons who enter the property of an owner without permission or privilege.

b. Duty of an Owner

An owner owes no duty to an undiscovered trespasser.

c. Exceptions

If an owner knows that trespassers frequent a limited portion of the property, the owner has a duty to warn of the dangers the trespassers would otherwise not discover.

2. Discovered Trespassers

a. Definition

A particular person who an owner knows or should know is trespassing on the owner's property.

b. Duty of an Owner

An owner must exercise reasonable care for the person's safety and warn of any dangers unknown to the person, but known to the owner.

Although courts agree this is the standard for artificial conditions on the land, the courts are divided as to whether this standard applies to natural conditions.

3. Child Trespassers

a. Definition

Traditionally, a child had to be lured onto the property by an artificial hazard for an owner to be liable; that is, the "attractive nuisance doctrine."

Under the modern view, a child-plaintiff must prove:
Mnemonic: **FRED**

    i. **F**requenting of the area by children is common and the owner knows of their tendency to enter the property.

    ii. **R**isks that the children are unable to appreciate make the condition likely to cause injury; their ability to appreciate the risk is decided by a subjective standard.

    iii. **E**xpense of protecting against the injury is slight compared to the risk.

    iv. **D**angerous conditions are present that the owner knows of or should know of.

  b. Duty of an Owner

An owner must exercise reasonable care to avoid risks of harm from conditions that are artificial. An owner does not have a duty to protect against natural conditions.

III. LESSOR AND LESSEE

  A. Duties of a Real Estate Lessee

    1. Liable for all damages caused on the property as an owner would be.

    2. Not liable for any harm caused in common areas.

  B. Duties of a Real Estate Lessor

    1. Generally, liability is passed from a lessor to a lessee.

    Exceptions:

      a. A lessor is liable for a defect present at the start of a lease that the lessor knows or should know of, and that a lessee has no reason to know of. This does not mean the lessor has a duty to inspect, but rather a duty to warn.

      b. A lessor is liable if the lessor knows the property will be open to the public and a defect exists when a lessee takes possession. A lessor in this case has a duty to inspect.

      c. A lessor is liable for any damages that result from an act the lessor voluntarily performs that is done negligently.

      d. A lessor is liable for a negligently repaired defect that the lessor is required to repair in the lease.

      e. A lessor is liable for damages that result from the lessor's improper maintenance of common areas.

    2. A lessor's duty is to the lessee and the lessee's guests and licensees.

IV. VENDORS OF LAND

Generally, vendors of land are not liable for harm caused by defects on the land after it is sold.

Exceptions:

A. A vendor is liable for concealing a defect that the vendor knew the buyer would not find.

B. A vendor that did not conceal a defect is still liable until the buyer has had a reasonable time to discover and correct the defect.

CASE CLIPS

Taylor v. Olsen (1978)

Facts: Taylor was injured when her car struck a tree that had fallen from Olsen's property onto a public road.
Issue: Is the level of care a possessor of land must use to prevent an unreasonable risk of harm different for urban and rural dwellers?
Rule: A possessor of land must exercise reasonable care, given the circumstances of the individual case, to prevent an unreasonable risk of harm. This applies whether they are urban or rural dwellers.
Note: This case rejects the traditional urban-rural distinction still followed by a majority of jurisdictions.

Salevan v. Wilmington Park, Inc. (1950)

Facts: While walking past the defendant's ballpark, Salevan was struck in the head by a baseball.
Issue: Do landowners in the usage of their land have a duty to protect persons passing by their land?
Rule: Landowners have a duty to exercise reasonable care in the use of their land so as to prevent injury to persons passing by the land.

Hayes v. Malkan (1970)

Facts: Hayes was injured when the car he was in crashed into the defendant's utility pole, located on private property near a public road.
Issue: Do landowners have a duty to protect those who use public lands from an unreasonable risk on their property if the object of risk is located near the public land?
Rule: Landowners owe no duty to protect persons on public lands from an unreasonable risk located on their property regardless of the risk's proximity to the public land.

Sheehan v. St. Paul Duluth Railway Co. (1896)

Facts: While walking on the defendant's railroad track, Sheehan's foot became caught in the rail and was severed by a passing train.
Issue: Do landowners owe duties of care to undiscovered trespassers?
Rule: Landowners owe no duty of care to trespassers whose presence is unknown to them.

10:34→11:04

Humphrey v. Twin State G. & E. Co. (1927)

Facts: While trespassing on the land of a third party, Humphrey was injured when he touched a fence that was in contact with electrical wires. The wires were negligently hung by the defendant.

Issue: Does a defendant who is permitted to use the land of another share the landowner's tort immunity toward trespassers?

Rule: Defendants are liable when their negligence causes injuries to a plaintiff who was trespassing on property belonging to a third party.

Barmore v. Elmore (1980)

Facts: Barmore went to Elmore's home to discuss lodge business. While there, he was attacked by Elmore's son, who had a history of mental illness.

Issue: Is a guest who is present for the purpose of conducting mutual business with a host considered to be an invitee or a licensee?

Rule: When a person is a guest in another's home to conduct mutual business, the host does not receive any personal benefit and the guest is considered a licensee. With licensees, a host only has a duty to warn of known dangers.

Note: A host has a duty to exercise reasonable care in keeping the premises reasonably safe for use by an invitee.

Campbell v. Weathers (1941)

Facts: The plaintiff, a frequent customer at the defendant's lunch counter, was injured on a day the plaintiff did not make a purchase.

Issue: Is one who enters a place of business, but has no intention of conducting business that day, considered a licensee or an invitee?

Rule: One who enters a place of business with an intention to do business then, or at some future time, is considered an invitee.

Whelan v. Van Natta (1964)

Facts: After the plaintiff purchased cigarettes at the defendant's grocery store, he asked if he could have an empty box. Directed to the back room, the plaintiff fell down an unseen stairwell.

Issue: Do visitors lose their status as invitees when they move beyond the scope of their invitation?

Rule: Visitors have the status of invitees only while on the part of the land to which their invitation extends. When they move beyond this area, invitees become trespassers or licensees, depending on whether they have the owner's consent.

Gladon v. Greater Cleveland Regional Transit Authority (1996)

Facts: P drank at a baseball game and became intoxicated. He took the train home, but got off at the wrong stop. At the station, he was attacked and mugged. He woke up sprawled on the tracks, not knowing how he got there. He was hit by a train when it came into the station.

Issue: What duty does a landowner owe to a business invitee who trespasses into areas not included in the invitation to come onto the land?

Rule: The landowner generally owes a business invitee a duty of reasonable care. When the invitee acts as a trespasser, however, the landowner owes him a duty only to refrain from engaging in wanton and reckless conduct.

Wilk v. Georges (1973)

Facts: The plaintiff slipped and fell while shopping in the defendant's store. The defendant had posted signs warning the floor was slippery.

Issue: Is a landowner's duty to protect invitees from an unreasonable risk of harm discharged by the posting of warning signs?

Rule: When a possessor of land can anticipate an unreasonable risk of harm to an invitee, the possessor must take reasonable and feasible steps to obviate such a risk beyond the mere posting of warning signs.

Boyd v. Racine Currency Exchange, Inc. (1973)

Facts: Boyd, a customer, was killed when the defendant's bank teller refused to give money to a robber who held a gun to Boyd's head.

Issue: Must a business proprietor honor the demands of a criminal to prevent an unreasonable risk to an invitee?

Rule: A business proprietor owes no duty to protect the welfare of an invitee by honoring the demands of a criminal.

Paubel v. Hitz (1936)

Facts: The plaintiff slipped on the sidewalk outside the defendant's place of business. Both parties knew that the sidewalk was slippery.

Issue: Are landowners required to warn an invitee of conditions that are obvious and known to the invitee?

Rule: Landowners owe an invitee a duty to maintain their premises so they are reasonably safe and to warn of unsafe conditions only if they are neither obvious nor known to the invitee.

Rowland v. Christian (1968)

Facts: Rowland, a social guest, was injured at Christian's house by a defective faucet Christian had known about prior to the accident.

Issue: Should the traditional distinctions among trespasser, invitee, and licensee be enforced?

Rule: An owner shall be judged by a reasonable person standard. The plaintiff's status as a trespasser, licensee, or invitee may have some bearing on the issue of liability, but it is not determinative.

Note: This is a minority view that only a few states have adopted.

Basso v. Miller (1976)

Facts: Basso, riding on the back of Miller's motorcycle, was injured in an accident caused by potholes in a public park. Basso sued Miller and the owner of the park.

Issue: What standard of care must landowners exercise in maintaining their property to avoid harm to all possible persons?

Rule: Landowners must maintain their property as a reasonable person would given the specific circumstances, including the likelihood of injury and the expense of protection against such injury. The court abandoned the distinctions among trespassers, invitees, and licensees.

Borders v. Roseberry (1975)

Facts: Borders slipped on the icy steps of a house that was owned by the defendant, but rented to a tenant.

Issue: Are landlords under an obligation or duty to the social guests of their tenants to repair or remedy hazardous conditions?

Rule: Landlords are not liable for injuries to others arising from a defective condition existing at the time of the lease, except for: (1) undisclosed conditions known to the lessor, but not to the lessee; (2) conditions that are dangerous to persons outside of the premises; (3) premises leased for a purpose involving admission to the public; (4) land the lessor retains control of that the lessee is entitled to use; (5) conditions the lessor contracts to repair (i.e., implied warranty); and (6) negligent repairs by lessor.

Pagelsdorf v. Safeco Ins. Co. of America (1979)

Facts: While helping a tenant in the defendant's building Pagelsdorf was injured when a wood railing of a balcony collapsed.

Issue: Do landlords owe a duty toward tenants and their visitors to exercise ordinary care in maintaining the premises?

Rule: Landlords must exercise ordinary care toward their tenants and others on the premises with permission.

O'Sullivan v. Shaw (2000)

Facts: P dove headfirst into the pool at the shallow end and suffered serious injury. P brought suit against D for negligence.
Issue: Does the landowner's duty to reasonably protect lawful visitors from dangerous conditions on the land govern in these circumstances?
Rule: When a dangerous condition on the land is "open and obvious," the landowner owes no duty of care, even to his lawful visitors.

Kline v. 1500 Massachusetts Ave. Apartment Corp. (1970)

Facts: Kline was injured when robbed in the lobby of her apartment building. The tenants had informed the defendant/landlord of previous incidents, but nothing was done.
Issue: Do landlords have an affirmative duty to protect their tenants from the foreseeable tortious acts of third parties?
Rule: Landlords must take reasonable steps to ensure the safety of their tenants from the tortious acts of third parties in areas where they have exclusive control.

Buch v. Amory Manufacturing Co. (1897)

Facts: Buch, age 8, had his hand crushed by dangerous machinery while trespassing on the defendant's property. The defendant's foreman warned Buch to leave before the accident, but did not make sure that he did.
Issue: Does a landowner have an affirmative duty to warn an infant trespasser of dangers on the property?
Rule: A landowner does not have a duty to warn a trespasser of a danger, even if the trespasser is a child.
Note: Today, a landlord's duties to trespassers have been expanded.

Robert Addie & Sons (Collieries), Ltd. v. Dumbreck (1928)

Facts: The defendant did not actively protect children who frequently played on his property. The plaintiff, age 4, was killed by machinery after being warned not to play in the area.
Issue: Must a landowner protect an infant trespasser from hazards on the landowner's property?
Rule: A landowner owes no duty to a trespasser other than refraining from willful injury.

Minnich v. Med-Waste, Inc. (2002)

Facts: P was a public safety officer at a university. While helping to load a truck with university refuse, he prevented the tractor-trailer from rolling away onto a public thoroughfare. In doing so, he sustained personal injuries. He brought suit against the negligent driver.

Issue: Are "first responders" (emergency personnel such as police officers, public safety officers, and firefighters) barred from suing tortfeasors when they suffer injuries during the course of their regular employment?

Rule: The state supreme court (SC) answered the certified question by rejecting the "firefighter's rule" and asserting that first responder tort claims should be subject to ordinary, nonpreclusive, and nondiscriminatory principles of tort liability. Emergency personnel can sue the person whose conduct caused their harm for a breach of the duty of ordinary care. There is no reason, under South Carolina law, to protect landowners or particular actors from the accountability of tort law. The multifarious rationales for the "firefighter's rule" are no longer responsive to contemporary social exigencies.

Strauss v. Belle Realty Co. (1985)

Facts: Strauss fell down in the common area of his apartment building during a city-wide power failure.

Issue: Does a public utility, contracting with a landlord, owe a duty of care to the landlord's tenants?

Rule: A utility does not owe a duty of care to a tenant because the utility has only contracted with the landlord.

Fitch v. Adler (1981)

Facts: Fitch, a guest/licensee in Adler's home, was injured when she walked off an outside deck after Adler had opened the deck doors. Adler had failed to warn her that the deck was without guardrails. Because of darkness Fitch was unable to see this dangerous condition.

Issue: Does the duty of a landowner to warn a licensee of concealed dangers apply when the licensee extends beyond the area of invite?

Rule: When the licensee extends beyond the specified area of invite, the licensee becomes a trespasser. A landowner owes no duty to warn of concealed dangers unless this area is reasonably thought to be extended because of the landowner's direct or implied actions.

Erickson v. Curtis Investment Co. (1989)

Facts: The plaintiff was attacked in Curtis Investment's parking garage. An expert for the plaintiff testified that the security measures taken by Curtis Investment were inadequate under the circumstances.

Issue: Does the owner-operator of a commercial parking garage have a duty to protect its customers from criminal actions by third parties?

Rule: An owner-operator of a commercial parking garage has a duty to use reasonable care under the circumstances to deter criminal activity that may cause harm to its customers. Circumstances to be considered include the cost of security, the risk of harm that the operator knows or should know, and the location of the garage.

Note: This is an exception to the general business enterprise rule that a merchant-customer relationship is not enough to impose a duty on the merchant to protect its customers.

CHAPTER 10

Damages

I. ACTUAL DAMAGES

Unlike intentional torts, there are no nominal damages awarded for negligence. A plaintiff has to show actual damages as part of a cause of action. This usually includes a required showing of some physical injury.

II. TYPES OF RECOVERABLE DAMAGES

A plaintiff who has sustained some physical injury can recover damages for all the harm sustained, which may include:

A. Medical Expenses

B. Lost Earnings

C. Future Earnings

The jury will often hear expert testimony regarding the value of the lost earning capacity and will approximate the value of future earnings lost, taking inflation and interest rates into account.

D. Pain and Suffering

This includes both amount of pain suffered up to the time of trial and an estimate of future pain.

E. Mental Distress

Includes fear and shock when injured, humiliation from disfigurement, impairment of activities, and anxiety over new life.

F. Property Damages

Can be measured either by the cost to repair the damaged item, or if repair is not possible, the fair market value of the destroyed property.

III. NONRECOVERABLE DAMAGES

A. Interest

One may not recover the interest that would have been earned on monetary damages from the date of the accident to the date of the verdict.

B. Attorney's Fees

IV. TAXATION AND DAMAGES

A. Tax Free

Damages for personal injuries are tax free, regardless of whether damages are awarded by a court judgment or received as part of a private settlement. Courts are split on the issue of whether a defendant is allowed to tell the jury that damages are tax free.

B. Calculation of Damages and Taxation

1. Past Earnings

Calculations for lost past earnings are based on the plaintiff's net earnings.

2. Future Earnings

Lost future earnings are calculated according to the plaintiff's tax bracket.

a. Ordinary Taxpayer — at gross

b. High Income Taxpayer — at net

c. Federal Rule — regardless of tax bracket, always based on net

V. COLLATERAL SOURCE RULE

The amount of damages is not reduced if the plaintiff recovered, or could recover, compensation from other sources such as insurance, disability benefits, or social security. Even if the plaintiff receives free medical care, the defendant has to compensate the plaintiff for the reasonable value of those benefits.

Rationale:

A. The plaintiff prepaid to receive these benefits. For example, it would be unfair to reduce a plaintiff's damages because the plaintiff has paid insurance premiums for numerous years.

B. Even if the plaintiff did not prepay, it is not right to aid the defendant who is a tortfeasor.

C. In many cases, the plaintiff is obligated to pay for the benefits received from a third party, such as an insurance company, out of the damages award. This is called subrogation.

VI. MITIGATION OF DAMAGES

A plaintiff cannot recover damages for injuries that a reasonably prudent person would have avoided. Usually this only applies to conduct after the accident. Some courts also look to conduct before the accident and will reduce damages because of a plaintiff's failure to take adequate precautions to reduce potential damages.

VII. PUNITIVE DAMAGES

Punitive damages are awarded as a punishment, meaning that they are always in excess of the actual harm suffered. They are only awarded in cases where a defendant has acted recklessly, wantonly, or willfully.

CASE CLIPS

Anderson v. Sears Roebuck & Co. (1974)

Facts: Helen Britain, a young child, was severely burned when a malfunctioning heater manufactured by Sears caused a fire in her home. The jury awarded Britain a $2 million award. Sears moved for remittitur to lower the award as legally excessive.

Issue: What criteria must a judge use to determine if a damage award is excessive?

Rule: In determining the reasonableness of damages a judge should determine the maximum amount a jury could reasonably award for each element of damages. The elements of personal damages are: past and future physical and mental pain, future medical expenses, loss of earning capacity, and permanent disability and disfigurement.

Helfend v. Southern California Rapid Transit Dist. (1970)

Facts: Helfend was awarded general and special damages for injuries sustained in an accident. His medical expenses were partially paid by insurance.

Issue: Should a tortfeasor, in an effort to reduce a damage award, be allowed to present the jury with evidence that the plaintiff has already been partially compensated?

Rule: A tortfeasor may not introduce evidence to prove that a plaintiff has been compensated by an independent collateral source such as insurance, pension, continued wages, or disability payments. This is an application of the "collateral source rule."

Mercado v. Ahmed (1992)

Facts: Taxi struck a 6-year-old boy who sustained such severe injuries that he would probably be institutionalized for the remainder of his life.

Issue: Can expert testimony be admitted as to the value of "hedonic damages" or damages for the inability to enjoy life's pleasures?

Rule: Expert testimony is excluded when it is manifestly inexpert. In this case, the would-be expert based his calculations on a number of disparate studies that failed to indicate any consensus in the field about damage measurement.

Zimmerman v. Ausland (1973)

Facts: The plaintiff received damages for a permanent knee injury. The defendant submitted evidence showing that the injury could be corrected using surgery.

Issue: May a plaintiff recover for a permanent injury if the permanent nature of the injury could have been avoided by the plaintiff?

Rule: The test to be applied in determining whether a plaintiff has unreasonably failed or refused to mitigate damages is whether, under the circumstances of the particular case, an ordinary prudent person would do so.

Gryc v. Dayton-Hudson Corp. (1980)

Facts: Gryc, age 4, was severely burned while wearing pajamas made of untreated flammable material. The jury awarded Gryc both compensatory and punitive damages.

Issue: May punitive damages be awarded to punish past misconduct and deter future misconduct?

Rule: Punitive damages may be awarded against a party who has acted in willful, wanton, or malicious disregard of the rights of others.

Pacific Mutual Life Ins. Co. v. Haslip (S. Ct. 1991)

Facts: Haslip made a claim against her health insurance and found that her policy had been cancelled because the agent had never forwarded the premiums to the provider. She obtained a verdict for both compensatory and punitive damages.

Issue: Under what circumstances may a punitive damages award be challenged?

Rule: Under traditional common law, the amount of the punitive damage award is initially determined by a jury with instructions to consider the gravity of the wrong and the need for deterrence, and is then reviewed by the court to ensure its reasonableness. This practice is not per se constitutional, as there are situations, notably when a jury is given instructions that allow for too much jury discretion, where an award may be constitutionally unacceptable.

State Farm Mutual Automobile Ins. Co. v. Campbell (2003)

Facts: Campbell caused a collision that resulted in severe personal injury. State Farm, his insurer, refused to settle with the victims, advised the insured that it would protect its interests, and pushed the matter to a jury verdict. The latter far exceeded the policy limits and the settlement to which the victims had been agreeable. In a subsequent action by Campbell against State Farm for bad faith settlement and fraud, various courts eventually award him $1 million in compensatory damages and $145 million in punitive damages.

Issue: Is the amount of the punitive damage award excessive in that it reflects passion, caprice, or irrationality?

Rule: According to the U.S. Supreme Court, the punitive amount was excessive and violated the Due Process Clause of the U.S. Constitution. There was a gross disproportionality between the potential harm suffered and the amount of the punitive damages, as well as with standard civil penalties in similar cases. Fundamental fairness prohibits arbitrary punishments even when D has engaged in reprehensible conduct.

Price v. Hartford Accident and Indemnity Co. (1972)

Facts: The Hartford Accident and Indemnity Co. refused to pay punitive damages arising from Price's participation in a drag race. Price's insurance policy covered "all" liabilities arising from his use of his car.

Issue: May an insurance company avoid liability for punitive damages?

Rule: An insurance company that takes premiums to cover "all" liability damages must pay for punitive damages.

Note: Courts are split on this issue.

Pavia v. State Farm Mutual Automobile Ins. Co. (1993)

Facts: Insurer refused to accept a settlement in the amount of the policy limits for a car accident caused by its insured. A jury returned a multimillion-dollar verdict, far in excess of the settlement proposal. P brought suit against insurer for "bad faith" settlement.

Issue: When do the circumstances of litigation indicate that an insurer has engaged in "bad faith" settlement?

Rule: The complaining party must establish that the insurer's conduct amounted to recklessness, that is, a "gross disregard" of the insured's interests in terms of the possible practical resolution of the claim and the realities of the litigation process.

Christopher v. United States (1965)

Facts: Christopher sought damages under the Federal Tort Claims Act for paralysis resulting from negligent treatment in a Veteran's Administration Hospital.

Issue: What types of compensation are available to an injured person?

Rule: An injured plaintiff can recover for pain and suffering, past and future lost income, and medical expenses.

Jackson v. Johns-Manville Corp. (1986)

Facts: Jackson suffered from asbestosis poisoning and established at trial that persons with asbestosis poisoning would likely get cancer.

Issue: May a plaintiff recover damages for the medical probability of developing an illness?
Rule: Once an injury becomes actionable (i.e., once some effect appears), a plaintiff can recover for the medical probability of developing an illness.

Feldman v. Allegheny Airlines, Inc. (1975)

Facts: A lower court ruled that inflation could be considered in calculating the damages for Feldman, who was killed in a plane crash.
Issue: May inflation be considered in assessing damages?
Rule: A court may include anticipated inflation in its damages award.

Sullivan v. Old Colony Street Railway (1908)

Facts: No facts stated.
Rule: Damage awards are monetary compensation for actual loss.

Zibbell v. Southern Pacific Co. (1911)

Facts: No facts stated.
Rule: "No rational being would change places with the injured man for an amount of gold that would fill the room of the court, yet no lawyer would contend that such is not the legal measure of damages."

McDougald v. Garber (1989)

Facts: During surgery, McDougald suffered severe brain damage, resulting in a permanent comatose condition. McDougald was awarded nonpecuniary damages for conscious pain and suffering as well as for loss of the pleasures and pursuits of life.
Issue 1: Is some degree of cognitive awareness a prerequisite to recovery for loss of enjoyment of life?
Rule 1: There must be some level of cognitive awareness by the plaintiff to recover for loss of enjoyment of life.
Issue 2: May damages for loss of enjoyment of life be considered separately from pain and suffering?
Rule 2: When considering nonpecuniary damage awards, compensation for loss of enjoyment of life is included as part of compensation for pain and suffering.

O'Shea v. Riverway Towing Co. (1982)

Facts: O'Shea fell while leaving the defendant's boat.
Issue: May inflation be computed when calculating lost future wages?

Rule: Inflation should be considered when computing lost future wages, but its effects should be balanced against interest earned on the settlement because inflation rates and interest rates are related.

Firestone v. Crown Center Redevelopment Corp. (1985)

Facts: Firestone was injured due to the defendant's negligent construction of a skywalk and was awarded $15 million in damages. Missouri law required Firestone to file a remittitur of $2.25 million to prevent the ordering of a new trial. This procedure was used in cases where a judge decided an excessive verdict was given against the weight of the evidence.
Issue: May a court require plaintiffs to diminish their damage awards, under the doctrine of remittitur, where the judge decided the verdict was excessive given the weight of the evidence?
Rule: The doctrine of remittitur is abolished. Judges may grant new trials, but may not require plaintiffs to diminish their damage awards where the judge decides the verdict was excessive.

Norfolk & Western Railway Co. v. Liepelt (1980)

Facts: In a wrongful death suit the trial court refused to allow the jury to be told that damages would be tax free.
Issue: Must a judge inform jurors that a plaintiff's damages award for a personal injury will be tax free?
Rule: A judge must permit a defendant to inform the jury that damages received in a personal injury award are not taxable.
Note: Courts are divided on this issue.

McGinley v. United States (1971)

Facts: McGinley refused to undergo surgery to alleviate pain incurred by an accident for which the defendant was responsible.
Issue: Does the duty to mitigate damages require that the injured party take all possible actions to alleviate its injuries?
Rule: A plaintiff has a duty to submit to reasonable medical treatment only; the test of reasonableness is determined by a jury.

Keans v. Bottiarelli (1994)

Facts: Keans was hospitalized when she kept bleeding after a tooth extraction. She suffered from a rare blood condition that affects clotting capacity. She informed the oral surgeon, but he did not consult Keans's hematologist. Keans, however, failed to fill a prescription and to contact the oral surgeon as her condition worsened.

Issue: Does Keans's failure to follow instructions and persist in contacting the dentist lessen her recovery for medical malpractice?

Rule: The injured patient has a duty to take reasonable steps to contain or mitigate the injury she suffered. A failure to act reasonably will reduce recovery for professional medical omissions.

Harding v. Town of Townshend (1871)

Facts: The trial court allowed the defendant's liability for damages to be reduced by the amount of money the plaintiff received from his insurance company.

Issue: Can testimony that a plaintiff was compensated from collateral sources be admitted in trial?

Rule: A court may not allow into evidence the fact that a plaintiff received payments from collateral sources.

Arambula v. Wells (1999)

Facts: P suffered personal injury in a car accident. Even though he was temporarily unable to work, his employer continued to pay him. D sought to eliminate P's recovery for lost wages.

Issue: Is P entitled to a windfall or double recovery?

Rule: The collateral source rule allows P to obtain lost wages from the tortfeasor even though his employer continued to pay him.

Fischer v. Johns-Manville Corp. (1986)

Facts: Fischer sued to recover damages for lung disease suffered as a result of exposure to asbestos supplied by the defendants.

Issue: May punitive damages be awarded in products liability actions?

Rule: Punitive damages may be awarded in a products liability action when a manufacturer, aware of a risk inherent in its product, fails to warn of such risk, and fails to act to reduce the risk.

Cheatham v. Pohle (2003)

Facts: Husband displays nude and other photos of former wife in public. She sues and is awarded punitive damages by the jury. The state statute on punitive damages requires that 75 percent of the punitive award go to a state fund for the public benefit.

Issue: Does the state regulation on punitive damages violate the "takings clause" of the state and federal constitution?

Rule: Punitive damages are quasi-criminal awards and are not attributed as a matter of right. They have no impact on the compensation of injury.

States can ban such damages entirely or impose, in effect, a heavy tax levy on them.

Seffert v. Los Angeles Transit Lines (1961)

Facts: The defendant's bus doors closed on Seffert, dragging her some distance. Seffert was awarded $187,903.75 in damages.
Issue: When can an appellate court reduce the amount of a verdict?
Rule: An appellate court can reduce a verdict only if it shocks the conscience and necessarily implies that the verdict must have been the result of passion and prejudice. An award will not be reduced just because it seems excessive.

Taylor v. Superior Court (1979)

Facts: Taylor was injured when he was struck by a car driven by an intoxicated driver who had numerous drunken driving convictions.
Issue: Does driving while intoxicated fulfill the malice requirement that is necessary to receive an award of punitive damages?
Rule: Malice implies an act conceived in a spirit of mischief or with criminal indifference toward obligations owed to others. Driving while intoxicated fulfills this malice requirement.

Coyne v. Campbell (1962)

Facts: Coyne, a medical doctor, was injured in a car accident. All of his medical expenses were provided gratuitously by his colleagues.
Issue: Does the collateral source rule allow a plaintiff to recover for damages even if the plaintiff did not actually pay the expenses?
Rule: Recovery for compensatory damages in a personal injury action is limited to actual pecuniary loss, and does not include free services.
Note: This is the minority view.

Montgomery Ward & Co. v. Anderson (1998)

Facts: Anderson fell in a Montgomery Ward store and was sent by the store to the hospital where she underwent surgery and other medical treatment. The latter amounted to $25,000, which the hospital said it would reduce by 50 percent. At trial, Montgomery Ward asserted that the actual costs should serve as the measure of damages.
Issue: Is the benefit conferred upon P by the hospital transferable to D and a proper consideration in measuring damages?
Rule: Discounted costs relating to medical services offered to the plaintiff are a collateral source and cannot be considered in calculating the damages owed by a tortfeasor to a plaintiff.

Holton v. Gibson (1960)

Facts: Holton was injured in a car accident, and sued Gibson for loss of future earning power.
Issue: Is loss of earning power an issue of fact for the jury to consider?
Rule: Even if a plaintiff shows no immediate loss in wages, the jury may properly decide whether future earning power has been curtailed when calculating damages.

Healy v. White (1977)

Facts: Healy sustained injuries in a car accident, resulting in brain dysfunction and epilepsy.
Issue: Can an expert witness express his opinion in terms of medical probabilities, without stating a conclusion with absolute certainty?
Rule: An expert witness is competent to express an opinion as long as that opinion is stated in terms of the probable, and not merely the possible.

Grayson v. Irvmar Realty Corp. (1959)

Facts: Grayson claimed loss of future earnings for an operatic career, although she had no professional operatic experience.
Issue: Can damages for future earnings be based on yet-to-be exploited talent?
Rule: Juries may award damages based on future earning potential of inchoate careers if the damages reflect genuine potentialities and not simply wishful thinking.

Walters v. Hitchcock (1985)

Facts: Walters sued Hitchcock for medical malpractice after Dr. Hitchcock removed a piece of her esophagus during a thyroid operation. Walters was awarded $2 million in damages.
Issue: When is a jury award for personal injury excessive?
Rule: An award for a personal injury is excessive when it "shocks the conscience."

Richardson v. Chapman (1997)

Facts: While driving a car, P was hit from behind by D's semi-trailer. D claimed that damages were excessive because of an inaccurate calculation by P's expert.
Issue: When is an award of damages deemed excessive?

Rule: Damages are excessive and subject to reduction when they represent unfair or unreasonable compensation of the victim or result from passion and shock the conscience.

Delaney v. The Empire Insurance Co. (1985)

Facts: Delaney was involved in a car accident that greatly aggravated a previously existing back condition.

Issue: Can a plaintiff recover for exacerbation of a preexisting condition?

Rule: A plaintiff may recover for exacerbation of a preexisting condition if the defendant's negligent conduct is a proximate cause of the exacerbation.

United States v. Olsen (2005)

Facts: Injured miners contended that careless federal inspectors contributed to a mining accident and brought suit against the federal government under the Federal Tort Claims Act.

Issue: Does the local or state government's amenability to suit under local law in similar circumstances also govern the liability of the federal government?

Rule: According to the U.S. Supreme Court, the United States authorized tort suits against itself (and waived its sovereign immunity) "only where local law would make a 'private person' liable in tort, not where local law would make 'a state or municipal entity' liable."

CHAPTER 11

Wrongful Death and Survival

I. UNDER COMMON LAW

A. A plaintiff's action against a defendant was extinguished when the plaintiff died.

B. Third parties that were harmed by a plaintiff's death were barred from bringing an action. Thus, there was no recovery in tort available to a plaintiff's survivors.

II. STATUTORY CHANGES

A. Survival Statutes
Survival statutes allow a decedent's cause of action to be continued by the decedent's estate. They allow recovery for the harm that the decedent suffered before death. This includes pain and suffering, medical care, lost income, and so on.

B. Wrongful Death Statutes
Wrongful death statutes allow a decedent's survivors to assert an action for damages based on the decedent's death. They allow recovery for damages that occurred after death. The survivors can sue for grief, loss of companionship, and so on.
Note: Any defenses that a defendant could have asserted against the decedent can also be used against the survivors.

C. Exception
Torts that invade a very personal interest will not survive death, such as defamation, invasion of privacy, and so on.

CASE CLIPS

Moragne v. States Marine Lines, Inc. (S. Ct. 1970)

Facts: An action for wrongful death was brought by a longshoreman's widow against her deceased husband's employer.
Issue: Can a wrongful death action be asserted for a maritime death absent an authorizing statute (i.e., is there a common law right to bring such a suit)?
Rule: (Harlan, J.) Wrongful death actions, made available by statute in all 50 states, are actionable under maritime common law.

Selders v. Armentrout (1973)

Facts: The plaintiffs brought a wrongful death action for their child.
Issue: Can parents recover for the loss of the "society, comfort, and companionship" of a minor child in a wrongful death action?
Rule: Parents can recover for the loss of "society, comfort and companionship" as well as for their pecuniary loss in a wrongful death action for the loss of a minor child.

Murphy v. Martin Oil Co. (1974)

Facts: Murphy brought both wrongful death and survivor actions after her husband died in a fire.
Issue: Can surviving spouses recover under both wrongful death and survivor statutes?
Rule: Surviving spouses can recover under both wrongful death and survivor statutes for the death of their spouse. To avoid double recovery, the latter is usually limited to compensation for lost wages and pain and suffering from the time of the accident to the time of death, and the former compensates for the future loss of the spouse.

Cassano v. Durham (1981)

Facts: Cassano asserted a wrongful death action after her lover died.
Issue: Can one who maintained a "live-in" relationship without marrying the decedent bring a wrongful death action?
Rule: A live-in plaintiff cannot be classified as a "surviving spouse" under intestacy laws. One must be legally married to assert an action under these acts.

Borer v. American Airlines, Inc. (1977)

Facts: Borer was injured by the defendant's negligence. Her children sued the defendant for loss of parental consortium.

Issue: May children sue to recover damages for the loss of the services, companionship, affection, and guidance of a parent?

Rule: There is no common law recovery by a child for the loss of parental consortium.

Note: The courts will allow a spouse to sue for loss of consortium.

CHAPTER 12

Defenses

I. CONTRIBUTORY NEGLIGENCE

A plaintiff whose negligence contributed proximately to cause the injury is completely barred from recovery.

A. Reasonable Person

A plaintiff is required to act as a reasonable person would to avoid being injured.

Exceptions:

1. Minors

A child plaintiff will be held to the standard of a reasonable child with the same age, intelligence, and experience.

2. Insane Persons

The courts are split as to whether an insane person should be judged according to the reasonable person standard. Courts are more willing to use a subjective standard to judge the contributory negligence, as opposed to negligence, of an insane person because the insane person has not caused injury to another person.

B. Unforeseeable Manner

If one's negligence creates a risk to oneself of a particular harm being brought about in a particular manner, the person is not contributorily negligent if the harm occurs in an unforeseeable manner.

Example: Rob warns Susan not to go in his room because she might cut herself on a broken window pane. Susan enters the room and is cut by a knife that was left on the floor. Although the cut she received was the same injury that was risked by her entry, she was not contributorily negligent because the harm was brought about in an unforeseeable manner, from the knife as opposed to the broken window pane.

C. Affirmative Defense

A defendant must specifically plead and prove a plaintiff's contributory negligence.

D. Perilous Situation
Remaining in a perilous situation may constitute contributory negligence.

E. Applicability
Contributory negligence does not apply to strict liability, intentional torts, or negligence per se.

F. Contributory Negligence vs. Failure to Mitigate
Generally, if one fails to mitigate damages after the accident has occurred, it is not contributory negligence. Usually, contributory negligence occurs before the accident, and the failure to mitigate damages occurs after the accident.

Exception: A plaintiff's failure to wear a seat belt while driving is not usually construed as contributory negligence, but rather as a failure to mitigate. Thus, damages will be lowered as opposed to barred.

II. LAST CLEAR CHANCE

A. Generally
This defense is actually a response to a defendant's claim that the plaintiff was contributorily negligent. If the plaintiff was contributorily negligent, but can show that the defendant still had the last clear chance to avoid causing the accident, then the plaintiff is not barred from recovering damages.

B. Applicability
The last clear chance doctrine applies whenever the defendant is aware of the plaintiff's danger and does not alleviate it, regardless of whether the plaintiff was helpless to avoid the danger or was inattentive to a means of avoiding the danger. If, however, the defendant did not know of the plaintiff's danger but should have, the last clear chance doctrine only applies if the plaintiff was helpless, as opposed to inattentive.

	Inattentive Defendant	Aware Defendant
Helpless Plaintiff	Last clear chance applies (Plaintiff recovers)	Last clear chance applies (Plaintiff recovers)
Inattentive Plaintiff	Last clear chance does not apply (Plaintiff does not recover)	Last clear chance applies (Plaintiff recovers)

III. COMPARATIVE NEGLIGENCE

A. Generally

This doctrine was developed in reaction to the all-or-nothing approach of contributory negligence. It rejects the all-or-nothing result and instead divides liability between the plaintiff and the defendant based on their relative degrees of fault.

There are two basic types of comparative negligence:

1. Pure Form — Minority View

A plaintiff can recover for damages caused by a defendant even if the plaintiff was more at fault in causing the accident. **Example:** Rob, a plaintiff, is 70 percent responsible for causing an accident. Susan, the defendant, is 30 percent responsible. Susan has to pay Rob 30 percent of the total damages.

2. Modified 50 Percent Rule — Majority View

Only a plaintiff who is equally or less negligent than a defendant can recover; that is, as long as the plaintiff is not more than 50 percent liable for causing the accident, the defendant has to pay a share of damages. But, if the plaintiff is 51 percent responsible then the defendant has no liability.

B. Policy Behind Comparative Negligence

1. The tort system is based on fault and the extent of each party's fault should govern the extent of its liability. Thus, a plaintiff should be allowed to recover damages even if there was contributory negligence.

2. Defendants have more of an incentive to be careful under a system of comparative negligence, as opposed to a system of contributory negligence, because a plaintiff's negligence does not bar recovery.

C. Apportionment of Liability

Usually, the percentage of fault assigned to the plaintiff is determined by examining the relative degree to which the plaintiff's conduct deviated from the standard of reasonableness, as opposed to how much it actually contributed to the accident.

IV. ASSUMPTION OF RISK

A. Generally

If the plaintiff had knowledge of and voluntarily assumed an unreasonable risk that the defendant created, the plaintiff is barred from any recovery.

There are two types of assumption of risk:

1. Express Assumption of Risk

The plaintiff may explicitly agree with the defendant, in advance of being injured, not to hold the defendant liable for any injuries. Express agreements will be enforced unless they are contrary to public policy.

Public policy issues to consider:

a. The relative bargaining power of the plaintiff and the defendant.

b. Whether the waiver of liability was apparent to the plaintiff, or would have been apparent to a reasonable person.

c. The scope of the waiver; for example, a waiver of liability for negligence will not waive liability for grossly negligent or intentionally tortious conduct.

2. Implied Assumption of Risk

Even in the absence of an express agreement, a plaintiff can still assume the risk if:

a. the plaintiff knows of the risk, and

b. the plaintiff's actions imply a voluntary assumption of the risk.

Examples:

a. Spectators are held to impliedly assume certain risks when they go to a sporting event and are injured as a natural and foreseeable result of the sport.

b. Firefighters and police officers cannot sue for injuries sustained in their lines of work because they knowingly and voluntarily undertake the risk.

B. Limitation on Assumption of Risk

1. Some courts treat assumption of the risk as a form of contributory negligence such that it is not a defense if the assumption of the risk was reasonable (i.e., not negligent).

2. In states that have adopted the comparative negligence doctrine, assumption of risk is not an absolute bar to recovery, but rather only a consideration to be taken into account when determining the plaintiff's degree of fault.

V. STATUTES OF LIMITATIONS

Broadly speaking, a statute of limitations puts a limit on the amount of time a plaintiff has to bring a lawsuit. They usually run from the time the plaintiff is injured.

An issue arises as to when the statute of limitations should begin in negligence actions where the plaintiff is injured but does not discover the injury until after the statute would have expired.

A. Traditional View

The statute begins to run at the time of the defendant's negligent act. The time of discovery of injury is irrelevant.

B. Modern Views (Malpractice)
1. Statute begins to run after the injury is discovered or would have been discovered by a reasonable person.
2. Statute begins to run after the physician-patient relationship is terminated.
3. Statute begins to run when the injury is discovered only in cases where a foreign object was left in the patient's body after surgery.
4. Statute begins to run after the injury and its possible cause is discovered.

VI. IMMUNITY

An immunity is a defense to liability in tort that is given to members of a protected class. The granting of immunity to a class of persons is based on their status or special relationship to the plaintiff.

A. Family Immunity
At common law there are two types of familial tort immunity: parent-child and husband-wife. The immunity granted is for personal injuries only.
1. Reasons for Granting Familial Immunity
   Mnemonic: **CLOT**
   a. Fear of **C**ollusion between family members.
   b. Fear of **L**itigation involving trivial disputes that would clog up the courts.
   c. **O**neness of husband and wife.
   d. To encourage peace and **T**ranquility within the family.
2. Exceptions
   a. The husband-wife immunity has been abolished or severely limited in a majority of states. The parent-child immunity has been abolished in about one-third of the states.
   b. There is no familial immunity for intentional torts.
   c. Spousal immunity does not apply to a tort that occurred before the marriage or to a suit commenced after the marriage is dissolved.
   d. Spousal immunity does not bar one from suing a party that is vicariously liable for a spouse's torts.
   e. Parent-child immunity does not apply if the child is an adult, the parent is a step-parent, or one party dies before the suit is begun.
3. Reasonable Parent Standard
   In states where parents have no tort immunity against their children, the parents' duty of care to the children is that of a reasonable parent. Courts will consider such factors as the

child's age, physical health, and intelligence; the number of children in the family; and the circumstances of the accident.

B. Charitable Immunity

At common law, charitable institutions were granted immunity from tort actions. Today, charitable immunity has either been abolished or severely limited.

1. Liability Insurance

The principle reason for abolishing this immunity is the widespread availability of liability insurance.

2. Limitations

In states that still maintain an immunity for charitable organizations, the following limitations are used:

a. Some have abolished it as to hospitals, but allow it for religious or other charitable organizations.

b. Some have allowed it to apply only if the plaintiff was a beneficiary of the charity.

C. Governmental Immunity

1. Federal Government

At common law, "the King could do no wrong" and was immune from all tort actions unless he consented to being sued. This rule was initially adopted in America. However, in 1946, with the passage of the Federal Tort Claims Act, the federal government waived its immunity in cases of "injury or loss of property or personal injury or death caused by the negligent or wrongful act or omission of any employee of the Government while acting within the scope of his office or employment" if the claim was of a nature that the United States would be liable if it were a private person.

Exceptions:

a. Intentional Torts

There is still immunity for intentional torts, except for assault, battery, false imprisonment or arrest, abuse of process, and malicious prosecution committed by investigative or law enforcement officers.

b. Discretionary Acts

There is still immunity for decisions made at the planning level, as distinguished from ministerial acts at the operational level. For example, if a government agency negligently harms a plaintiff because of improper agency procedures, there is no liability because the procedures are formulated at the planning level.

2. State Government

The traditional state government immunity is gradually disappearing. The main reasons for this change are the availability of liability insurance and the inappropriateness today of the idea that "the King can do no wrong."

   a. In states that have not abolished immunity, it extends to state agencies such as jails, social services, and health agencies.

   b. States that have abolished a general governmental immunity still retain immunity for state courts and legislatures.

3. Local Governments

Traditionally, local governments have had at least a limited immunity protecting them from liability arising out of governmental as opposed to proprietary functions. However, because of the difficulty in distinguishing between these functions, many courts have abolished the immunity either completely or at least in cases where the city/local government is insured against liability.

   a. Governmental Functions

   These usually involve police and fire departments, health, education, and other functions traditionally carried out by the government.

   b. Proprietary Functions

   These are functions that tend to produce revenues, such as utilities or airports. Generally, these are functions that could be performed by the private sector.

   c. Standard of Care

   Where local governments do not have any immunity at all, the standard of care that is applicable to them is lower than that used generally in tort.

4. Public Officials

Apart from the immunity conferred on governments, a public official who is acting within the scope of official duties is privileged against tort actions for any damages that result from discretionary conduct.

Judges, legislators, and senior administrative officials have a broader immunity than other public officials. Judges and legislators, acting within the scope of their duties, are not liable even if they acted maliciously or to further their own interests. Senior officials lose their immunity if they act in bad faith.

CASE CLIPS

Butterfield v. Forrester (1809)

Facts: The plaintiff was thrown from his horse when the horse hit a pole left in the road by the defendant. The plaintiff was riding very fast and evidence suggested that the pole could have been seen from 100 yards away.

Issue: May a defendant's negligence be excused by a plaintiff's failure to exercise ordinary care?

Rule: A plaintiff is barred from recovering damages caused by another's negligence when the exercise of ordinary care by the plaintiff could have prevented the accident.

Davies v. Mann (1842)

Facts: Mann's wagon struck Davies's donkey, which was negligently left on a public highway.

Issue: Is a negligent plaintiff barred from recovery?

Rule: A plaintiff whose negligence was not the immediate cause of an accident may recover if a defendant using due care could have avoided the accident.

Note: The "last clear chance doctrine" will allow a contributorily negligent plaintiff to recover if a defendant negligently failed to use the last clear chance to avoid the accident.

McIntyre v. Balentine (1992)

Facts: McIntyre and Balentine were involved in a motor vehicle accident. McIntyre brought a negligence action against Balentine, who answered that the plaintiff was contributorily negligent.

Issue: Should the system of contributory negligence be replaced by one of comparative fault?

Rule: While replacing the all-or-nothing rule of comparative negligence, Tennessee, instead of totally abandoning the fault-based system, opted for the "49 percent rule." Under this system, the amount of damages recoverable is reduced in proportion to the percentage of the total negligence attributable to the plaintiff.

Note: Forty-six states, including Tennessee, have adopted comparative fault, 11 by judicial means, and 34 through the legislature.

Li v. Yellow Cab Co. of California (1975)

Facts: Li negligently made a left-hand turn at an intersection, hitting a driver for Yellow Cab who was speeding through a yellow traffic light.

Issue: Is a contributorily negligent plaintiff completely barred from recovery?

Rule: When both parties have been negligent, liability shall be apportioned according to their relative degrees of fault (pure comparative negligence).

Note: There is no need for the last clear chance doctrine under a system of pure comparative negligence.

Winterstein v. Wilcom (1972)

Facts: Winterstein signed a release before racing his car on Wilcom's race track. Winterstein was injured when he hit an object that was negligently left on the track by Wilcom.

Issue: May a party contract to expressly assume the risk of harm?

Rule: Parties can agree that one party will assume the risk of injury as long as the parties have equal bargaining power, the issue did not involve an essential public service such as a utility, and the injury was not a result of gross negligence or an intentional tort.

Dalury v. S-K-I, Ltd. (1995)

Facts: P signed a release form that exculpated the ski resort from any liability for injuries or property damages he sustained owing to conditions on the property. P was injured when he ran into a metal pole that fenced off the line for the lift.

Issue: Does the release form absolve the resort from liability for P's personal injury?

Rule: Public policy can prohibit the enforcement of an exculpatory provision even if it is clear and express when the business enterprise is in a better position to curtail the risks of the activity.

Seigneur v. National Fitness Institute, Inc. (2002)

Facts: P joined a fitness club and signed an agreement exculpating the club from liability for injuries due to would-be acts of negligence. Under the agreement, the patron assumed the risk of any injury that might befall her in the use of the club. She was injured when she used the club's weight machine for an initial evaluation. She sued.

Issue: Can the exculpatory provision in the contract shield the club from liability for a member's personal injury?

Rule: As long as the exculpatory clause is clear and specific, it is effective in having the patron assume the risk of personal injury occasioned by its use of the club and its facilities.

Hildebrand v. Minyard (1972)

Facts: Hildebrand parked a vehicle in a roadway, partially blocking the flow of traffic. Minyard negligently drove his tractor into Hildebrand's vehicle, killing Hildebrand.

Issue: When has a party impliedly assumed the risk of injury?

Rule: Implied assumption of risk entails a risk to the plaintiff caused by the defendant or the defendant's property, knowledge and appreciation of the magnitude of the risk on the part of the plaintiff, and the plaintiff's voluntary decision to remain in the area of risk.

Note: The failure to fully appreciate and comprehend the consequences of one's own acts is not a matter of assumption of risk, but rather a matter of contributory negligence.

Murphy v. Steeplechase Amusement Co. (1929)

Facts: Murphy fell while riding an amusement park ride that dropped people onto cushions.

Issue: May one recover for an injury received from a perceived risk?

Rule: One who takes part in a sport accepts its inherent, obvious, and necessary dangers.

Rush v. Commercial Realty Co. (1929)

Facts: Rush was injured when she fell through the poorly maintained floor of her apartment's outhouse.

Issue: Does use of a known defective facility constitute assumption of risk if the actor could not have avoided its use?

Rule: The assumption of risk defense does not apply when a plaintiff had "no choice" but to assume the risk.

LeRoy Fibre Co. v. Chicago, Milwaukee & St. Paul Railway (S. Ct. 1914)

Facts: LeRoy Fibre Co. asserted an action for the value of flax burned when a spark flew out of the defendant's negligently operated locomotive. The railroad company claimed that the storage of the flax on the plaintiff's property next to the tracks was contributorily negligent.

Issue: May the use of one's property be limited by the chance that a neighbor may be negligent?

Rule: (McKenna, J.) The right to use one's own property cannot be limited by the wrongs of another.

Siragusa v. Swedish Hospital (1962)

Facts: Siragusa was injured at work by a metal hook on a door.
Issue: Does an employee "assume the risk" of an unsafe work area by staying on the job?
Rule: An employer who negligently fails to provide employees with reasonably safe working conditions cannot assert the defense of "assumption of the risk."

Blackburn v. Dorta (1977)

Facts: Not stated.
Issue: Does implied assumption of risk remain an absolute bar to recovery in comparative negligence jurisdictions?
Rule: The affirmative defense of implied assumption of risk is merged into the defense of contributory negligence; thus the principles of comparative negligence apply in all cases where such defense is asserted.

McIntyre v. Balentine (1992)

Facts: Pickup truck and tractor collide. Both drivers are intoxicated and deemed at fault for the accident. One driver's claim for personal injury was rejected on the basis of contributory negligence.
Issue: Does contributory negligence still act as an absolute bar (in Tennessee) to recovery in personal injury cases?
Rule: Contributory negligence has outlasted its former significance in the attribution of legal liability. It is no longer an actionable defense. In most states, it has been replaced by comparative negligence.

Spier v. Barker (1974)

Facts: Spier suffered extensive injuries because she was not wearing a seat belt when Barker's truck negligently hit her car.
Issue: May damages be reduced for a plaintiff who failed to use a seat belt?
Rule: If a plaintiff failed to mitigate damages by wearing a seat belt, damages should be apportioned such that the defendant is only liable for those that would have occurred had the plaintiff been wearing a seat belt.

Teeters v. Currey (1974)

Facts: Teeters became pregnant over two years after her doctor performed an operation to prevent future pregnancies. She instituted a suit against her physician approximately 11 months after discovering her pregnancy; there was a one-year statute of limitations for such injuries.

Issue: Does the statute of limitations in a malpractice action begin to run from the date of an injury or from the date of its discovery?

Rule: The statute of limitations for a malpractice action commences when the patient discovers, or in the exercise of reasonable care and diligence, should have discovered the resulting injury.

Note: The majority of courts use this "discovery rule."

Levandoski v. Cone (2004)

Facts: P, a police officer, was severely injured when he fell off a rock ledge during a chase to apprehend D. D had refused to stop running after the officer ordered him to do so. P sued D for personal injury on the basis of negligence. D invoked the "firefighter rule."

Issue: Can the "firefighter rule" prevent a policeman from recovering damages for negligence from a tortfeasor who is not the owner or possessor of the property on which he is injured?

Rule: The "firefighter rule" limits a landowner's liability to a first responder to the degree of care owed to a licensee. The limitation applies because of the usually urgent circumstances of the first responders' entry onto the land and to shift the burden of compensation to the municipality that hires and trains the security and emergency personnel. The rule is restricted to premises liability cases and is inapplicable in the instant case.

Freehe v. Freehe (1972)

Facts: The defendant negligently failed to warn her husband of her tractor's unsafe condition.

Issue: Is interspousal tort immunity still applicable?

Rule: The rule of interspousal immunity in personal injury cases is abandoned.

Note: Most courts accept this rule, but retain interfamily immunity in parent-child suits.

Anderson v. Stream (1980)

Facts: The Andersons' child was hit by Stream's car while playing. Stream sought indemnity from the Andersons for negligently allowing their child to wander without supervision.

Issue: Is the doctrine of parental immunity necessary to protect parental authority and discretion?

Rule: The application of a "reasonable parent" standard adequately respects parental authority and discretion, rendering the doctrine of parental immunity unnecessary.

Renko v. McLean (1997)

Facts: While driving, mother rear-ended another vehicle. Her daughter, a passenger in her car, suffered serious injury as a result. Once she reached 18, the daughter filed suit against her mother for the injuries.
Issue: Given the introduction of compulsory automobile liability insurance, is there now an exception to the parent-child immunity doctrine that allows the daughter to sue the mother in the foregoing circumstances?
Rule: Despite the existence of automobile liability insurance, there is no exception (in Maryland) to the parent-child immunity doctrine because its abrogation would result in family financial discord and make raising children more difficult.

Broadbent v. Broadbent (1995)

Facts: Mother left her toddler son near the pool to answer a telephone call. The child fell into the pool and was severely brain injured as a result. Father brought suit against the mother.
Issue: Does the doctrine of parental immunity or intrafamily tort immunity foreclose the possibility of suit?
Rule: Under state law (Arizona), parental immunity is no longer applicable; as a result, parental conduct is assessed by reference to what a reasonable person would have done in the circumstances.

Abernathy v. Sisters of St. Mary's (1969)

Facts: Abernathy was injured when an employee of the defendant's hospital failed to assist him as he moved from his bed to the bathroom.
Issue: Is a benevolent, religious, nonprofit corporation and charitable institution immune from liability for its torts?
Rule: A nongovernmental charitable institution is liable for its own negligence and for the negligence of its agents and employees acting within the scope of their employment.

Ayala v. Philadelphia Board of Public Education (1973)

Facts: Ayala's arm was injured by a shredding machine at the trade school he attended.
Issue: Can a local government be held responsible for injuries resulting from its negligence?

Rule: Local governmental units (e.g., municipal corporations and quasi-corporations) are not immune from tort liability.

Riss v. City of New York (1968)

Facts: Riss was blinded and maimed by a party who had repeatedly threatened her. Her repeated requests for police protection had been denied.

Issue: Is a municipality liable for the negligent failure to protect a citizen from crime?

Rule: Local governments, through their police departments, may not be held liable in the absence of legislation for failure to protect members of the public from external hazards and the activities of criminal wrongdoers.

Lauer v. City of New York (2000)

Facts: The New York City Medical Examiner (ME) issued a faulty autopsy report, leading police to consider P a prime suspect in a homicide. The ME then discovered the true cause of death, but failed to correct the initial report or inform law enforcement authorities. P sued for negligent infliction of emotional distress.

Issue: Is the municipality accountable, through the actions of one of its agents, for the harm suffered by P?

Rule: The public cannot sue municipalities for the performance of public functions unless a statute creates a duty owed to particular individuals or a class of individuals.

DeLong v. Erie County (1982)

Facts: DeLong was stabbed to death because the local police department made an error in writing her address and did not follow standard verification procedures during an emergency call.

Issue: Is a municipality immune from damages caused by the misfeasance of its employees?

Rule: A municipality loses its governmental immunity where a municipal agent undertakes responsibilities to a particular person and exposes the person, without adequate protection, to risks.

Fitch v. United States (1975)

Facts: Fitch was drafted into the army and sent to Vietnam because of a clerical error. He sued under the Federal Tort Claims Act.

Issue: Can a person sue the federal government for misrepresentation?

Rule: Although the Federal Tort Claims Act waives the federal government's immunity for the torts of its employees acting within the scope of their employment, the Act also provides that the courts may not consider "any claim arising out of . . . misrepresentation."

Cope v. Scott (1995)

Facts: P had an accident on a busy road maintained by the National Park Service. P alleged that the Park Service negligently maintained the condition of the road and failed to post sufficient safety warnings.
Issue: Is an action against the National Park Service precluded by the immunity that flows from the discretionary judgment exception to governmental immunity?
Rule: There is nothing discretionary or public-policy-implicating about the maintenance of a road and the posting of safety signs. P has the right to try to convince a jury that the Park Service's conduct was negligent.

Hicks v. State (1975)

Facts: Hicks brought a wrongful death action asserting the state's negligent failure to maintain a bridge.
Issue: Is the state protected from negligence suits by the doctrine of "sovereign immunity?"
Rule: The doctrine of sovereign immunity is abolished.

Deuser v. Vecera (1998)

Facts: Deuser acted in a lewd and offensive manner on the grounds of a national park. Two park rangers arrested him and brought him to the local police. The latter eventually released him, leaving him in a parking lot with no money or means of transportation. He then wandered onto the highway where he was struck by a vehicle and killed.
Issue: Is the United States government liable for Deuser's would-be wrongful death because of the actions of the park rangers?
Rule: Deuser's arrest by park rangers fell within the discretionary function exception to the government's civil liability for injuries to others occasioned by its employees' negligence.

Dalehite v. United States (S. Ct. 1953)

Facts: Dalehite was injured in an explosion at a fertilizer plant that was negligently supervised by the federal government.
Issue: Does the Federal Tort Claims Act allow governmental liability for negligence at the operational (but not at the planning) level?

Rule: (Reed, J.) The Federal Tort Claims Act allows recovery of damages caused by negligent plans, specifications, or schedules of operations. Acts of subordinates in carrying out the operations of the government in accordance with official directions are not actionable.

Geier v. Am. Honda Motor Co., Inc. (2002)

Facts: P sustained severe injuries when her vehicle hit a tree. She sued the manufacturer because it failed to install airbags and other safety equipment in the car.
Issue: Is the lawsuit tenable in light of the Federal Motor Vehicle Safety Standard Act that gives car manufacturers the discretion to install airbags?
Rule: According to the U.S. Supreme Court, airbag lawsuits are preempted by federal law.

Pierce v. Yakima Valley Memorial Hospital Association (1953)

Facts: The plaintiff brought a malpractice action against a charitable hospital in which the plaintiff was a paying patient.
Issue: Is a charitable organization immune from liability for injuries caused by the negligent conduct of its employees?
Rule: The doctrine of charitable immunity is abolished.

Friedman v. State of New York (1986)

Facts: Friedman's car was involved in an accident after it was sideswiped and flung into oncoming traffic. There was no road divider, although the state had previously decided that one was needed.
Issue: Is a state liable for failing to remedy a known dangerous situation?
Rule: The state may be held liable for its failure to remedy a dangerous situation of which it was aware, unless it has a legitimate state interest in doing so.

Clark v. Boston & Maine Railroad (1935)

Facts: Clark was injured when he stood on the defendant's railroad tracks with his back to an oncoming train.
Issue: Is a contributorily negligent plaintiff necessarily barred from recovering against a negligent defendant?
Rule: Under the "last clear chance" doctrine a negligent plaintiff may recover from a subsequently negligent defendant who could have avoided the accident. The plaintiff has the burden of proving that the defendant had the last clear chance to avoid the accident.

Lovell v. Oahe Electric Cooperative (1986)

Facts: Lovell was awarded damages under the state's comparative negligence statute, which allowed a plaintiff who was only slightly negligent to recover damages reduced in proportion to the amount of the plaintiff's contributory negligence.

Issue: Must a judge direct a verdict for a defendant when a plaintiff's negligence was greater than the defendant's?

Rule: When the facts show beyond a reasonable doubt that a plaintiff's negligence was greater than the defendant's, it is the function of the court to find in favor of the defendant.

Farwell v. The Boston and Worcester Rail Road Corp. (1842)

Facts: Farwell, the defendant's employee, was injured when the defendant's train derailed due to another employee's negligence.

Issue: Does one assume the risks inherent in one's employment?

Rule: A party who is employed for compensation takes upon himself the natural risks and perils incident to the performance of his job.

Note: Today it is unlikely that a court would allow this result because of a general policy against the "contracting away" of liability.

Lamson v. American Axe & Tool Co. (1900)

Facts: Lamson, a hatchet painter, complained that the racks on which the hatchets were hung to dry were dangerous. He was told to use the racks or lose his job. Lamson was injured by a falling hatchet.

Issue: Does an employee impliedly assume a risk when the employee continues working, fully aware of a potential danger of the job?

Rule: An employee has assumed the risk and may not recover for an injury if the employee continues working despite the employer's refusal to correct a potential hazard identified by the employee.

Clayards v. Dethick (1848)

Facts: The plaintiff's horse died when it fell in a ditch dug by the defendant. The plaintiff knew of the ditch because he had passed it earlier in the day and was warned by the defendant's employees.

Issue: Has one assumed the risk of another's negligence when one proceeds despite warnings of the risk?

Rule: One does not assume the risk of another's negligence by proceeding despite knowledge of the risk, unless the danger was so great that no sensible person would have incurred it.

Jefferson County Bank of Lakewood v. Armored Motors Service (1961)

Facts: Jefferson County Bank sued Armored Motors Service after the money they were transporting was stolen. Although both parties agreed by contract to limit the defendant's liability, Jefferson sued for an amount in excess of the agreed upon amount.

Issue: Can one limit liability for negligence through contract?

Rule: Liability for the negligent acts of a bailee can be contractually limited if both parties have a thorough understanding of the contract's provisions and equal bargaining power.

McConville v. State Farm Mutual Automobile Insurance Co. (1962)

Facts: The plaintiff, a passenger in the defendant's car, sued the defendant and her insurer for injuries sustained in a car accident.

Issue: Does a guest/passenger assume the risk of negligence by the host/driver?

Rule: The driver of an automobile owes a guest the same duty of care as to other persons. The guest is not implied to have assumed the risk of negligent driving.

Salinas v. Vierstra (1985)

Facts: Salinas lost his tort action when a jury accepted his employer's defense that Salinas had assumed the risk inherent in his employment. This defense conflicted with the state's comparative negligence laws.

Issue: Is the doctrine of assumption of risk still valid?

Rule: Except where an individual expressly consents to contractually assume the risk involved, the assumption of risk defense no longer has any legal effect. Issues of nonexpress assumption of risk are decided by using principles of comparative negligence.

Tunkl v. Regents of the University of California (1963)

Facts: Tunkl signed a form releasing a charitable hospital from any liability for negligent acts. This was a condition of admission.

Issue: Is an agreement to relieve a hospital of liability for negligent acts valid?

Rule: Public interest will void an agreement limiting a hospital's liability for negligence.

Beems v. Chicago, Rock Island & Peoria R.R. Co. (1882)

Facts: Beems died while trying to uncouple two railroad cars of a moving train. Beems had signaled the other workers to slow down the train, but they failed to do so. The court rejected the defendants' argument that Beems was contributorily negligent.
Issue: What is the effect of a court's rejection of a contributory negligence defense?
Rule: A negligent defendant will be completely liable if the plaintiff is found to be free of contributory negligence.

Gyerman v. United States Lines Co. (1972)

Facts: Gyerman, a longshoreman, was injured while unloading sacks that he knew were stacked dangerously.
Issue: Which party has the burden of proving the elements of contributory negligence?
Rule: The defendant has the burden of proving that the plaintiff's own negligence contributed to the injury.

Derheim v. N. Fiorito Co. (1972)

Facts: The plaintiff was not wearing his seat belt when he was injured in a collision caused by the defendant's negligence.
Issue: Is the failure to wear a seat belt contributory negligence?
Rule: Failure to use a seat belt is not contributory negligence because it is not the cause of an accident.

Kumkumian v. City of New York (1953)

Facts: Kumkumian was found dead under a subway car that had made an emergency stop after the engineer had twice attempted to drive over the track, but was unable to because of the plaintiff's body on the tracks. These attempts to drive on probably killed the plaintiff.
Issue: May a negligent plaintiff recover damages against a negligent defendant when the defendant had a chance to avoid the accident?
Rule: Under the last clear chance doctrine, a plaintiff's negligence is not the proximate cause of the plaintiff's injury when a negligent defendant had the last clear chance to avoid the accident.

Meistrich v. Casino Arena Attractions, Inc. (1959)

Facts: Meistrich continued to skate on the defendant's ice rink after noticing that its corners were too slippery for ordinary skaters.

Issue: Are assumption of risk and contributory negligence distinct and independent defenses?

Rule: Assumption of risk is not a separate defense from contributory negligence. If a plaintiff impliedly assumes a risk, the plaintiff is considered to be contributorily negligent.

Obstetrics & Gynecologists v. Pepper (1985)

Facts: Treatment at a medical clinic was conditioned on the signing of an irrevocable arbitration agreement expressly waiving the right to a trial. Pepper was injured by a drug prescribed by the medical clinic. She did not recall signing the agreement or having it explained by an employee of the medical clinic.

Issue: Is an arbitration clause of an adhesion contract enforceable against the adhering party?

Rule: Although an adhesion contract is enforceable if it falls within the reasonable expectations of the weaker party and is not unduly oppressive, courts will not enforce a contractual provision limiting the duties or liabilities of a stronger party absent plain and clear notification of the terms of the contract and an understanding consent to such terms by the weaker party.

American Motorcycle Association v. Superior Court (1978)

Facts: The plaintiff was injured in a motorcycle race for novices that was negligently organized by the defendants, the American Motorcycle Association. The defendants filed a crossclaim against the plaintiff's parents for their negligent supervision of their child.

Issue: Can the indemnity doctrine be modified to allow only partial, proportional indemnity among concurrent tortfeasors?

Rule: Under the doctrine of partial equitable indemnity, the apportionment of loss among codefendants on pure comparative principles is permitted.

Berkovitz by Berkovitz v. United States (S. Ct. 1988)

Facts: Berkovitz was injured by a dose of a contaminated polio vaccine. The defendants, having approved the production and release of that vaccine, asserted the "discretionary function" exception.

Issue: When may government officials invoke the discretionary function exception to avoid liability for decisions that involve the permissible exercise of policy judgment?

Rule: (Marshall, J.) The discretionary function exception will be barred as a defense to liability only where the organization's policy leaves no room for an official to exercise discretion, or if the act does not involve the exercise of discretion.

Harlow v. Fitzgerald (S. Ct. 1982)

Facts: The defendants, aides to President Nixon, were instrumental in influencing the President to fire Harlow, an Air Force employee who had testified about huge cost overruns in the Air Force.
Issue: Are senior aides and advisors to the President of the United States entitled to immunity for damages caused by official acts?
Rule: (Powell, J.) Presidential aides are not immune for official acts if they knew or reasonably should have known that the actions they took within their sphere of official responsibility violated the constitutional rights of the plaintiff, or if they maliciously intended to deprive the plaintiff of constitutional rights.

Brown v. San Francisco Ball Club, Inc. (1950)

Facts: Brown was struck by a wildly thrown baseball while she was sitting in the stands behind first base.
Issue: Are the dangers inherent in attending a baseball game so obvious that a spectator impliedly "assumes the risk?"
Rule: By voluntarily entering into a baseball stadium as a spectator, one accepts the reasonable risks and hazards inherent and incidental to the sport.

Verduce v. Board of Higher Education (1959)

Facts: Verduce fell down a staircase when she exited the stage without looking down during an opera rehearsal. The director had told her not to look down when exiting or she would be fired.
Issue: Can one recover for injuries resulting from a known danger?
Rule: A person must exercise reasonable care in regard to one's own safety. Ignoring a known danger for personal motives is no excuse.

Santangelo v. State of New York (1988)

Facts: The plaintiffs, police officers, were injured while capturing a mental patient who was negligently allowed to escape from a state hospital.
Issue: May a police officer injured in the line of duty sue a party who negligently created the need for their services?
Rule: Because it is the duty of the police to deal on behalf of the public with emergencies created by negligence, they may not sue a party who has negligently created the need for their services.
Note: Firefighters may not sue those who negligently caused a fire.

Gonzalez v. Garcia (1977)

Facts: The plaintiff was injured while he was a passenger in a car driven by a driver he knew to be intoxicated.

Issue: What effect does the adoption of comparative negligence have upon the defense of implied assumption of the risk?

Rule: Adoption of a comparative negligence standard results in the merger of implied assumption of risk and comparative negligence. Express assumption of risk still remains as a separate defense.

D'Amario v. Ford Motor Co. (2001)

Facts: P's son was a passenger in a car that veered off the road and hit a tree. The driver of the car was intoxicated and going at a high rate of speed. The car caught fire upon impact. P alleged that the fire was due to a faulty relay switch.

Issue: Does comparative fault apply in automobile crash worthiness cases?

Rule: The Florida state Supreme Court adhered to the minority view and held that victim negligence was irrelevant as to whether the manufacturer created a vehicle with a defective design. In effect, crashworthiness cases involve two separate events and two separable causes of action: the initial crash caused by the negligent driver, which then leads to the safety issue of how well the car was conceived from an engineering perspective. Distinct tortfeasors thereby are held liable for the injuries they actually cause. Evidence about the driver's recklessness might also be prejudicial to P's case against the manufacturer.

Turner v. Jordan (1997)

Facts: A nurse was severely beaten by a patient who was in treatment with a psychiatrist at the same facility. The psychiatrist knew of the patient's violent propensities.

Issue: Does comparative fault allow for the uneven distribution of liability between the patient and the psychiatrist and, if so, can most or all of the liability be attributed to the psychiatrist?

Rule: There is a split among courts on this issue. Some courts allow all forms of fault (intentional, reckless, and negligent) to be compared and assessed together. Other courts, such as the one in this case, do not allow the "mixing and matching" of different forms of fault, even though one may proceed reasonably forseeably from another. These courts find it difficult to apportion responsibility among qualitatively different behaviors. This approach could, however, discourage merely negligent actors from complying with the basic duty of care.

Albritton v. Neighborhood Centers Association for Child Development (1984)

Facts: Albritton's daughter was allegedly injured at the defendant's day care center. The defendant was a nonprofit corporation.

Issue: Is the doctrine of charitable immunity valid in Ohio?

Rule: There is no immunity for charitable organizations in Ohio. Allowing immunity forces injured parties to make a contribution to the charity that caused the injury and often results in other governmental assistance agencies and other charities bearing the burden of the loss. Further, the fear that charitable organizations will cease to exist if immunity is abolished is unfounded.

Winn v. Gilroy (1984)

Facts: The plaintiff sued her husband after her two children were killed in a car accident caused by her husband's drunk driving.

Issue: May a parent be liable to a child for injuries caused?

Rule: Although general familial tort immunity has been abolished, parents still retain some privilege due to the special relationship they have with their children. However, where parents have failed to fulfill the general duty of ordinary care to avoid foreseeable injury, they may be liable.

CHAPTER 13

Imputed Negligence

I. VICARIOUS LIABILITY

The doctrine of vicarious liability imputes the wrongful conduct of a tortfeasor to a third person who is considered to be responsible for the tortfeasor's actions. This responsibility arises out of a special relationship, for example, in employment relationships, family relationships or joint ventures.

One of the motivating factors of this doctrine is the need to find a defendant who can compensate the plaintiff.

A. Respondeat Superior

1. Employer-Employee

Under the doctrine of respondeat superior, an employer is liable for the torts that employees commit while acting within the scope of their employment. An employee is considered to be a worker who is subject to the control of the employer.

2. Scope of Employment

All actions that are closely connected to an employee's work that are done with a purpose to advance an employer's business interests are within the scope of employment. Actions that are expressly prohibited by an employer are not automatically outside the scope of employment. Rather, the court will consider both the fact that they were prohibited, and whether they were performed for the employer's benefit.

a. Commuting to Work

Traveling between work and home is outside the scope of employment.

b. Frolic and Detour During Business Trips

An employee who makes a detour for personal reasons while on a business trip and causes damages:

i. Traditionally, an employer was liable only if the accident occurred while an employee was on the way back to the business route after ending the personal visit.

  ii. Today, courts will hold an employer liable if the detour is reasonably foreseeable. One factor to consider in foreseeability is the distance of the detour.

 3. Intentional Torts

 An employer is liable for intentional torts by an employee if they were done for the benefit of the employer's business. However, if an employee acted for personal reasons, the employer is not liable. Some courts allow liability only if the intentional tort was reasonably foreseeable by the employer.

B. Independent Contractors

Independent contractors are workers who are not subject to the control of the employer. They decide for themselves how to do the work. An employer is not held liable for a tort committed by an independent contractor unless:

Mnemonic: **NUN**

 1. **N**ondelegable

 Public policy makes the duty nondelegable.

 2. **U**ltrahazardous

 The work involved ultrahazardous activities.

 3. **N**egligence

 An employer negligently selects an incompetent independent contractor.

C. Joint Enterprise

All members of a joint venture are vicariously liable for the torts of each other.

Mnemonic: **MAC**

 1. **M**utuality of Control

 Each member must have an equal say on the issue of how things are done. This is not necessarily equal physical control, but at least a situation where all have equal influence.

 2. **A**greement

 The members must be acting in concert by some express or implied agreement.

 3. **C**ommon Pecuniary Purpose

 All the members must have a common pecuniary purpose. Merely sharing expenses or a social interest is not enough.

D. Bailments and Other Bases

 1. Automobile Owner and Driver

 Generally, an automobile owner is not vicariously liable for the conduct of another person who drives the car. However, this rule is subject to exceptions.

  a. Permissive Use/Auto Consent Statutes

  Some states have enacted statutes that make a car owner vicariously liable for the tortious conduct of any person that drives the car with the owner's consent. Of course the driver has to act reasonably within the scope of the owner's consent. For example, Rob lends his car to Susan to go to a movie, then Susan drives 2,000 miles: no consent.

If an owner lends a car to a driver who in turn lends it to another, the owner will be liable for damages by the second driver if the first driver was in the car at the time of the accident.

b. Family Purpose

In the absence of a statute, some courts will hold an owner of a family car vicariously liable for the torts committed by immediate family or household members driving with express or implied permission. A family purpose exists anytime any family member benefits from the use of the car.

c. Bailee

If there is no permissive use statute, a bailor is not vicariously liable for a bailee's negligent conduct unless the bailor was negligent in allowing the bailment.

2. Parent-Child

Parents are usually not vicariously liable for the negligence of their children.

Exceptions:

a. The parent was negligent.

b. The child was acting as a family agent.

II. IMPUTED CONTRIBUTORY NEGLIGENCE

Contributory negligence can be vicariously transferred between parties just like ordinary negligence.

For example, Susan, Brett's employee, is involved in an accident with Rob. If Susan is contributorily negligent, Brett is also considered to have been contributorily negligent. Thus, Brett would be barred from recovery for damages to his car in an action against Rob.

However, in situations where vicarious liability exists because of consent statutes or the family purpose doctrine, the courts will usually not impute contributory negligence.

CASE CLIPS

Lundberg v. State (1969)

Facts: Lundberg was killed in an accident involving a state employee who was driving home from work.

Issue: May employers be held vicariously liable under respondeat superior for a wrongful death caused by an employee's negligence while commuting?

Rule: Employees who drive to and from work are not acting within the scope of their employment. Thus employers are not liable under respondeat superior for an employee's negligence while commuting.

Bussard v. Minimed, Inc. (2003)

Facts: Employee became ill at work when she inhaled fumes at Minimed facility. She was dizzy and went home early. On route, she rear-ended P's car at a stoplight. P sued both the employee and her employer, the latter on the basis of vicarious liability.

Issues: Does returning home early after falling ill at work due to workplace conditions come within the worker's scope of employment, making the employer vicariously liable for the consequences of her conduct?

Rule: Ordinarily, commuting to and from work is not part of an employee's employment responsibilities. Such travel, however, can engender employer liability if the employee's need to return home resulted from workplace conditions and created a reasonably foreseeable risk of harm to others. The elements of the exception were met in this case.

Fruit v. Schreiner (1972)

Facts: Schreiner was injured by Fruit, who was driving back to his home from a business convention.

Issue: Is the doctrine of respondeat superior applicable when an employee travels to a social function with the intention of making a business connection?

Rule: When part of one's motivation to attend a social function is business related, the function is within the scope of employment and an employer is liable under the doctrine of respondeat superior.

Murrell v. Goertz (1979)

Facts: Goertz, a newspaper delivery boy, injured Murrell, a customer, in a fight over damage caused by thrown newspapers.

Issue: What factors are used to determine whether an individual is an independent contractor or an employee?

Rule: If an individual has the right to control the physical details of the work, the individual will be considered an independent contractor, not an employee. Employers are not liable under respondeat superior for the actions of independent contractors.

Maloney v. Rath (1968)

Facts: Rath was involved in an accident due to his negligently repaired brakes. The defect was unknown to him.

Issue: May a defendant delegate the duty of reasonable care to an agent?

Rule: Where grave harm or death may result from negligence, the duty of care is unlikely to be delegable.

Popejoy v. Steinle (1991)

Facts: Steinle got into a car accident on the way to purchasing a cow for her daughter. Popejoy alleged that the trip was actually a joint venture between Steinle and her husband, in an attempt to reach his estate to obtain damages for recurring injuries from the accident.

Issue: Does the running of household errands constitute a joint venture between a husband and wife so as to make each liable for the other's actions?

Rule: Where there is no financial or business purpose to a trip, a joint venture does not exist, and one spouse cannot be found to be vicariously liable for any alleged negligence committed by the other.

Shuck v. Means (1974)

Facts: Shuck was injured in a car accident caused by the defendant's negligent driving of a car rented by the defendant's friend. A statute provided for the vicarious liability of a car's owner for any negligent driver who is expressly or impliedly authorized to drive the car.

Issue: Is a lessor liable for damages caused by the negligent use of its property by a person other than the lessee in violation of a contract?

Rule: A lessor is vicariously liable if its property is negligently used by a third party when a consent statute provides for such liability, even though such use by a third party is in violation of the leasing contract.

Note: The court, by using the "consent" doctrine, bypassed the traditional rule of no vicarious liability between a lessor and lessee. The court considered this an unbroken "chain of consent" despite limits in the contract against such actions.

Smalich v. Westfall (1970)

Facts: Smalich was killed while a passenger in her own car, which was negligently driven by Westfall. The driver of the car they hit was also driving negligently. The lower court imputed Westfall's contributory negligence to Smalich, thereby barring her right to recovery.
Issue: Must the contributory negligence of a driver always be imputed to the car's owner?
Rule: A plaintiff is not barred from recovering against a negligent defendant by the contributory negligence of a third party unless the plaintiff's relationship with the third party would make him vicariously liable as a defendant for the party's negligent actions. Only a finding of a master-servant relationship or a joint enterprise would create such liability.

Ira S. Bushey & Sons, Inc. v. United States (1968)

Facts: An inebriated Coast Guard sailor returning to his ship from shore leave accidentally damaged the plaintiff's drydock controls.
Issue: Can an employer be vicariously liable for torts committed by an employee that were not made to further the employer's interest?
Rule: An employer will be held vicariously liable for foreseeable torts that are committed by employees, even if the torts do not occur while the employer's interest was being advanced.

Becker v. Interstate Properties (1977)

Facts: Becker was injured in a construction accident caused by the defendant's subcontractor, who was not properly insured.
Issue: May an employer be held vicariously liable for the torts of an independent subcontractor?
Rule: An employer may be held vicariously liable for the torts of an independent subcontractor if the employer did not exercise ordinary care in selecting the subcontractor.

O'Shea v. Welch (2003)

Facts: Store manager collides with another vehicle while he is en route to the district office to deliver NFL tickets to other managers in the company. The manager tried to turn suddenly into a gas station to get an estimate from a mechanic for the maintenance of his vehicle. In doing so, he hit P's car.
Issue: Could a jury reasonably conclude that the manager's activities were related to, and arose from, his employment responsibilities and that his conduct, as a result, implicated the employer's liability?

Rule: Under the "slight deviation" rule, vicarious liability can extend to actions that are reasonably incidental to employment.

Jackson v. Jackson (1974)

Facts: Jackson brought an action for malicious prosecution against the partners of the law firm representing her estranged husband.
Issue: Are all partners in a law firm liable for the actions of one of the partners in the law firm?
Rule: Partners are held vicariously liable for wrongful acts by other partners that are in furtherance of business.
Note: Actions such as malicious prosecution are not considered in furtherance of a law firm's business.

Howard v. Zimmerman (1926)

Facts: The defendant borrowed his father's car and went for a joyride with his friend. His friend drove the car negligently and hit the plaintiff.
Issue: May a person who is not in an authority position over a party be held vicariously liable for the negligence of that party?
Rule: When two persons are involved in a joint enterprise with equal authority and a common goal, one can be held vicariously liable for the negligence of the other.

Weber v. Stokely-Van Camp Inc. (1966)

Facts: The plaintiff was injured in a car accident when his employee, who was driving for business reasons, negligently hit another car. The driver of the other car was also negligent.
Issue: Must contributory negligence be imputed between two parties who have a relationship that would give rise to vicarious liability?
Rule: Contributory negligence is not imputed between two parties if the party who is vicariously liable does not control the other party's minute to minute decisions.

Hardy v. Brantley (1985)

Facts: Plaintiff was killed when his perforated duodenal ulcer was misdiagnosed by an emergency room physician and went untreated.
Issue: When can a provider of services be held vicariously liable for the conduct of its agents?
Rule: A provider of services is vicariously liable for the conduct of its agents when a person engages the services promoted by the provider without regard to the identity of the agent who is contracted to provide that service. The injuries must be proximately caused by the negligence of the agent.

CHAPTER 14

Strict Liability

I. HARM CAUSED BY ANIMALS

A. Trespassing Animals

If an animal trespasses on a plaintiff's land and causes damages, the animal's owner is strictly liable. However, if the owner is walking the animal along a public road and it strays onto the adjoining land, the owner is not strictly liable.

B. Dangerous Animals

An owner is strictly liable for any harm that a dangerous animal causes if:

1. the harm results from a dangerous propensity that is characteristic of the animal's species or a dangerous propensity particular to the animal that the owner knew or should have known; and
2. the victim did not contribute to the animal's behavior.

C. Domestic Animals

An owner is strictly liable only if the owner knew or should have known that the animal had dangerous propensities.

D. First Bite Rule

The owner is liable for the second time that the animal bites somebody but not the first time it bites if it never showed such a propensity to bite before.

II. ULTRAHAZARDOUS ACTIVITIES

There is strict liability for activities that involve an inherent and substantial risk of harm. Generally, if a defendant engages in such an activity, the defendant is strictly liable for any harm caused.

A. Limitations

1. Strict liability extends only to foreseeable plaintiffs who are injured by a kind of risk that made the activity ultrahazardous. For example, radiation is the foreseeable risk of a nuclear reactor. However, if a wall of the reactor collapses because of an earthquake,

strict liability would not be applied because that is not the risk that makes a reactor dangerous.

2. The defendant is not liable if the plaintiff is hurt because of the plaintiff's abnormal sensitivity.

B. Determination

Some factors to consider when determining whether an activity is ultrahazardous are:

1. the degree of risk of harm to persons or property.
2. the seriousness of the harm that could result.
3. whether the activity cannot be performed with complete safety.
4. whether the activity is commonly engaged in.
5. the location at which the activity is performed.
6. the value to the community versus the activity's dangerous attributes.

C. Examples

Some examples of ultrahazardous activities include the operation of nuclear reactors, the use and storage of explosives, and the spraying of crops.

Note: The operation of an airplane is not considered to be an ultrahazardous activity, but some courts will rule that strict liability for ground damage from aviation accidents is applicable.

D. Defenses

1. Contributory Negligence

   Contributory negligence is not a defense unless the party knew of the abnormally dangerous activity.

2. Assumption of Risk

   If the party unreasonably exposed itself to the risk, fully aware of its existence, the defendant will not be liable.

3. Comparative Negligence

   Comparative negligence will be used to reduce damages.

CASE CLIPS

Rylands v. Fletcher (1865-1868)

Facts: The defendant had a reservoir constructed close to the plaintiff's coal mines. When the reservoir filled, water broke through an abandoned mine shaft and flooded the plaintiff's mines. Although the contractors and engineers were negligent, the defendant was not personally negligent.
Issue: May a person be liable for damages caused despite the use of due care?
Rule in the Exchequer (1865): Unless damages are immediate, there can be no trespass. Unless the act is unlawful, there can be no nuisance. Unless there is negligence, there can be no liability.
Rule in the Exchequer Chamber (1866): One who brings anything on land that is likely to do mischief if it escapes is strictly liable for damages that are the natural consequence of its escape.
Rule in the House of Lords (1868): One is strictly liable for damages resulting from the dangerous nonnatural use of land.

Bridges v. The Kentucky Stone Co., Inc. (1981)

Facts: Webb, an employee of Kentucky Stone, stole dynamite from Kentucky Stone's plant and blasted Bridges's home.
Issue: Is the storage of explosives an ultrahazardous activity?
Rule: Whether storage of explosives in any particular circumstance is an "ultrahazardous activity" must be determined on a case-by-case basis.

Yukon Equipment, Inc. v. Fireman's Fund Insurance Co. (1978)

Facts: Thieves broke into Yukon's explosives warehouse and blew it up to destroy evidence of their crime. Fireman's sued to recover the damage that occurred to adjoining property, claiming that Yukon was strictly liable.
Issue: Is the storage of explosives an ultrahazardous activity?
Rule: The storage of explosives is inherently ultrahazardous, regardless of the storage location.

Indiana Harbor Belt R.R. Co. v. American Cyanimid Co. (1990)

Facts: A train car carrying chemicals arrived at plaintiff's yard where some of the chemicals leaked.

Issue: Should the shipper of a hazardous chemical be strictly liable for the consequences of a spill or other accident, while the chemicals are being transported?

Rule: Strict liability creates an incentive to be a more careful party. The greater the risk and the cost, were an accident to occur, the stronger the case for strict liability. To be strictly liable, one must prove that the transportation of a chemical through populated areas is so hazardous that even with due care an accident would occur.

Langan v. Valicopters, Inc. (1977)

Facts: Valicopters, a crop-dusting company, sprayed a field adjoining Langan's organic farm. Because some of the pesticide landed on Langan's crops, he was unable to sell his produce because it was no longer "organic."

Issue: Is a party strictly liable for damage that is proximately caused by the aerial spraying of pesticides?

Rule: Aerial spraying of pesticides is by its very nature an abnormally dangerous activity and strict liability applies to all damages it causes.

Note: The Restatement (Second) of Torts §520 lists six factors to determine "abnormally dangerous" activities: (1) high degree of risk of harm, (2) likelihood that harm will be great, (3) inability to eliminate risk by use of reasonable care, (4) not a common activity, (5) location where activity is carried on, and (6) the value of activity to the community. These six factors are weighed together and don't have to be met individually.

Foster v. Preston Mill Co. (1954)

Facts: Blasting by the Preston Mill Co. frightened Foster's minks and caused them to kill their kittens.

Issue: Is one strictly liable for all damages caused by an ultrahazardous activity?

Rule: One conducting an ultrahazardous activity is not strictly liable for damages incident to a plaintiff's extraordinary and unusual use of land where such damages are not a result of the risk that made the activity ultrahazardous.

Golden v. Amory (1952)

Facts: A hurricane caused water in the defendant's dike to overflow, damaging the plaintiff's property.

Issue: Is one strictly liable for damages caused by an act of God?

Rule: Although strict liability is usually imposed on those who bring on their lands anything likely to do mischief if it escapes, it will not apply when an injury results from an act of God.

Baker v. Snell (1908)

Facts: The defendant's dog, known to have a propensity to bite, bit the plaintiff after the defendant's servant mischievously let the dog loose.

Issue: Must negligence be shown to make an animal owner liable for injuries inflicted by the animal?

Rule: An owner of an animal that is known to be dangerous is strictly liable for the animal's actions, even if the immediate cause of damage is the act of a third party.

Sandy v. Bushey (1925)

Facts: The plaintiff was kicked by the defendant's horse while trespassing. The defendant knew his horse had vicious tendencies.

Issue 1: Is an owner of an animal strictly liable for its actions?

Rule 1: An owner of an animal is strictly liable for injuries caused by the animal if the owner has knowledge of the animal's vicious propensities.

Issue 2: Is contributory negligence a defense to strict liability?

Rule 2: Contributory negligence is only a defense to negligence claims. Although a plaintiff's slight negligence or want of due care is insufficient to relieve a defendant of strict liability, a plaintiff who unnecessarily and voluntarily brings an injury upon himself is not entitled to recovery.

Marshall v. Ranne (1974)

Facts: Marshall's hand was severely injured by Ranne's vicious hog. Marshall knew of the hog's tendencies but failed to protect himself.

Issue: Does contributory negligence bar recovery for damages in an action based on strict liability involving a vicious animal?

Rule: The defense of contributory negligence is not available in strict liability actions for injuries caused by a vicious animal, unless the plaintiff's negligence directly allowed the animal to escape from the defendant's land.

Shipley v. Fifty Associates (1870)

Facts: The plaintiff was injured when ice and snow that had naturally accumulated on the defendant's roof slid off and hit her in the head.

Issue: Is one strictly liable for damages caused by one's property?

Rule: One is strictly liable for damages caused by one's property (i.e., one has a duty to use the property in such a way that others will not be harmed).

Siegler v. Kuhlman (1973)

Facts: The trailer of Kuhlman's truck disengaged and spilled gasoline on the road. The plaintiff was killed when the gas caught fire. The reason for the trailer's disengagement was unknown.

Issue: Is a defendant liable for injuries proximately caused by an inherently dangerous activity despite an absence of negligence?

Rule: Inherently dangerous activities are subject to strict liability.

Koos v. Roth (1982)

Facts: The defendant, a commercial grass seed producer, regularly burned his field after the seed was harvested. Without any negligence on the defendant's part, the plaintiff's adjoining field caught fire.

Issue: Is a party who engages in an activity that is not inherently dangerous liable in the absence of negligence if the activity was conducted in an abnormal manner?

Rule: An individual who engages in an activity in a manner that creates an uncontrollable danger of serious harm beyond the ordinary risks associated with that activity is strictly liable.

PSI Energy, Inc. v. Roberts (2003)

Facts: Roberts was employed by AC and S, who, in turn, worked as an independent contractor for PSI. As part of his work for AC and S and PSI, Roberts frequently came into contact with asbestos. When he developed mesothelioma, he sued his employer and their employer on a vicarious liability basis.

Issue: Is vicarious liability a proper bridge by which to reach PSI Energy as a potentially liable tortfeasor?

Rule: Working with insulation that contains asbestos does not constitute an "inherently dangerous" activity; therefore, vicarious liability against the employer of the employer is not warranted.

Chavez v. Southern Pacific Transportation Co. (1976)

Facts: Eighteen boxcars loaded with government-owned bombs exploded while being transported by Southern Pacific Transportation.

Issue: Is a party strictly liable for damages that result from an ultrahazardous activity when the party is obligated by law to perform the activity?

Rule: Parties who engage in ultrahazardous activities are strictly liable for damages caused by those activities, regardless of whether the party was obligated by law to engage in the activity.

Lubin v. Iowa City (1964)

Facts: Iowa City's underground water main broke, flooding the basement of Lubin's store. As a matter of policy, Iowa City did not inspect its pipes for repairs until they broke.
Issue: Is a party strictly liable when it deliberately fails to maintain its property?
Rule: Strict liability may be imposed on a party who deliberately keeps property that was not inherently dangerous in an inherently dangerous manner.

Bierman v. City of New York (1969)

Facts: Bierman's home was damaged by a water main break. She was unable to show any negligence on the part of the defendant.
Issue: May the rule of strict liability be applied to achieve the social goal of spreading a risk among many persons?
Rule: Cost spreading is a valid social goal and a valid reason to apply strict liability.

McLane v. Northwest Natural Gas Co. (1970)

Facts: Gas leaked from Northwest Natural's gas tanks and exploded despite extensive precautions taken to avoid an accident.
Issue: Is an activity considered ultrahazardous when the risk of an accident is small?
Rule: The principal factor determining if an activity is ultrahazardous is whether the activity creates an additional risk to others that cannot be alleviated, and that arises from the extraordinary, exceptional, or abnormal nature of the activity.

Miller v. Civil Constructors, Inc. (1995)

Facts: P was injured when he was hit by a stray bullet that ricocheted from a gravel pit where police officers were engaged in firing practice. P sued the owners of the pit on the basis of strict liability.
Issue: Does the use of firearms constitute an ultrahazardous activity to which no-fault liability principles apply?
Result: The use of firearms and guns is governed by negligence principles and a duty of reasonable care in the circumstances. Reasonable care is sufficient to attenuate the risks associated with the commonplace use of guns in society.

Maye v. Tappan (1863)

Facts: Maye and Tappan owned adjacent gold mines. Tappan entered Maye's mine and removed gold, erroneously believing he was still on his own property.
Issue: Has a trespass occurred when a party believed it was on its own property?
Rule: The intent required for a trespass is the intent to do the physical act of the trespass, and not the intent to trespass.

Madsen v. East Jordan Irrigation Co. (1942)

Facts: The defendant's blasting caused Madsen's minks to panic and kill their young.
Issue: Is one who is engaged in an ultrahazardous activity strictly liable for indirect damages?
Rule: Parties engaged in ultrahazardous activities are strictly liable for direct, but not indirect damages.

Sullivan v. Dunham (1900)

Facts: Sullivan was killed by fragments from a tree that the defendant was using dynamite to remove.
Issue: Must negligence be proven to recover for a trespass to the body resulting from a dangerous activity?
Rule: A person is strictly liable for trespass damages proximately caused by the person's involvement in a dangerous activity.

Turner v. Big Lake Oil Co. (1936)

Facts: Polluted water from Big Lake's wells escaped and poisoned land and water on Turner's property.
Issue: Can a person be held strictly liable for escape of water confined on one's land?
Rule: A plaintiff must prove negligence to establish liability for damage caused by water escaping from a defendant's land.
Note: This holding, which rejects the Rylands rule, is the view in a minority of states.

CHAPTER 15

Products Liability

Products liability refers to the liability of a seller or manufacturer whose product causes damage to a buyer, user, or even a bystander because it was defectively made.

I. NEGLIGENCE

A plaintiff can use ordinary negligence principles to hold a manufacturer liable for a defective product. At one time there was a requirement that a plaintiff be in privity with the seller, but that was abolished in MacPherson v. Buick Motor Co. A plaintiff may recover for personal injury and property damages.

A. Manufacturer's Duty of Care

Plaintiffs may bring negligence actions against manufacturers if the manufacturers fail to properly ensure that:

1. the products are designed in a reasonably safe way;
2. the manufacturing system is reasonably error-free;
3. the products are reasonably tested/inspected;
4. the products are packaged and shipped with reasonable safety;
5. the components used are reasonably competent.

B. Retailer

It is very difficult to hold the retailer of a product liable under a negligence theory. Usually retailers do not have a duty to inspect the products they sell. However, a retailer who knows or should know that a product was unreasonably defective has a duty to warn.

C. Bystanders

Bystanders may be able to sue a manufacturer if they can show that they were foreseeable plaintiffs.

II. WARRANTY

Where a manufacturer of a product is not negligent, a party may still recover damages from the seller if it can be shown that the seller of the product made representations or warranties as to the quality of the product that prove to be false, regardless of whether it was known to be false. This applies to both implied and express warranties.

A. Express Warranty (UCC)

An express warranty is not limited by privity; it extends to all members of a class that a seller intended to reach with the warranty. However, a warranty does not extend to resale if the manufacturer did not expect the product to be resold.

An express warranty can be made in several ways:

1. a seller describes the product in a certain way;
2. a seller uses a sample or model to show clients; or
3. there is a written statement or clause in a contract.

B. Implied Warranty

A warranty may be implied, even absent an express one, from the fact that goods are being offered for sale.

1. Implied Warranty of Merchantability

All products that are packaged in labeled containers are assumed to be fit for the ordinary purpose for which they are intended. This warranty applies if:

a. the seller is regularly engaged in the sale of the product;
b. the product is food and drink; or
c. the warranty is implied by the act of a seller in offering to sell the product.

2. Implied Warranty of Fitness for a Particular Purpose

This warranty is breached only if a seller misrepresents to a buyer, even unintentionally, that a product is suitable for a specific use for which it is not suitable, and the buyer, relying on the misrepresentation, is injured.

3. Privity

There is no requirement of privity between a buyer and a seller. An implied warranty runs with a product to any buyer. The courts allow other parties to sue by one of two legal fictions that create privity.

a. Horizontal Privity

Most states allow a warranty to extend to a buyer's family and guests. For example, Rob buys a car from Buick and lets Susan, his sister, drive the car. Susan crashes because the brakes are defective. Susan can sue Buick for breach of the implied warranty of merchantability.

b. Vertical Privity
Vertical privity extends to any foreseeable people using the product.

C. Defenses
Mnemonic: <u>D</u>efensive <u>T</u>ypes <u>C</u>onsciously <u>A</u>void <u>L</u>iability
1. <u>D</u>isclaimers
   a. Express
   If a manufacturer uses a disclaimer of merchantability, it must be both apparent and specific to defeat the warranties.
   b. Implied
   If a good is sold "as is," this is viewed as an implied disclaimer of warranties.
2. <u>T</u>imeliness
   A buyer who fails to give timely notification of a defect is barred from recovery.
3. <u>C</u>omparative Negligence
   Some jurisdictions allow comparative negligence.
4. <u>A</u>ssumption of Risk
   Use of goods that are known to be defective will relieve a seller of liability.
5. <u>L</u>imitation of Liability
   A manufacturer can place limits on the extent it must replace and repair defective products. This is only acceptable for business goods, as opposed to consumer goods.

D. Damages
1. Personal Injury
   A plaintiff can recover for personal injuries regardless of whether the plaintiff was in privity with the seller.
2. Property Damage
   A plaintiff not in privity with a seller will not recover for property damage in most states under an implied warranty, but will recover in most states under an express warranty.
3. Intangible Harm
   a. Direct Purchasers
   For an intangible harm, a direct purchaser will recover:
      i. The decreased value of the product due to the defect.
      ii. Any consequential damages a defendant had reason to expect at the time of sale.
   b. Users or Bystanders
   Under an implied warranty the majority of the courts will deny recovery to a user or a bystander for an intangible harm. Under an express warranty they may recover for an intangible harm, but it is unlikely they will be able to prove the warranty existed.

E. Advantage of Warranty-Based Actions Over Tort-Based Actions
   1. If a plaintiff suffered purely economic harm, it is not usually recoverable under strict liability.
   2. The statute of limitations is longer for a warranty action than for a tort action.
   3. A plaintiff who is in direct privity with a defendant has an easier case under a warranty action because it is relatively easy to establish a duty and a breach.

III. STRICT PRODUCTS LIABILITY

A manufacturer is strictly liable if it places a defective product in the market that causes injury to others. There are several policy reasons for holding a manufacturer of a defective product strictly liable.
A. Better Position
   A manufacturer is in a better position to anticipate and avoid defects.
B. Loss Spreading
   A manufacturer can better spread the costs by charging all its customers more and using the money to compensate a plaintiff.
C. Encourage Research
   Holding manufacturers liable will give them the incentive to develop safer products.
D. Difficulty of Proof
   It is almost impossible for a plaintiff to prove a defendant was at fault given the complex technologies and procedures of modern production.
E. Reciprocal Risk
   This is the rationale that a manufacturer marketed the product and therefore should be held responsible.

IV. TYPES OF DEFECTS

There are three general types of product defects for which a manufacturer may be held strictly liable.
A. Construction/Manufacturing Defects [Restatement 2d §402(a)]
   A manufacturing defect involves a product that is normally safe, but because of a mistake or error was defectively constructed.
   1. A manufacturer is strictly liable when it sells a product in a defective condition that is unreasonably dangerous to a consumer or a consumer's property if:
      a. the seller is regularly engaged in the business of selling this product; and

        b. the product reaches the ultimate consumer without any substantial change in the condition in which it was sold.

    2. No privity is required between the manufacturer and the plaintiff. However, the manufacturer is not liable if the plaintiff used the product in an abnormal manner.

    3. Generally, a plaintiff has to prove that:

        a. the defendant manufactured the product;

        b. the product was defective;

        Some courts require a plaintiff to show that it was unreasonably unsafe, that is, dangerous beyond what ordinary users would expect. Others allow res ipsa loquitur to be used to infer defectiveness.

        c. the product was both the actual and proximate cause of the plaintiff's injury; and

        d. the defect existed at the time the product left the defendant's factory/control.

        Courts will usually allow an inference of this fact.

B. Design Defects

Design defects involve products that are manufactured according to plan, but are defective because they were improperly planned.

    1. Types of Design Defects

        a. Structural Defect

        There is a structural defect if the product is not as durable as a reasonable person would expect. There is no requirement of super durability, but the product must pass a reasonableness standard.

        b. Lack of Safety Features

        It is no excuse that a competitor's product also lacks safety features. However, courts may excuse a lack of safety features if the burden of installing them exceeds the potential loss.

        c. Suitability for Foreseeable Unintended Use

        A product does not have to be designed to be safe for every possible use, but some misuses of a product are foreseeable, and a manufacturer must take reasonable precautions to protect against those misuses.

    2. A Plaintiff's Burden Is to Prove:

        a. the design was defective and caused the plaintiff's injury;

        b. there was a practical, safer alternative design.

    3. Cost-Benefit Analysis

Does the inherent risk of a defective design outweigh its benefits? Consider:

        a. the gravity of the inherent risk;

        b. the likelihood that danger will occur;

        c. the mechanical feasibility of a safer alternative design;

      d. the financial cost of an improved design;

      e. the obviousness of the dangers; and

      f. the public expectations of a danger.

      Some courts will instead consider whether the product was as safe as a reasonable consumer would expect it to be when used for an intended or foreseeable unintended purpose.

   4. Defenses

      a. The plaintiff used the product in an unforeseeable, unintended manner.

      b. The product did not cause the injuries.

      c. The plaintiff knew of the defective design, but ignored it.

      d. Comparative negligence: compare the defective design and the plaintiff's negligence to reduce the defendant's damage liability.

C. Unavoidably Unsafe Products

Almost like a subgroup of manufacturing defects, the products included in this category are incapable of being made safe for their intended and ordinary use.

If a product is unavoidably unsafe, but its benefits exceed its costs, a manufacturer is relieved of liability if it properly prepares, tests, and labels the product.

   1. Manufacturers are negligent if they:

      a. knew or should have known of the product's inherent dangers had they exercised reasonable care given the technology at the time the product was sold; and

      b. fail to adequately warn all foreseeable users.

   2. Obvious Dangers

      There is no general duty to warn against obvious dangers or against misuse of a product.

   3. Prescription Drugs

      A manufacturer of prescription drugs only has to warn a physician, who can use personal discretion in deciding whether to warn users.

CASE CLIPS

MacPherson v. Buick Motor Co. (1916)

Facts: MacPherson was injured when his car's defective wheel broke into fragments. He had bought the car from a dealer who had bought it from Buick Motors, the manufacturer of the car. A reasonable safety inspection would have revealed the defect in the wheel.

Issue: Is a manufacturer liable to one who is not a direct purchaser?

Rule: Manufacturers of products that are "reasonably certain to place life and limb in peril when negligently made" owe a duty of reasonable care to all foreseeable users.

Baxter v. Ford Motor Co. (1932)

Facts: Baxter purchased an automobile from Ford that they claimed was equipped with a windshield that was "shatterproof." He was later injured when the windshield shattered.

Issue: Does a manufacturer's representations create an implied or express warranty to a third party that is not a direct purchaser?

Rule: A manufacturer's representations create an express warranty to an indirect buyer if they are made with the intention of attracting consumers and the buyer actually relies on the representation.

Crocker v. Winthrop Laboratories (1974)

Facts: Crocker became addicted to a drug manufactured by Winthrop Laboratories that they represented as nonaddictive.

Issue: Are manufacturers liable for the breach of an express warranty they honestly believe to be true?

Rule: Manufacturers are liable for breaching an express warranty if it is found to be false even if they reasonably believed it to be true, and could not have possibly known that it was false.

Henningsen v. Bloomfield Motors Inc. (1960)

Facts: Henningsen was injured when her car's defective steering gear caused it to crash. When Henningsen's husband bought the car he signed a standard waiver of all warranties against the defendants.

Issue: When is an express waiver limiting a manufacturer's liability under the implied warranty of merchantability valid?

Rule: A waiver is valid unless the court finds the two parties are in a position of gross inequality of bargaining power.

Greenman v. Yuba Power Products, Inc. (1963)

Facts: The plaintiff was injured by a tool negligently manufactured by the defendants, but did not notify the defendants of the breach of warranty within a "reasonable time" as required by state law.
Issue: Does a failure to notify a manufacturer of a breach of warranty within the statute of limitations bar recovery in tort?
Rule: Manufacturers of products that are expected to be used without inspection are strictly liable in tort. Limiting provisions of state law will not bar recovery.

Rix v. General Motors Corp. (1986)

Facts: Rix was injured when the pickup truck he was driving was hit from behind by a General Motors truck.
Issue: Can a manufacturer be found to be strictly liable for placing a product with manufacturing and design defects into the stream of commerce?
Rule: A party is strictly liable when a manufacturer/seller sells a product that was in a defective condition unreasonably dangerous to a consumer or user, when the product was expected to and did reach the ultimate consumer without change in the condition it was in at the time it was sold, and when the defect condition in the product proximately caused injury to the plaintiff.

Phillips v. Kimwood Machine Co. (1974)

Facts: Phillips was injured by a machine he claimed was unreasonably dangerous because it had no protective device against accidents.
Issue: Can a manufacturer be held strictly liable for a product that is considered unreasonably dangerous?
Rule: A product is unreasonably dangerous, and a manufacturer is held strictly liable, if the seller would be considered negligent to sell the product knowing the risk involved.
Note: Under the Restatement, a product is unreasonably dangerous when it is dangerous beyond the expectations of an ordinary consumer.

Prentis v. Yale Mfg. Co. (1984)

Facts: Prentis was injured when he fell from a forklift manufactured by the defendant. Prentis claimed the forklift was negligently designed because it did not provide the operator with a seat or platform.
Issue: When are manufacturers liable for "design defects?"

Rule: Manufacturers are liable for designs defects only if they were negligent in designing their products. Under a risk-utility analysis, a design is defective only when its risk of harm outweighs its utility.

Note: This is different from cases of "product defects," where strict liability applies. Product defects involve products that are properly designed, but improperly manufactured.

Honda of Am. Mfg., Inc. v. Norman (2003)

Facts: When the Normans' daughter submerged her car, she was unable to exit the vehicle because of the malfunction of her automatic seat belt. She drowned. On appeal, Honda argued that the Normans failed to establish that there was a safer alternative design for seat belts.

Issue: What evidentiary elements must be established to find that a product was defectively designed and unreasonably dangerous?

Rule: There must be proof that there was a safer alternative design that would have reduced the risk of injury significantly without compromising the product's utility. Further, the alternative must have been possible from a technological standpoint and cost efficient at the time the product was put into the stream of commerce. Finally, the alternative seat belt system would not have lessened the utility of the product for "intended users." The Normans only satisfied the first few aspects of these requirements.

Soule v. General Motors Corp. (1994)

Facts: P's car collided on a wet road with a car that skidded into her lane. The impact caused the driver's side wheel to crush the "toe pan," the collapse of which fractured P's ankles. P alleged design defectiveness in the body of the car.

Issue: Is the application of the "ordinary consumer expectations" test suitable in a design defect case?

Rule: The correct standard is to determine whether the design embodies "excessive preventable danger."

O'Brien v. Muskin Corp. (1983)

Facts: O'Brien sustained head injuries when he dove into a pool. He sued the pool's manufacturer for defectively designing the pool.

Issue: Can a risk-benefit analysis be used on a product that is not defective, but is unavoidably dangerous by its nature?

Rule: In determining liability for an unavoidably dangerous product a jury may evaluate the risk of harm versus the utility of the product.

Hood v. Ryobi America Corp. (1999)

Facts: P purchased a saw made by D. Both the body of the saw and the owner's manual warned consumers not to remove the blade guards. P disregarded the warnings, removed the guards, and was injured by a blade that dislodged from the saw.

Issue: Is a manufactured product defectively designed when it fails to provide adequate warnings against likely dangers?

Rule: A manufacturer owes a duty to provide adequate warnings and instructions with a product. In the instant case, the warnings were sufficient as a matter of law.

Brown v. Superior Court (Abbott Laboratories) (1988)

Facts: The trial court determined that the defendants could be held liable for their failure to warn of any known or knowable side effects of DES, not for the alleged defect in the drug.

Issue: Can manufacturers of prescription drugs be held strictly liable for a defectively designed product?

Rule: A manufacturer is not strictly liable for injuries caused by a prescription drug so long as the drug was properly prepared and contained warnings of either known or knowable dangers at the time of distribution. Were strict liability employed, the public interest in the development and marketing of new drugs would be substantially impaired.

Roysdon v. R.J. Reynolds Tobacco Co. (1985)

Facts: Roysdon sued the defendant, a cigarette manufacturer, for severe vascular disease that resulted from a lifetime of smoking.

Issue: When is a product considered unreasonably dangerous?

Rule: A product is unreasonably dangerous if it is "dangerous to an extent beyond what would be contemplated by an ordinary consumer."

McCarthy v. Olin Corp. (1997)

Facts: A deranged person opened fire in a train, killing 6 and injuring 19 others, including P. The shooter used special bullets with enhanced wounding properties.

Issue: Was the design of the bullets defective because of their increased wounding impact on targets?

Rule: The design defectiveness of a product arises from flaws that make it unreasonably dangerous for its intended use. The bullets effectively did what they were designed to do. They, therefore, were not unreasonably hazardous for achieving their purpose. Moreover, there is no cause of action that applies to products that are unreasonably designed per se.

Anderson v. Owens-Corning Fiberglas Corp. (1991)

Facts: Anderson alleged that he contracted lung ailments through exposure to products containing asbestos manufactured by defendant.

Issue: Can a defendant present evidence of the state of the art, that is, evidence that the particular risk was neither known nor knowable by the application of scientific knowledge available at the time of manufacture and/or distribution, in a products liability action based on an alleged failure to warn of a risk of harm?

Rule: A defendant in a strict products liability action based on an alleged failure to warn of a risk of harm may present evidence of the state of the art, that is, evidence that the particular risk was neither known nor knowable by the application of scientific knowledge available at the time of manufacture and/or distribution.

Parish v. Jumpking, Inc. (2006)

Facts: P attempted to back somersault on a trampoline and fell on his head. He became a quadriplegic as a result of the fall. He sued the manufacturer of the trampoline.

Issue: Does a trampoline have a "manifestly dangerous" design when it leads to serious injury of a user?

Rule: Multiple express warnings, which existed in this case, eliminate claims of "manifestly dangerous" design. Moreover, to establish the latter, P must show a reasonable alternative design.

Woodill v. Parke Davis & Co. (1980)

Facts: Use of the defendant's drug during childbirth caused birth defects in Woodill's son. No warning was given because the defendant did not know of the possibility of these complications.

Issue: Is a defendant strictly liable for failure to warn of a product's risk if the defendant did not know of the danger?

Rule: A manufacturer that fails to warn of a product's risk will be liable only if the plaintiff proves that the manufacturer knew or should have known of the danger.

Note: This is known as the "state of the art defense."

Vasallo v. Baxter Healthcare Corp. (1998)

Facts: P's silicone breast implants ruptured and caused personal injury. P sued the manufacturer for negligent design and negligent warnings of possible product dangers. She also claimed that the warnings breached the implied warranty of merchantability.

Issue: Is the manufacturer liable to warn against all dangers that might accompany the use of a product?
Rule: Under the Restatement (Third) of Torts and the Products Liability Restatement, the manufacturer has no duty to warn of risks that were not reasonably foreseeable at the time of sale or that could not be discovered by reasonable testing.

Beshada v. Johns-Manville Products Corp. (1982)

Facts: The plaintiffs contracted lung disease from asbestos produced by the defendants. The defendants argued that they could not warn of its dangers because they were unknown at the time of marketing.
Issue: Can one who fails to warn of a product risk claim that the danger was undiscoverable at the time the product was marketed?
Rule: Strict liability is imposed on those who fail to warn of a product's risk despite the fact that the "state of scientific knowledge" at the time made discovery of these dangers impossible.
Note: This rejects the "state of the art defense."

Gray v. Badger Mining Corp (2004)

Facts: P developed silicosis of the lungs after working for his employer for 45 years. He sued the supplier of sand for its failure to warn him of the dangers of silica dust.
Issue: Does the supplier of a product to a company owe a duty to warn the company's employees of the dangers of the product as the ultimate users?
Rule: The supplier has a duty to warn ultimate users of the product of the likely harm that can result from the intended use of the product, including the provision of instructions on how to use the product.

MacDonald v. Ortho Pharmaceutical Corp. (1985)

Facts: MacDonald was injured when she took contraceptive pills prescribed by her doctor and manufactured by the defendant. The defendant had given a warning about the product's dangers to the prescribing doctor, but did not give one to the consumer directly.
Issue: Does a manufacturer of contraceptive pills have a duty to directly warn the user of the product's risks?
Rule: A manufacturer of contraceptive pills has a duty to warn the ultimate users of the dangers of its product.
Note: This is an exception to the general rule that manufacturers of prescription drugs need only warn the doctor of any dangers that exist.

Edwards v. Basel Pharmaceuticals (1997)

Facts: P's husband died from a nicotine-induced heart attack. He smoked cigarettes while using the Habitrol nicotine patch. P sued the manufacturer for its failure to warn consumers adequately of the dangers of smoking and overuse of the product.

Issue: Does the communication of the dangers to a "learned intermediary" (i.e., a physician) bar the action against the manufacturer for failure to warn?

Rule: FDA regulations mandate that warnings be communicated to the ultimate user as well as the physician. The requirement constitutes an exception to the "learned intermediary rule."

Sheckells v. AGV Corp. (1993)

Facts: P lost control of his motorcycle and suffered serious head trauma even though he was wearing a helmet. He sued the helmet manufacturer for defective design and failure to warn.

Issue: What duty is incumbent upon a manufacturer in terms of warning against possible or likely dangers of a product?

Rule: Product manufacturers do not owe users or consumers a duty to warn of dangers that are obvious or of which the P had, or should have had, knowledge after using the product.

Friedman v. General Motors Corp. (1975)

Facts: Friedman's car lunged forward and crashed when he started it with its gear in the drive position. An expert for Friedman suggested at trial that the gear shift was probably damaged.

Issue: What must a plaintiff prove in a products liability action?

Rule: To sustain a products liability action against a manufacturer, a plaintiff must prove that the product was defective, that the defect existed at the time the product left the manufacturer, and the defect was the direct and proximate cause of the accident and the injuries.

Two Rivers Co. v. Curtiss Breeding Service (1980)

Facts: Two Rivers Co. purchased defective bull semen from the defendants that caused the death of four of their cattle's offspring.

Issue: Can a products liability action be brought for economic loss caused by a product that was not unreasonably unsafe?

Rule: Economic damages do not warrant strict products liability where the product is not found to be unreasonably unsafe, even if it is defective.

When a product does not fulfill one's expectations, suit should instead be brought under the UCC for breach of contract.

East River Steamship Corp. v. Transamerica Delaval (S. Ct. 1986)

Facts: The plaintiff chartered a supertanker that suffered engine damage. They sued the manufacturer for the cost of engine repairs and for lost income while the ship was out of service.
Issue: Is a manufacturer of a commercial product liable in tort for damages to the product itself?
Rule: (Blackmun, J.) A manufacturer in a commercial relationship has no duty under either a negligence or strict products liability theory to prevent a product from injuring itself.
Note: A manufacturer may be liable, however, under contract law.

Pennsylvania Glass Sand Corp. v. Caterpillar Tractor Co. (1981)

Facts: The plaintiff's machine, manufactured by Caterpillar Tractor Co., caught fire. The plaintiff claimed that the machine had a design defect and brought a tort action to recover the value of the machine.
Issue: Is property that is damaged because of its own defective design considered to be economic loss or "property damage?"
Rule: Damage to property caused by its faulty design is "property damage" and recoverable in tort. Had the defect caused a loss in the value of the product, a contract action would be appropriate.

Daly v. General Motors Corp. (1978)

Facts: Daly, intoxicated and not wearing his seat belt, was thrown from his car in an accident because of a defective door latch. He would not have been thrown from his car had he worn his seat belt.
Issue: Will a plaintiff's comparative negligence reduce a products liability damage award?
Rule: Damages in strict liability actions for defective products can be reduced by a plaintiff's failure to exercise reasonable care to the extent that the lack of care contributed to the plaintiff's injury.

General Motors Corp. v. Sanchez (1999)

Facts: Sanchez was crushed to death when his truck backrolled. He left the truck running while he opened a gate. His estate claimed that the transmission was defectively designed and that GM failed to provide an adequate warning of product defects.

Issue: What legal obligations are imposed on the user or consumer of products in terms of the possible dangers that can arise from the use of products?

Rule: Although a consumer may have no duty to discover or guard against product defects, the consumer's conduct in relation to the causation of injury is subject to the principle of comparative fault.

Henderson v. Ford Motor Co. (1974)

Facts: Henderson's Ford automobile crashed when the negligently designed gas filter prevented her from reducing speed.

Issue: Is a manufacturer obligated to construct its product in the best possible way?

Rule: Manufacturers must produce their products so that they are not unreasonably unsafe. However, they are under no obligation to use the most durable design.

Ford Motor Co. v. Matthews (1974)

Facts: Matthews's tractor ran over him when he started it in gear, despite the presence of a safety device. The defendant alleged that Matthews had misused the product by his actions.

Issue: May parties recover damages caused by their misuse of defectively manufactured products?

Rule: Manufacturers must anticipate reasonably foreseeable misuse of their products and make the product safe against such misuse.

King v. Collagen Corp. (1993)

Facts: King received an injection of a cosmetic medical device marketed by Collagen Corp., which underwent a premarketing approval and a post-approval regulatory process through which the Food and Drug Administration approves and regulates medical devices. She alleged that the medical device caused her to develop an autoimmune disease.

Issue: Where a federal statute regulates a particular activity, may an individual sue the party being regulated under state law?

Rule: A state cause of action is preempted where there is express or implied Congressional intent to do so. One must look at the language of the statute to determine whether a plaintiff's liability claims give rise to state law requirements that add or alter federal requirements. If the requirements are conflicting, the product liability claim may not be pursued.

Peterson v. Lou Bachrodt Chevrolet Co. (1975)

Facts: The plaintiffs were injured by a defective used car.
Issue: Does strict products liability extend to a seller who was not involved with the original production and marketing of a product?
Rule: Strict liability will not be imposed on a seller of a product who neither created the risk nor reaped the profit by placing the product in the stream of commerce.

Price v. Shell Oil Co. (1970)

Facts: Price was injured while working on a truck that his employer had leased from the defendant.
Issue: Are bailors and lessors of property strictly liable for injuries caused by their leased property?
Rule: The doctrine of strict liability in tort, already applicable to sellers of personal property, is also applicable to bailors and lessors of such property. The distributor of property is strictly liable regardless of who retains title to the property.

Becker v. IRM Corp. (1985)

Facts: Becker sued his landlord when he was cut by an untempered glass door that shattered. This defect was unknown to the defendant.
Issue: Is a landlord strictly liable to a tenant for a latent defect in the rental premises?
Rule: A landlord is strictly liable in tort for injuries to a tenant that result from a latent defect in the premises if the defect existed at the time the premises were originally let.

Hector v. Cedars-Sinai Medical Ctr. (1986)

Facts: Plaintiff alleged that she received a personal injury that resulted from the implantation of a defective pacemaker. The hospital was not in the business of recommending, selling, distributing, or testing pacemakers. It does, however, maintain pre- and postoperative care, nursing care, a surgical operating room, and technicians.
Issue: Can a hospital, in the provision of services, be held liable for injuries to patients for products necessary to their treatment, even if the hospital neither knew nor could have known about the defect?
Rule: When a hospital acts as a provider of services, it is not subject to strict liability for injuries caused by a defective product provided to a patient during the course of treatment.

Royer v. Catholic Medical Center (1999)

Facts: Royer underwent knee replacement surgery at CMC and the prosthesis turned out to be defective, necessitating a second procedure.
Issue: Is a health care provider liable for the defects in the prosthetic implants it provides to patients?
Rule: The provision of prosthetic devices to patients in a surgical setting does not represent participation in a commercial sale. The medical center provides health care services and products are an indirect part of that activity.

Escola v. Coca Cola Bottling Co. (1944)

Facts: The plaintiff was injured when a soft drink bottle exploded in her hand. She asserted an action based on res ipsa loquitur.
Issue: Must a manufacturer's negligence be proven in an action to recover damages caused by a defective product?
Rule: A manufacturer is strictly liable if the defect in its product caused the plaintiff's injuries, the defect was present when the product left the manufacturer's control, and the plaintiff did not unreasonably misuse the product.

Elmore v. American Motors Corp. (1969)

Facts: A defective drive shaft manufactured by the defendant fell off Elmore's car, injuring Elmore and killing another person.
Issue: Is a manufacturer strictly liable for damages caused to a bystander by its defective product?
Rule: Consumers and bystanders may recover for injuries proximately caused by a defective product; strict liability may not be restricted by privity of contract.

Goldberg v. Kollsman Instrument Corp. (1963)

Facts: Goldberg was killed in an airplane crash that was caused by the airplane's defective altimeter, which the defendants manufactured but did not assemble.
Issue: Is a manufacturer of a defective component part strictly liable for injuries to parties not in privity with the manufacturer?
Rule: A component manufacturer is not strictly liable to parties not in privity with it. However, an assembler or final manufacturer is strictly liable for injuries caused by its product if the component was negligently made when it left the party's control and the injured party was a reasonably foreseeable user.

Heaton v. Ford Motor Co. (1967)

Facts: Heaton's new pickup truck tipped over when the rivets in the wheel came apart after he drove over a six-inch rock.
Issue: What standard is used to determine whether a manufacturer is liable for its defective product when the plaintiff has not shown the manufacturer to be negligent?
Rule: If a product deviates from the standard of performance that would be reasonably expected by users of the product, a manufacturer will be liable even if no evidence of negligence is presented.

Barker v. Lull Engineering Co. (1978)

Facts: Barker was injured while operating the defendant's defectively designed high-lift loader.
Issue: When is the design of a product considered defective?
Rule: A product's design is considered defective if either the dangers inherent in the product's design outweigh the product's usefulness, or if the product was less safe than the ordinary consumer would expect when used in an intended or reasonably foreseeable manner.

Hammond v. International Harvester Co. (1982)

Facts: Hammond lost his life while operating heavy equipment that his employer had purchased from the defendant. At the employer's request, the defendant had removed a standard safety device that, if not removed, would most likely have prevented the accident.
Issue: Is a manufacturer strictly liable for a design defect when the design of the product was altered due to a purchaser's request?
Rule: If a manufacturer fails to provide a product with every element necessary to make it safe, the product's design is considered defective and the manufacturer is strictly liable. A request by a purchaser to alter the product's design does not relieve the manufacturer of liability.

Jones v. Ryobi, Ltd. (1994)

Facts: P sued the manufacturer of a printing press when her hand was crushed by the mechanism of the press while she was operating it at work. P's employer had removed a plastic guard and disabled a shut-off switch to enhance the efficiency of the press. These adjustments were commonplace in the trade.
Issue: Can a buyer's foreseeable modification of a product eliminate the manufacturer's responsibility for personal injuries suffered by the users of the product?

Rule: An injured party must establish that its injury results from a defect in the product at the time of sale. Subsequent modification by the purchaser, even if likely and anticipated, does not relieve the manufacturer of liability for the harm caused by its product.

Feldman v. Lederle Laboratories (1984)

Facts: Feldman was not warned that the antibiotic she used would discolor her teeth. The manufacturer knew of the possibility of such side effects but did not provide warnings until four years later.
Issue: Is a manufacturer assumed to be aware of reasonably obtainable information about its product?
Rule: A manufacturer is generally assumed to know all reasonably obtainable general information about its product, but may avoid liability for an accident if it can prove that it lacked the information that would have prevented the accident.

Findlay v. Copeland Lumber Co. (1973)

Facts: Findlay was injured when he fell off the defendant's defectively manufactured ladder. Findlay was negligent in using the ladder.
Issue: Does contributory negligence defeat a products liability action based on strict liability?
Rule: Contributory negligence does not preclude recovery in a strict product liability action so long as the plaintiff did not assume the risk of the product defect.

Micallef v. Miehle Co. (1976)

Facts: Micallef was injured when he stuck his hand into a fast-moving printing press to remove an object despite knowing of the danger. The machine had no safety guards to protect against such dangers.
Issue: Must a manufacturer install a safety device to protect users from an obvious danger?
Rule: A manufacturer is not relieved of its duty to protect users from an unreasonable danger because the danger is obvious.

Acosta v. Honda Motor Co., Ltd. (1983)

Facts: Acosta was injured when the rear wheel of his motorcycle came loose. He was awarded punitive damages in a products liability suit.
Issue: Are punitive damages appropriate to products liability actions?

Rule: Where a plaintiff proves by clear and convincing evidence that the defendant's conduct was outrageous, punitive damages may be awarded in products liability actions.

Grimshaw v. Ford Motor Co. (1981)

Facts: Grimshaw was awarded punitive damages when her Ford Pinto burst into flames after being struck by another car. Ford was aware that its Pintos could not withstand high-speed accidents, but failed to warn its consumers or remedy the problem.
Issue: Can punitive damages be awarded against a manufacturer for the defective design of its product?
Rule: Punitive damages may be awarded against companies that manufacture or mass produce products when evidence of malice in designing the product is presented.

McCabe v. Liggett Drug Co. (1953)

Facts: The plaintiff was injured by an exploding coffee maker, which was purchased from the defendant.
Issue: Does an implied warranty of merchantability accompany a product when it is purchased?
Rule: When a product is purchased it is accompanied by an implied warranty that the product is reasonably suitable for its intended use.

Murphy v. E.R. Squibb & Sons, Inc. (1985)

Facts: Murphy suffered injuries after taking a defective drug sold to her by the defendant, a pharmacist.
Issue: Are those who provide professional services strictly liable for alleged defects in products they sell?
Rule: Unlike sales retailers, those who provide professional services to their customers are not strictly liable for the products they sell that are related to the service they provide.

Pouncey v. Ford Motor Co. (1972)

Facts: Pouncey was injured when a blade flew off his car's radiator. At trial he used expert testimony to suggest that the blade flew off because of metal fatigue that was reasonably foreseeable.
Issue: May negligence in the construction of a product be inferred from circumstantial evidence?
Rule: A jury may use circumstantial evidence to infer a manufacturer's negligence in constructing a product.

Volkswagen of America, Inc. v. Young (1974)

Facts: The plaintiff was killed when his car's seat was separated from the car after the car was hit.

Issue: Must an automobile's design include precautions to prevent injuries in the event of an accident to fulfill the requirement that a product be fit for its "intended use?"

Rule: An automobile manufacturer is liable for a design defect that the manufacturer could have reasonably foreseen would cause or increase injuries on impact, and that is not patent or obvious to the user.

Cann v. Ford Motor Co. (1981)

Facts: The plaintiffs were injured when their car shifted itself into reverse because of a design defect. Ford redesigned its cars to avoid such accidents in the future.

Issue: Can a plaintiff introduce evidence of a defendant's remedial measures subsequent to the accident as proof that the product was defectively designed?

Rule: Evidence of postaccident remedial repairs by a manufacturer is not admissible to prove the existence of a design defect.

Camacho v. Honda Motor Co., Ltd. (1987)

Facts: Camacho's leg was injured after he was involved in a motorcycle accident. The motorcycle did not have crash bars that were available on other types of motorcycles at the time of its purchase.

Issue: Is the unreasonably dangerous and defective nature of a product's design determined by the ordinary consumer's contemplation of open and obvious danger?

Rule: The unreasonableness of a product's design is not determined by consumer expectation, but is primarily determined by technical, scientific information. Factors to be considered are (1) the usefulness of the product, (2) the safety of the product, (3) the availability of a safer alternative product of comparable utility, (4) the manufacturer's ability to make the product safer without affecting its utility, (5) the user's awareness of the product's inherently dangerous nature, and (6) the manufacturer's ability to spread losses or to carry liability insurance.

Hahn v. Sterling Drug, Inc. (1986)

Facts: Hahn's daughter was seriously injured after ingesting an "over-the-counter topical analgesic" manufactured by Sterling Drug. The trial court granted a directed verdict to Sterling concerning the adequacy of the warnings provided.

Issue: May a court direct a verdict concerning the adequacy of a manufacturer's warning?

Rule: The adequacy of a manufacturer's warning is a question of fact and must be submitted to a jury.

Huber v. Niagara Machine and Tool Works (1988)

Facts: Huber's hand got caught in a mechanical power press when his foot slipped and hit a foot-operated starter switch that had its safety devices removed. The foot switch had been manufactured and sold with the safety devices.

Issue: Does a manufacturer have a duty to warn users about dangers related to the misuse and modification of its products?

Rule: If a product is safe when sold, the manufacturer does not have to warn about the dangers related to the product's misuse or modification, unless such misuse or modification is foreseeable.

Liriano v. Hobart Corp. (1998)

Facts: P lost limbs when using a meat grinder to perform his job. The owner of the supermarket removed a safety guard from the grinder. The machine provided no warning of the danger of using it without the safety device.

Issue: Is the seller or maker of a product liable for its failure to warn of the dangers even though the structure of the product has been modified by a third party?

Rule: Manufacturers have a duty to warn of the possible misuse of their products, as well as their foreseeable modification by users.

White v. Wyeth Laboratories, Inc. (1988)

Facts: White, an infant, suffered permanent brain damage after being injected with a DPT vaccine manufactured by Wyeth Laboratories.

Issue 1: Are all prescription drugs considered "unavoidably unsafe" such that their manufacturers are immune from strict liability conditioned on the proper preparation of the drug and the proper provision of directions and warnings?

Rule 1: Prescription drugs, vaccines, or like products are not "unavoidably unsafe" per se; they are only "unavoidably unsafe" if no alternative design exists that effectively accomplishes the same purpose with less risk.

Issue 2: What constitutes adequate warning for an "unavoidably unsafe" product?

Rule 2: A manufacturer of an unavoidably unsafe prescription drug provides adequate warning when it reasonably discloses all risks inherent in the use of the drug of which the manufacturer, being held to the standard of an expert in the field, knew or should have known to exist.

Hoven v. Kelble (1977)

Facts: The plaintiff suffered a heart attack while undergoing a lung biopsy by the defendant.
Issue: Does the doctrine of strict products liability apply to improper medical care?
Rule: The doctrine of strict products liability does not apply to medical services.

Hauter v. Zogarts (1975)

Facts: Hauter was injured by a golf practice set that advertised that the "completely safe ball will not hit player." The manufacturer argued that it was understood that no device could protect a person from the normal hazards of golf.
Issue: Can a manufacturer modify an implied or express warranty?
Rule: A manufacturer's attempts to modify an implied or express warranty will not be effective unless the manufacturer can prove that the disclaimer was clear to all relevant parties.

McCormack v. Hankscraft Co. (1967)

Facts: McCormack was severely burned when she tipped over and spilled the scalding water from a vaporizer manufactured by Hankscraft.
Issue: When is a manufacturer liable for a defective design of a product?
Rule: A manufacturer can be held liable for defective product design if the manufacturer knows or should have known of the danger to the consumer; the manufacturer fails to warn the consumer of the danger; and the dangers inherent in the use of the product are not immediately obvious to the consumer.

Troja v. Black & Decker Manufacturing Co. (1985)

Facts: Troja accidentally amputated his thumb while operating a radial arm saw manufactured by Black & Decker. Troja claimed that the saw was defectively designed, and should have included some additional safety mechanisms.
Issue: Must evidence of a reasonable safer alternative be presented in an action based on design defect?
Rule: In an action for defective design, where a risk is not "inherently unreasonable," a plaintiff is required to show there is a reasonable, safer

design alternative. The court will evaluate the reasonableness of the design alternative using a risk-utility balancing analysis.

Green v. Sterling Extruder Corp. (1984)

Facts: Green's hand was crushed while operating a machine manufactured by the defendant. A trial jury found that Green was 75 percent negligent. The court entered judgment in favor of the defendant on a comparative negligence basis.

Issue: Is comparative negligence applicable in an action for strict products liability?

Rule: A plaintiff's contributory negligence does not act as a bar to recovery in strict products liability, except when that plaintiff's conduct amounts to an unreasonable and voluntary exposure to a known risk.

CHAPTER 16

Nuisance

I. INTRODUCTION

A. Interest Protected

The interest protected by nuisance is one's use and enjoyment of one's property, whereas trespass only protects one's interest in the possession of property.

B. Intent Requirement

A party must be aware of the harmful effects of its conduct. However, reckless, negligent, or ultrahazardous interference with a party's use of its land might suffice to show intent. The two types of nuisance are public and private.

II. PUBLIC NUISANCE

An interference with a right that is common to the general public or community. The elements of a public nuisance are:

A. Substantial Harm

Nuisance requires a substantial harm. This is unlike trespass where nominal damages are awarded even if no harm is done.

B. Injury to the Public at Large

C. Personal Harm Is Separate from Public

If an individual party wants to recover damages that it suffered from a public nuisance, it must show that it suffered a different kind of harm than the general public.

III. PRIVATE NUISANCE

A substantial and unreasonable interference with a party's use or enjoyment of its land. The elements of a private nuisance are:

A. Possessory Interest

The plaintiff must have a possessory interest in the land; for example, a person who stays at a friend's house cannot sue a factory that pollutes the friend's lawn. However, a tenant has a sufficient possessory interest.

B. Substantial Interference
1. A nominal injury is not enough; the plaintiff must be actually and substantially discomforted.
2. Whether an interference is substantial is determined by its effect on an average person; an extrasensitive person will not recover.
C. Unreasonable Interference
1. In determining unreasonableness, a court will balance the harm to the plaintiff against the benefits of the defendant's conduct to the community.
2. The Restatement (2d) suggests an alternative test, providing that plaintiffs should also be reimbursed if the harm to the plaintiff is substantial or the harm outweighs the utility of the interference to the defendant.
3. Regardless of the test used, the court will consider such factors as the character of the neighborhood, land values, and the nature of the parties.

IV. REMEDIES

A plaintiff has three possible remedies against a nuisance.
Mnemonic: **AID**
A. **A**batement by Self-Help
A party is allowed to use reasonable force to cure the nuisance after the defendant refuses a request to do so.
B. **I**njunction
An injunction will only be granted if the party succeeds in proving that its injuries outweigh the community's benefits from the defendant's activity. If successful, the party can shut down the defendant's operations and stop the nuisance.
C. **D**amages
Damages may be awarded for past and future harm in the case of ongoing or permanent nuisances.

V. DEFENSES

Mnemonic: **CARGO**
A. **C**ontributory Negligence
Contributory negligence only applies if the plaintiff claims that the defendant negligently created the nuisance.
Note: There are other ways to fulfill the intent requirement; that is, intentional, reckless or ultrahazardous conduct.
B. **A**ssumption of **R**isk
Assumption of risk applies if the defendant engaged in negligent or ultrahazardous conduct. If the plaintiff acted unreasonably

despite knowledge of a nuisance, the plaintiff will be barred from recovery.

A variation of assumption of risk that the courts recognize is when the plaintiff "comes to the nuisance."

1. Old Rule

   If the defendant came to an area before the plaintiff, the plaintiff was barred from recovery.

2. Restatement (2d)

   Coming to the nuisance is only one factor to look at in the balancing test.

C. Governmental Authority

   Conformity to local zoning laws and regulations is persuasive, although not conclusive, evidence that an activity is not a nuisance.

D. Others Are Liable

   When several parties combine to produce a nuisance, each party is only liable for the portion of damages it actually caused.

CASE CLIPS

Philadelphia Electric Co. v. Hercules, Inc. (1985)

Facts: Philadelphia Electric was forced to clean up chemicals spilled by the previous owner of its recently purchased plant. It sued for the cost of the cleanup under a private nuisance theory.

Issue 1: Is the purchaser of real property entitled to recover damages from the seller on a private nuisance theory for the negative conditions existing on the land?

Rule 1: One who sells real property is not liable to the purchaser in nuisance for defects present on the property at the time of transfer. Private nuisance actions are meant to protect the interests of neighbors, not purchasers.

Issue 2: May a private actor bring a tort suit for a public nuisance?

Rule 2: To bring a private action for public nuisance a party must have suffered a harm different in kind from that suffered by the general public. The particular damage must have been produced from the exercising of the public right that was the subject of interference.

Note: A public nuisance is generally prosecuted by the state as a low-grade criminal offense.

Morgan v. High Penn Oil Co. (1953)

Facts: Morgan brought a private nuisance action against High Penn Oil, whose refinery emitted nauseating gases and odors.

Issue: If a party is conducting an otherwise lawful act, can there be a nuisance in the absence of negligence?

Rule: A nuisance "per se" (at law) is an act, occupation, or structure that is a nuisance at all times and under any circumstance, regardless of location or surroundings. Nuisances "per accidens" (in fact) are those that become nuisances by reason of their location, or the manner in which they are constructed, maintained, or operated. A nuisance "per accidens" need not be the result of negligence; it may be either intentional or unintentional.

Carpenter v. The Double R Cattle Co., Inc. (1985)

Facts: When a neighboring rancher expanded its feedlot to accommodate 9,000 cattle, the increase in manure, odor, and water pollution prompted Carpenter to bring a nuisance action.

Issue: Is a party liable in nuisance if the utility of the conduct complained of outweighs the gravity of harm?

Rule: There is no nuisance if the utility of the conduct outweighs the gravity of the harm it causes.

Note: This rule is the "balancing test" applied by some jurisdictions.

Winget v. Winn-Dixie Stores, Inc. (1963)

Facts: Winget, a homeowner, sued a neighboring Winn-Dixie supermarket for nuisance, complaining of crowding, noise, and fumes from cars and garbage trucks; a decrease in their property value; and general disturbance of peace and quiet. The supermarket was zoned for such use.

Issue: Are the usual and normal by-products of a lawfully located business actionable as a private nuisance?

Rule: There must be an injury to a legal right to bring a nuisance suit; mere annoyance or disturbance is not sufficient. Normal, usual, and necessary acts of a properly zoned business are not actionable.

Boomer v. Atlantic Cement Co., Inc. (1970)

Facts: Dirt, smoke, and vibrations emanating from the defendant's cement plant were a nuisance to the plant's neighbors.

Issue: Can a monetary award be substituted for an injunction in nuisance action?

Rule: If the effects of an injunction are significantly more severe than the effects of a nuisance to the plaintiff, a court may grant an injunction conditioned on the payment of permanent damages to the plaintiff. This payment would compensate for the total present and future economic loss to the plaintiff's property caused by the defendant's operations.

Spur Industries, Inc. v. Del E. Webb Development Co. (1972)

Facts: Del Webb developed a residential area near Spur's feedlot where more than 20,000 cattle produced more than a million pounds of wet manure per day. Del Webb sued for nuisance, seeking an injunction. In addition to Del Webb, the residents of Del Webb's development were harmed by the nuisance.

Issue: May a plaintiff who has "come to the nuisance" be granted an injunction to abate the nuisance?

Rule: A plaintiff who has "come to the nuisance" ordinarily would not be granted injunctive relief. However, if the nuisance adversely affects innocent third parties as a result of the plaintiff having come to the nuisance, injunctive relief will be granted, but the plaintiff will have to indemnify the defendant for having caused the need for an injunction.

Timmons v. Reed (1977)

Facts: The defendant's oil plant emitted boiling water into a roadside ditch, causing dense fog on the roadway. Although Timmons had driven over the same stretch of road every day and was aware of the fog near the plant, he collided with a truck.

Issue: Is contributory negligence a defense to a nuisance action?

Rule: The defense of contributory negligence is available in a nuisance action based on negligence, but not for a nuisance action based on intentional conduct or strict liability.

Wheat v. Freeman Coal Mining Corp. (1974)

Facts: Wheat brought a nuisance action against the defendant, a coal mine, for emitting dust and smoke onto his property.

Issue 1: What are the elements of a nuisance action?

Rule 1: Nuisance is an injury that is caused by an intentional and unreasonable act, and is determined by weighing the gravity of injury against the utility of the conduct.

Issue 2: How are damages measured in a nuisance action?

Rule 2: The measure of damages in a nuisance action is the value of the discomfort and deprivation of the healthful use of the land.

Nicholson v. Connecticut Half-Way House, Inc. (1966)

Facts: The plaintiffs brought a nuisance action to prevent the Connecticut Half-Way House from using a house as a residence for paroled convicts.

Issue: Are fears of future harm sufficient to merit an injunction in apprehension of a possible nuisance?

Rule: No injunction should ever be granted merely because of the fears and apprehension of future harm.

Atkinson v. Bernard, Inc. (1960)

Facts: Homeowners living near a small airport brought an action to enjoin flights from flying over their property. They argued that the airplanes trespassed on their airspace, creating noise and vibrations that substantially interfered with the use and enjoyment of their property.

Issue: Is an action to enjoin airport operations properly brought under the theory of nuisance or trespass?

Rule: Suits to enjoin all or part of the operations of an airport should be brought under the theory of nuisance rather than trespass.

Railroad Commission of Texas v. Manziel (1962)

Facts: The plaintiff sued to prevent the defendants from injecting salt water in their well to improve oil yield. The plaintiff claimed that the salt water would seep underground onto his property.
Issue: Is the subsurface invasion of land a trespass?
Rule: The traditional rules concerning the surface invasion of land do not apply to subsurface invasions. Public policy must be considered when determining if a subsurface invasion is a trespass.
Note: The court's determination that no trespass occurred was based on the need to ensure adequate oil production.

Martin v. Reynolds Metals Co. (1959)

Facts: Chemicals spewed from Reynolds Metals Company's plant caused the poisoning of Martin's cattle.
Issue: Does air pollution give rise to an action in trespass or in nuisance?
Rule: Damage caused by air pollutants entering one's property may be recovered in a suit based on trespass. There is no requirement that the invading object be seen.

Whalen v. Union Bag & Paper Co. (1913)

Facts: Union Bag's pulp plant discharged pollutants into a stream that passed by Whalen's property.
Issue: Can an injunction to prohibit a nuisance be denied merely because the defendant's loss will be greater than the plaintiff's benefit?
Rule: An injunction should not be set aside merely because the abatement of the nuisance causes the defendant far greater loss than it benefits the plaintiff.

State Department of Environmental Protection v. Ventron Corp. (1983)

Facts: The defendants operated a mercury processing plant that dumped untreated toxic waste underground, polluting state waterways.
Issue: Is the storage of toxic waste an abnormally dangerous activity for which a landowner may be held strictly liable?
Rule: Mercury and other toxic wastes are abnormally dangerous and their disposal is an abnormally dangerous activity. Consequently, landowners are strictly liable for harm caused by toxic wastes that are stored on their property.

Jost v. Dairyland Power Cooperative (1970)

Facts: Jost and other neighbors of a Dairyland coal plant brought a nuisance suit to recover monetary damages for damaged crops and loss in the market value of their farmlands.

Issue: May damages be awarded for the permanent loss in market value of land due to a continuing nuisance?

Rule: A landowner is entitled to compensation for damages caused by permanent and continuing nuisances. The value of the damages that may be awarded is reflected in the diminution of the market value of the landowner's property.

Copart Industries, Inc. v. Consolidated Edison Co. of New York, Inc. (1977)

Facts: Copart Industries lost its car servicing business when the cars it worked on became discolored and pitted as a result of noxious emissions from Consolidated Edison's adjoining power plant. Copart brought a nuisance action grounded in negligence.

Issue: What type of conduct creates nuisance liability?

Rule: A defendant may be liable for nuisance for either negligent or intentional conduct.

532 Madison Ave. Gourmet Foods, Inc. v. Finlandia Center, Inc. (2001)

Facts: Consolidated cases involving suits by businesses against the owner of commercial buildings because of the City's response to problems with construction projects resulted in closure of streets and difficulty accessing the buildings. The loss of commercial traffic resulted in a substantial decline of profits.

Issue: Does the commercial landlord's duty of reasonable care include the losses suffered by business establishments occasioned by a public nuisance?

Rule: Ps failed to make a case that they suffered special losses as a result of the public nuisance that differed from the losses suffered by the public at large.

Bamford v. Turnley (1862)

Facts: The defendant built a kiln and began making bricks in a residential neighborhood. The plaintiff sued for nuisance.

Issue: May activity on one's own land that is not wantonly or maliciously conducted be enjoined where it causes a diminution of the enjoyment of a neighbor's land?

Rule: One may be enjoined from conducting activities only if the activities are not necessary for the common and ordinary use and occupation of land.

Fontainebleau Hotel Corp. v. Forty-Five Twenty-Five, Inc. (1959)

Facts: The Eden Roc Hotel brought a private nuisance action to prevent the Fontainebleau Hotel from building an addition to its Miami Beach hotel that would block air and sunlight from the Eden Roc. There was evidence to indicate that the actions of the Fontainebleau were motivated partly by malice.

Issue: Can landowners be enjoined from using their land in a manner injurious to their neighbors if there is evidence of malicious intentions?

Rule: Landowners may use their property in any reasonable and lawful manner, even if motivated by spite, so long as they do not thereby deprive the adjoining landowners of any right of enjoyment of their property that is recognized and protected by law.

Note: The law does not recognize a right to light and air; consequently, it is not a nuisance to block them.

Rodgers v. Elliott (1888)

Facts: The defendant refused to stop ringing a church bell after the plaintiff's physician advised him that the noise would cause the plaintiff to have convulsions. The plaintiff brought a nuisance action seeking an injunction.

Issue: Can one be liable in nuisance to an abnormally sensitive plaintiff?

Rule: The standard of whether an activity is a nuisance is judged by its effect on an average person, not its effect on an ultrasensitive plaintiff.

Bennett v. Stanley (2001)

Facts: A 5-year-old drowned in the neighbor's pool after he trespassed onto the property. The pool had been neglected and was filled with rain water and plant growth. The young boy had been attracted by the frogs in the pool. His mother drowned trying to save him.

Issue: Is recovery for the death of the child precluded by the child's status as a trespasser?

Rule: Children of "tender years" have a special status in tort law and are entitled to greater protection because of their inexperience. The condition of D's pool created an attractive nuisance for children and, therefore, an unreasonable risk of harm. Young children do not perceive or understand the dangers that inhere in commonplace situations.

Ensign v. Walls (1948)

Facts: Neighboring homeowners brought a nuisance action to close the defendant's dog kennel because of odors and noise emanating from it. The homeowners had moved to the neighborhood after the kennel was established.

Issue: Is a party liable for a nuisance if it was conducting the offending activities before the plaintiffs acquired their property interests (i.e., the plaintiffs "came to the nuisance")?

Rule: A nuisance may be abated even though it predated the plaintiffs' property interests. The defense of "coming to the nuisance" is not absolute. Public policy concerns over health and safety may override it.

Anonymous (1535)

Facts: The plaintiff brought a private nuisance action to prevent the defendant from continually blocking a public highway and preventing its use.

Issue: Can a private action in nuisance be brought to recover damages suffered by the general public?

Rule: A party may assert a private action in nuisance for public damages only if the party has suffered greater damages than ordinary members of the public.

Waschak v. Moffat (1954)

Facts: Gas and fumes from the defendant's coal processing plant caused the paint on Waschak's house to turn from white to black.

Issue: Can a plaintiff recover damages for nuisance from a defendant's reasonable use of land?

Rule: An action for nuisance will lie when there is an unreasonable use of land such that the social utility of the defendant's conduct is outweighed by its harmful effects. To award damages for nuisance a defendant's conduct must not only be unreasonable but also either intentional, negligent, or ultrahazardous.

Crushed Stone Co. v. Moore (1962)

Facts: Crushed Stone operated a quarry that created excessive dust, noise, vibrations, and so on, and interfered with Moore's use and enjoyment of his property.

Issue 1: May a court issue an injunction against a nuisance when the detriment to the defendant will outweigh the benefit to the plaintiff?

Rule 1: Where the harm caused by a nuisance is substantial and irremediable, and an award of damages is an inadequate remedy, a court may issue an injunction against a nuisance notwithstanding a great disparity in the economic consequences of the injunction.

Issue 2: May a nuisance be enjoined by a plaintiff who has purchased property near an already existing nuisance?

Rule 2: A nuisance may be enjoined by a plaintiff who "comes to a nuisance" if that plaintiff had no actual knowledge of the harmful effects of the defendant's conduct.

CHAPTER 17

Defamation

I. NATURE OF A DEFAMATORY COMMUNICATION

The tort of defamation attempts to protect a person's reputation and relationships with others by making another liable who ridicules, vilifies, or humiliates a person in the eyes of the public by use of an oral or written communication.

II. LIBEL AND SLANDER

Mnemonic: **L**ibel is **L**etter, **S**lander is **S**poken

A. Libel

A recorded defamatory statement: written, recorded, computer tape, photograph, movie, and so on.

1. Radio and TV
   a. Written Script
      All courts will consider defamatory remarks made on TV or radio to be libel if they are read off a prepared script.
   b. Ad Lib
      If defamatory remarks are not read from a script, the courts are split between whether it is libel or slander.
2. Damages
   General damages are presumed from libel; a plaintiff does not have to prove special damages unless the libel concerns an issue of public importance. See Ch. 17, VI, A.

B. Slander

A spoken defamatory statement.

1. Damages
   A plaintiff is generally required to prove special damages. See Ch. 17, VI, B.

2. Slander Per Se
An exception to damages rule for slander is that damages will be
presumed if the slander involves one of these topics:
Mnemonic: **CAB RIDE**
a. Criminal Act
If it is implied that a plaintiff has committed a crime.
b. Business Reputation
If a plaintiff's professional reputation has been slandered.
c. Impurity
If a defendant implies that a woman is unchaste.
d. Disease Exposed
If a defendant implies that a plaintiff has a disease.

III. PUBLICATION

Publication occurs when a defamatory statement is conveyed and
understood by a third person.
A. Repetition
Each repetition of a defamatory statement creates a new cause of
action for defamation.
Exception: Single Publication Rule
An entire edition of a book, newspaper, or magazine is treated as
one publication even though the defamatory statement is repeated
numerous times. The time of publication occurs when the product
is first offered for sale.
B. Republisher
Each person who either says or repeats a defamatory statement is
liable for defamation.
C. Understanding
For a publication to occur, the third party who receives it must
understand it in its defamatory context.
For example, if Susan makes a defamatory statement to Rob, who
does not understand English, there is no publication. However, if
Brett overhears and understands Susan, then a publication has
occurred.

IV. BASIS OF LIABILITY

For libel or slander to occur the following elements must exist:
Mnemonic: **DIP FAD**
A. Defamatory and False Statements
1. A plaintiff does not have to prove that the statement is false, but
truth will be an absolute defense.
2. A statement is defamatory if it tends to detract from a plaintiff's
reputation.

3. A statement is actionable whether it is defamatory on its face or is only defamatory with additional knowledge.
4. A statement is defamatory even if it was not believed. A plaintiff, however, will have to prove special damages.
5. A statement must have an element of disgrace in the eyes of at least one respectable segment of society to be considered defamatory. A plaintiff has to show disapproval by a number of relatively respectable people based on the statement.
6. If the statement could have more than one meaning, a judge will determine whether one meaning could possibly be defamatory; if it may, a jury will decide if anybody actually interpreted the statement in a defamatory manner.
7. Opinions are not defamatory.
B. Identifying a Plaintiff as the Object of the Statement
  1. Groups
     A statement that defames a group that is greater than about 25 members is not defamatory.
  2. Dead Persons
     Negative statements about a dead person are not defamatory.
  3. Corporations
     Corporations can be defamed, but can only recover for monetary losses.
  4. Unnamed Plaintiffs
     Statements can be defamatory even if a plaintiff is not directly mentioned by name.
C. Publication
   See Ch. 17, III.
D. Fault
   A defendant must act either intentionally or negligently; there is no strict liability for defamation. The intent that is required is the intent to publish.
  1. Public Figures
     A public figure is one who has achieved fame or notoriety, or at least voluntarily enters the public spotlight. Recovery is available only if the defendant acted with malice, or with knowledge that the statements are false or made with reckless disregard as to their truth.
  2. Private Persons
     Recovery is available if a defendant acted maliciously or negligently.
     a. If a plaintiff does not show malice, the plaintiff has to prove special damages.
     b. If a plaintiff shows malice, damages will be presumed and punitive damages are allowed.
E. Actual Damages
   See Ch. 17, VI.

V. DEFENSES

A. Truth

Truth is an absolute defense.

B. Plaintiff's Consent

C. Privilege

1. Absolute Privileges

No liability even if a defendant acted with malice.

a. Judicial and Legislative Proceedings

All those involved in these proceedings are privileged to make any defamatory remark that is related to the proceedings.

b. Government Officials

Any official statement made by a government official is privileged. This applies to all federal officials. Courts are split on whether all state officials are protected.

c. Husband and Wife

Communications between spouses are privileged.

2. Qualified Privileges

The following statements are privileged if they are made without malice:

a. Reports of a Public Proceeding

Example: Reporting of trials, congressional hearings, and so on.

b. Fair Criticism

Example: Movie reviews and articles of general interest.

c. Statements Involving the Public Interest

Example: An article that identifies criminals.

d. Statements Made for the Interest of the Maker

e. Statements Made in the Common Interest

Example: Defamatory statements made by a loan company to a bank concerning a prospective loan applicant.

f. Statements Made for the Interest of the Recipient

Example: Defamatory statements made by a person's former employer to the person's new employer.

VI. REMEDIES

A. General/Presumed Damages

Damages presumed by law; a plaintiff does not have to prove special damages.

B. Special Damages

A plaintiff who must prove special damages must specifically prove pecuniary loss.

C. Recoverable Damages
 1. Punitive
    In cases of malice only.
 2. Damages to Reputation
    These include economic harm.
 3. Damages to Feelings
    These include medical bills for a plaintiff's emotional distress.

CASE CLIPS

Belli v. Orlando Daily Newspapers, Inc. (1967)

Facts: The defendant published a false statement that alleged Belli, a prominent lawyer, bought clothes and charged them to his hotel room at the expense of the Florida Bar Association.

Issue: Should a judge or a jury rule on defamation if a statement has more than one interpretation?

Rule: When a statement has more than one possible interpretation, a judge determines if at least one of those interpretations could be defamatory. If so, a jury then determines if the recipient did in fact interpret the statement in that way.

Grant v. Reader's Digest Association (1945)

Facts: Grant sued Reader's Digest for libel after their article claimed that he was a legislative agent for the Massachusetts Communist Party.

Issue: Has one's reputation been injured when a false allegation is written that, if believed, will hurt one's reputation only among people with a certain viewpoint?

Rule: A false allegation is defamatory even if a person's reputation is only lowered among a group of "wrong-thinking" people.

Kilian v. Doubleday & Co., Inc. (1951)

Facts: Kilian sued Doubleday for libel for a story they published that detailed alleged acts of cruelty by him during World War II. Kilian was convicted of similar activities, but Doubleday could not prove that the exact incidents had occurred.

Issue: Has the defense of truth been satisfied in a defamation action by a showing of events that are similar in character and nature to the ones recounted?

Rule: A defense of truth will succeed only when it is proven that the activities of the alleged defamation substantially occurred. Proof that a plaintiff committed acts similar to those recounted will not suffice.

Neiman-Marcus v. Lait (1952)

Facts: Neiman-Marcus and several employees sued the defendants for publishing a book that claimed some of Neiman-Marcus's saleswomen were "call-girls" and most of their salesmen were "fairies."

Issue: Can individual members of a group assert an action for defamation for statements made against the group as a whole?

Rule: When a group or class that is defamed is large, none can sue individually even though the language used encompasses all of the individuals. When a group or class that is defamed is small and each and every member is referred to, any individual member can sue.

Bindrim v. Mitchell (1979)

Facts: Mitchell enrolled in Bindrim's nude-therapy program and signed an agreement not to photograph, write about, or disclose what transpired. Mitchell wrote a novel based on her experience and gave Bindrim, the group therapy leader, a fictitious name.
Issue: May a person receive compensation for defamation even when the person was portrayed as a fictional character?
Rule: A publication is considered defamatory if a reasonable person would understand that a fictional character described was, in fact, the plaintiff.

Shor v. Billingsley (1956)

Facts: During a radio telecast the defendant, the host of the show, ad libbed, "I wish I had as much money as he [the plaintiff] owes."
Issue: Is defamation that occurred in a telecast considered libel or slander?
Rule: Defamation by radio, television, or movie is libelous because of its great potential for dissemination, regardless of whether a prepared script was used.

Terwilliger v. Wands (1858)

Facts: Terwilliger told a third party that Wands was having sexual relations with a married woman. Wands, upon hearing of Terwilliger's gossip, fell ill and was unable to work.
Issue: What type of damages must be shown in a defamation suit based on slander?
Rule: A plaintiff must show special damages to recover for slander (i.e., pecuniary damages). Illness and other nonpecuniary damages are insufficient to invoke liability.

Economopoulos v. A.G. Pollard Co. (1914)

Facts: A.G. Pollard's employee, speaking Greek, incorrectly accused Economopoulos of stealing a handkerchief. The accusation was only overheard by persons who did not understand Greek.
Issue: Does publication, the communication of defamatory words to someone other than the defamed, exist when a third person heard but did not understand a slanderous statement?

Rule: Publication does not occur when a third party to a defamatory communication does not understand the language of the defamer.

Ogden v. Association of the United States Army (1959)

Facts: The defendant published a book containing an alleged libel of the plaintiff. The suit was brought three years after the book was first published, beyond the state's one-year statute of limitations for libel.

Issue: In a libel action, does every sale or delivery of a publication containing a defamatory statement create a separate cause of action, or does one cause of action arise at the time of the first publication?

Rule: Under the "single publication rule," a publication containing defamatory statements gives rise to only one cause of action for libel, which accrues at the time of the original publication. A state's statute of limitations runs from that date.

Bromage v. Prosser (1825)

Facts: Not stated.

Issue: Is one liable for slander if it is not a malicious action?

Rule: An ordinary slander action will succeed if the defendant spoke falsely. It is not necessary to prove an "actual malicious action."

E Hulton & Co. v. Jones (1910)

Facts: The defendant published a story about a married man and his mistress. Jones, unbeknownst to the defendant, had a name similar to the man's in the article and people thought the article was about him.

Issue: Does lack of intent to injure defeat a defamation action?

Rule: Defendants are liable for libel when they defame other people regardless of whether they actually intended to defame those specific people. The main issue is how a statement is understood by others.

New York Times Co. v. Sullivan (S. Ct. 1964)

Facts: Sullivan, a Police Commissioner in Montgomery, Alabama, sued the New York Times Co. for libel after they carried an advertisement that criticized the actions of the Montgomery police. Some of the statements made in the advertisement were erroneous.

Issue: May public officials sue for libel?

Rule: (Brennan, J.) Public officials cannot recover damages for false defamatory statements unless they can prove that the statements were made with "actual malice" (i.e., with knowledge that they were false or with reckless disregard of whether they were false or not).

Concurrence: (Black, J.) Public officials are categorically denied any action of defamation insofar as their public conduct is concerned.

St. Amant v. Thompson (S. Ct. 1968)

Facts: St. Amant falsely charged Thompson, a deputy sheriff, with criminal conduct during a political speech. St. Amant received the accusations from a union member without checking their veracity.

Issue: What is the definition of "reckless disregard?"

Rule: (White, J.) In a defamation suit, a statement is published with "reckless disregard" only if the defendant published it despite the fact that there were serious doubts as to its authenticity.

Dissent: (Fortas, J.) A defendant has a duty to check the reliability of a statement (i.e., make a good faith effort) before publishing it.

Masson v. New Yorker Magazine (S. Ct. 1991)

Facts: Masson claimed that an article written about him contained defamatory material. A number of passages had been altered when the author converted her tape recorded interviews into the finished work.

Issue: How much alteration will be permitted in meaning between an author's words and those of the subject before an issue of fact for a jury as to falsity is created?

Rule: If an author alters a speaker's words but effects no material change in meaning, the speaker suffers no compensable defamation of character. Where, however, an alteration results in a material change in the meaning of the conveyed statement, an issue of fact is created as to falsity.

Edwards v. National Audubon Society, Inc. (1977)

Facts: Arbib published an article claiming that scientists who argued for the continued use of DDT were "being paid to lie." Arbib told the defendants the names of five scientists, but said he was unsure if they lied. The defendants printed the five names in their newspaper.

Issue: If an organization accurately reports a statement against a public figure even though the organization may have serious doubts of the statement's accuracy, is the report protected under the First Amendment of the Constitution?

Rule: When an organization reports serious charges against a public figure, the First Amendment protects the accurate reporting of those charges regardless of the reporter's views regarding their validity.

Gertz v. Robert Welch, Inc. (S. Ct. 1974)

Facts: Gertz was defamed as a "Leninist" by the defendant in a magazine article. The defendants claimed Gertz, a reputable lawyer, was a public figure and thus they had a privilege to criticize him.

Issue 1: When is a person considered a public figure?

Rule 1: (Powell, J.) When there is clear evidence of general fame or notoriety in a community, or a pervasive involvement in the affairs of society, a person is considered a public figure. A person is not a public figure merely because of an involvement in a matter of public interest.

Issue 2: Can a private figure recover presumed and punitive damages against media defendants for libel in a matter of public concern?

Rule 2: Plaintiffs, in an action for libel involving a matter of public concern, can recover presumed and punitive damages only if they are able to prove actual malice by the media defendants.

Note: Of the four dissenters, two would impose greater restrictions and two would impose lesser restrictions on defamation actions.

Dun & Bradstreet, Inc. v. Greenmoss Builders, Inc. (S. Ct. 1985)

Facts: Dun & Bradstreet, a supplier of confidential credit reports, erroneously reported that the plaintiff had filed for bankruptcy. The plaintiff sued for libel seeking punitive and compensatory damages.

Issue: May presumed and punitive damages be awarded in an action for libel that does not involve a matter of public concern?

Rule: (Powell, J.) A private individual may recover presumed and punitive damages for false and defamatory statements absent a showing of actual malice if the matter does not involve a public issue.

Dissent: (Brennan, J.) A private individual may recover presumed and punitive damages only if actual malice is shown, regardless of whether it was a matter involving public or private concern.

Philadelphia Newspapers, Inc. v. Hepps (S. Ct. 1986)

Facts: The defendant published a newspaper article accusing Hepps of using organized crime links to influence governmental processes.

Issue: Which party in a defamation action has the burden of proving the truth of the statements in question?

Rule: (O'Connor, J.) A plaintiff has the burden of proof to show falsity, as well as fault, before recovering damages for defamation in a matter of public concern. In a matter of private concern, however, a defendant must prove the veracity of the statements.

Dissent: (Stevens, J.) A plaintiff must only prove fault, not falsity to recover damages for defamation in a matter of public concern.

Flamm v. Am. Assoc. of Univ. Women (2000)

Facts: AAUW directory of attorneys who handled gender discrimination cases distributed to members described P as an "ambulance chaser" who was likely to take only "slam dunk cases." P sued for libel per se.
Issue: Is there a likelihood that the pejorative statements in the directory could be interpreted as representations of objective fact by its users?
Rule: P bears the burden of establishing that the statements made are "provably false." The term "ambulance chaser" could reasonably be construed as implying unethical professional conduct.

Milkovich v. Lorain Journal Co. (S. Ct. 1990)

Facts: The defendant published an article that opined and implied that Milkovich had perjured himself.
Issue: Are statements of opinion given special constitutional protection under the First Amendment?
Rule: There is no separate constitutional privilege to make defamatory statements of opinion. An opinion is defamatory if a reasonable jury could find that the opinion implied a fact concerning the defendant and the implied fact can be proven false.

Irwin v. Ashurst (1938)

Facts: Irwin, a witness in a criminal trial, sued the judge for allowing the trial to be broadcast and the defense counsel for calling her a dope fiend. She had used morphine for medical purposes in the past.
Issue: Is a judge or an attorney liable for defamation emanating from their actions during a trial?
Rule: A judge has absolute immunity from liability for defamation that occurs in the course of a judicial proceeding. An attorney has absolute immunity from liability for all communication that is relevant to a trial. If it is irrelevant, it must be malicious to invoke liability.

Kennedy v. Cannon (1962)

Facts: Cannon, the attorney for a man accused of raping Kennedy, was sued for slander after telling a reporter Kennedy had consented.
Issue: Does an attorney's immunity from liability for defamation extend to statements made outside the court?

Rule: An attorney's privilege against defamation for statements made during a trial does not extend to statements made outside the court.

Sindorf v. Jacron Sales Co. Inc. (1975)
Jacron Sales Co., Inc. v. Sindorf (1976)

Facts: Sindorf left the defendant's employment to work for Tool Box Corporation. The defendant called Tool Box, a competitor and friend of the defendant's, and told him that Sindorf was less than honest.
Issue: When does one have a conditional privilege to defame?
Rule: A defamatory communication is conditionally privileged when the occasion shows that a communicating party and a recipient have a mutual interest in the subject matter. This conditional privilege is defeated if the defendant acts with malice.

Watt v. Longsdon (1930)

Facts: Longsdon, Watt's supervisor, received a letter from Watt's co-worker that contained false statements about Watt. Longsdon showed the letter to the chairman of the company as well as to Watt's wife.
Issue: Under what circumstances do privileged defamatory statements become actionable?
Rule: Privileged defamatory statements lose their privilege when they exceed the limits of their duty or when they are made with malice.

Western Union Telegraph Co. v. Lesesne (1952)

Facts: Western Union delivered a defamatory telegram to Lesesne.
Issue: Is a telegram company liable for defamation on the grounds that delivery of a telegram is publication?
Rule: Delivery of a libelous telegram to a person defamed does not constitute publication even if the message reached the hands of a third person, unless the telegraph company expected or should have reasonably expected that the telegram would reach the third person.

Old Dominion Branch No. 496, National Association of Letter Carriers v. Austin (S. Ct. 1974)

Facts: Austin's name was listed in a union newsletter's "List of Scabs," a list of letter carriers who had failed to pay their union dues.
Issue: Are defamatory statements made by a union attempting to organize workers privileged?

Rule: (Marshall, J.) Under federal labor law, loose language and undefined slogans are considered part of the give-and-take in economic and political controversies and are privileged statements.

Janklow v. Newsweek, Inc. (1986)

Facts: Newsweek published an article that implied Janklow, a former attorney general, once prosecuted a case out of revenge. Newsweek argued that it was not liable for defamation because the article stated opinion only, not fact.

Issue: How does a court determine if a statement is fact or opinion?

Rule: To determine if a statement should be interpreted as fact or opinion, a court must look at four factors: (1) the precision and the specificity of the statement, (2) the verifiability of the statement, (3) the literary context of the statement, and (4) the public context in which the statement was made (i.e., private person vs. public figure).

Harte-Hanks Communications, Inc. v. Connaughton (1989)

Facts: Prior to an election, newspaper carried a front-page story adverse to the candidate it opposed. The account contained allegations of bribing witnesses to testify against an official in the incumbent's office.

Issue: What procedure must an appellate court follow to determine whether the news account reflected a reckless disregard of the truth and actual malice?

Rule: The U.S. Supreme Court ruled that the appellate court must undertake a "plenary review" of the entire record to make a determination.

New England Tractor-Trailer Training of Connecticut, Inc. v. Globe Newspaper Co. (1985)

Facts: The Globe published a series of articles that were critical of vocational schools in general and of NETT-MASS specifically. Although the plaintiffs, NETT-CONN, were not mentioned specifically in the article, they argued that they were defamed because NETT-MASS and NETT-CONN were part of the same company.

Issue: In a defamation action, must a plaintiff prove that the defendant had a subjective intent to defame the plaintiff?

Rule: In a defamation suit, a plaintiff must prove that the defendant intended its words to refer to the plaintiff, that the defendant's words could reasonably be interpreted to refer to the plaintiff, and that the defendant was negligent in publishing them in such a way.

Farnsworth v. Hyde (1973)

Facts: Hyde wrote a book about Farnsworth's character, describing Farnsworth as the laziest man in the world.
Issue: When is a statement considered defamatory?
Rule: Defamation is actionable when statements cause a plaintiff to be subjected to hate or ridicule, and diminish the respect in which the plaintiff is held by a substantial number of people in the community.

Khawar v. Globe International, Inc. (1998)

Facts: Globe tabloid published a book review of a book alleging that P had assassinated RFK. P sued Globe for defamation.
Issue: Can actual malice be established in the republication of a third-party's false statements?
Rule: Actual malice can be found in the circumstances of republication if there were "obvious reasons to doubt" the truth or accuracy of the claims made.

Cinquanta v. Burdett (1963)

Facts: The defendant shouted to the plaintiff, his employer, "I don't like doing business with crooks. You're a deadbeat." The plaintiff sued for slander and recovered damages for slander per se.
Issue: What determines whether a statement is slander per se?
Rule: To determine if words are actionable as slander per se, they must be taken in the context and in light of all the circumstances attendant upon the utterances.

Taylor v. Perkins (1607)

Facts: The defendant said to the plaintiff, "Thou art a leprous knave." The plaintiff sued for defamation.
Issue: Is a verbal statement that a plaintiff has a disease actionable?
Rule: A verbal statement that an individual has a disease is an actionable defamatory utterance.

American Broadcasting-Paramount Theatres, Inc. v. Simpson (1962)

Facts: The plaintiff, one of two guards who transferred Al Capone between prisons, objected to a TV episode of *The Untouchables* in which a guard is bribed while transferring Capone between prisons.
Issue 1: Are TV broadcasts classified as libel or slander?

Rule 1: Defamation occurring during a radio or TV broadcast falls under the laws of libel.

Issue 2: If it is falsely said that one of two persons has committed a crime, do both have a cause of action for defamation?

Rule 2: Any member of a small group that is defamed has a cause of action in libel.

Bottomley v. F.W. Woolworth & Co., Ltd. (1932)

Facts: The defendant, a retail store, sold a magazine that defamed Bottomley without knowing of the magazine's defamatory content.

Issue: Is a retailer liable for the sale of defamatory material?

Rule: A retailer is not liable for the sale of defamatory material if it did not know of the libel, it had no reason to know of the libel, and it was not negligent in failing to know of the libel.

Carafano v. Metrosplash. Com, Inc. (2003)

Facts: An unidentified person posed as an actress on an online dating service. As that persona, the individual posted a personal profile of the actress and information of a sexual kind. This resulted in sexually oriented harassment of the real actress and her family. She sued the dating service for defamation.

Issue: Can the online dating service be held liable for defamation when false information is posted about another person and the service fails to verify the information?

Rule: The immunity provision of the federal Communications Decency Act shields the dating service from liability for defamation as long as the published falsehoods were provided by another party.

Dunlap v. Wayne (1986)

Facts: Dunlap sought payments from Wayne for services rendered. Wayne's lawyer wrote to Dunlap's lawyer stating that Wayne refused to pay because the payment was a kick-back. Dunlap saw the letter.

Issue: Are statements of opinion on private affairs actionable as defamation?

Rule: A defamatory communication may consist of a statement in the form of an opinion, but a statement of this nature is actionable only if it implies the allegation of undisclosed defamatory facts as the basis for the opinion.

Broadway Approvals Ltd. v. Odhams Press, Ltd. (1965)

Facts: The plaintiff used questionable marketing techniques to sell stamps by mail order. Odhams Press wrote a highly critical newspaper article about the plaintiff, intentionally omitting favorable facts.
Issue: Is the defense of fair comment defeated if the party acted maliciously?
Rule: An honest and fair expression of opinion on a matter of public interest is not actionable even though it is untrue and unjustified unless the publisher acted with malice.

Dairy Stores, Inc. v. Sentinel Publishing Co., Inc. (1986)

Facts: After conducting chemical analyses on the plaintiff's product, Sentinel published articles that the plaintiff's bottled water was not pure spring water, as the plaintiff had advertised.
Issue: Does the fair comment privilege apply to statements of fact with respect to matters of legitimate public concern?
Rule: The fair comment privilege extends to statements of fact regarding matters of public concern.

McGranahan v. Dahar (1979)

Facts: During a trial, Dahar implied that McGranahan, who was not involved in the trial, had improperly granted a tax abatement to property in which McGranahan held a financial interest.
Issue: Are statements made during the course of a trial that are relevant to the trial considered to be defamatory if they are false?
Rule: Relevant statements made during a judicial proceeding cannot be defamatory because they are absolutely privileged.

Chamberlain v. Mathis (1986)

Facts: Mathis, the Director of the State Department of Health Services, made several negative statements concerning Chamberlain's job performance.
Issue: Does a government official have immunity from liability for defamatory statements made while exercising a discretionary function?
Rule: A government official is entitled to qualified immunity for defamatory statements unless the official acted outside his discretionary functions, or with malice.

Retail Credit Co. v. Russell (1975)

Facts: Retail Credit's files on the plaintiff contained incorrect defamatory material that was not changed despite repeated requests.

Issue: Is a credit reporting agency privileged to make a libelous statement?
Rule: A credit reporting agency has no privilege to make libelous statements.
Note: This is the minority rule.

Mims v. Metropolitan Life Insurance Co. (1952)

Facts: Mims, who had worked for Metropolitan Life for 32 years, suspected that he was dismissed because he did not contribute a dollar to a political campaign. Metropolitan Life sent Mims a letter that falsely accused him of inefficiency and unsatisfactory production.
Issue: Has a defamatory statement been published if the only persons who heard it were those who wrote the statement and the defamed person?
Rule: There has been no publication if the only communication of the defamatory material was among the principal actors themselves and not a third party (i.e., a party other than the one defamed).
Note: Although the employees who produce the defamatory material on behalf of the corporation are considered to be one entity, if another corporate employee not involved in the activity saw or heard the defamatory material, publication would have occurred.

Parmiter v. Coupland (1840)

Facts: No facts stated.
Issue: What constitutes libel?
Rule: A publication without justification or lawful excuse that is calculated to injure the reputation of another by exposing that person to hatred, contempt, or ridicule is libel.

Youssoupoff v. Metro-Goldwyn-Mayer Pictures (1934)

Facts: The plaintiff claimed she was defamed in a fictional movie made by the defendants, which incorrectly portrayed a character closely resembling her as being raped.
Issue: When is a defamatory portrayal of a character actionable?
Rule: A portrayal of a character is actionable when a jury could reasonably find that a considerable number of reasonable people would identify the character portrayed with the plaintiff and would consider the portrayal defamatory.

St. Amant v. Thompson (1968)

Facts: St. Amant delivered a political speech on television in which he contended that a deputy sheriff had engaged in criminal activity.

He believed the statement to be right, but did not investigate the facts to verify their accuracy.

Issue: Does the failure to investigate the circumstances constitute a "reckless disregard" of the truth and actual malice under N.Y. Times v. Sullivan?

Rule: The U.S. Supreme Court held that actual malice required the defendant to have "serious doubts as to the truth" of the assertion. St. Amant had no awareness of the likely falsehood of his statement about the deputy sheriff.

Burton v. Crowell Publishing Co. (1936)

Facts: The plaintiff was paid to pose for a picture that was used in the defendant's advertisement. Due to an error, the picture was distorted, making the plaintiff look "grotesque and obscene."

Issue: Is a mistaken distortion of one's photograph defamation?

Rule: Portraying a person in a manner that subjects the person to ridicule is actionable even if it resulted from a mistake.

Good Government Group of Seal Beach, Inc. v. Superior Court of Los Angeles County (1978)

Facts: The defendant, a local newsletter, published an article criticizing the plaintiff, a city councilman, claiming that he had extorted $100,000 from a land development company in exchange for a building permit.

Issue: Is inflammatory rhetoric in the form of an opinion defamation?

Rule: Epithets, fiery rhetoric, or hyperboles stated as opinion are not actionable.

Ellsworth v. Martindale-Hubbell Law Directory, Inc. (1938)

Facts: The plaintiff, a lawyer, was listed in the defendant's directory of law firms, but not rated. He had been rated in past editions.

Issue 1: Are words considered libelous if their negative connotations are not directly apparent?

Rule 1: When words are libel per se (i.e., libel on their face), the courts will presume damages, but when extrinsic facts are needed to establish libel, the words are said to be liable per quod and damages are not awarded unless a plaintiff specifically proves special damages.

Issue 2: Is a general loss of customers considered special damages?

Rule 2: A general decline of business resulting from the nature of a defendant's words is sufficient to establish special damages.

Faulk v. Aware, Inc. (1962)

Facts: The defendants blacklisted Faulk, a radio and TV performer, as a communist, causing him financial loss. Faulk recovered $4.75 million in damages for libel.

Issue: Under what circumstances may a judge overturn a jury damage award in a defamation action?

Rule: A judge may overturn a jury's award of compensatory and punitive damages in a defamation action only if the judge rules that the award was not reasonable.

Faulk v. Aware, Inc. (1963)

Facts: Same as above.

Issue: How should punitive damages be apportioned between multiple defendants?

Rule: Punitive damages should be apportioned between multiple defendants based on their degree of culpability.

Brown & Williamson Tobacco Corp. v. Jacobson (1983)

Facts: The defendants broadcasted a damaging story about the plaintiffs based on a summary of a government report. The plaintiffs alleged that the summary was not an accurate reflection of that report.

Issue: Under what circumstances might a jury reasonably consider a summary of information unfair?

Rule: A rational jury might consider a summary unfair where the libelous effect of the summary exceeds the effect the information would have if read verbatim; that is, if it has a "greater sting."

Carr v. Hood (1808)

Facts: The defendant wrote a book that was a parody and satire of the plaintiff's book.

Issue: Is ridicule of a literary work actionable?

Rule: Criticisms of the professional abilities of persons who have placed themselves in the public eye is privileged.

Curtis Publishing Co. v. Butts; Associated Press v. Walker (S. Ct. 1967)

Facts: These two cases involved the defamation of public figures by the press. In the first case, Butts, a college football coach, was falsely accused of "fixing" a game. In the second case, Walker was alleged to have led a riot against national guardsmen who were escorting black students as part of a racial integration program. Both defendants claimed a privilege because the plaintiffs were public figures.

Issue: What is the standard of care that journalists must adhere to when reporting on issues involving public figures?

Rule: (Harlan, J.) A public figure who is not a public official can recover damages for a defamatory falsehood on a showing of highly unreasonable conduct constituting an extreme departure from the ordinary standards of investigation and reporting.

Romaine v. Kallinger (1988)

Facts: The defendant published a nonfiction book that stated that Romaine knew "a junkie . . . who was doing time in prison."

Issue 1: Is it defamatory as a matter of law to allege that one knows a criminal?

Rule 1: Whereas a false attribution of criminality is defamatory as a matter of law, an allegation that one merely knows a criminal is not.

Issue 2: When may the question of a statement's defamatory nature be submitted to a jury?

Rule 2: The question of a statement's defamatory nature may be submitted to a jury if a court determines that the statement when read by reasonable persons of ordinary intelligence is susceptible to two different meanings, one of which is defamatory.

Matherson v. Marchello (1984)

Facts: The defendants made defamatory statements about Matherson and his wife on a radio talk show.

Issue: Is defamation by radio considered to be libel or slander?

Rule: Defamation that is broadcast by means of radio or television is classified as libel.

Medico v. Time, Inc. (1981)

Facts: Time magazine published an article based on an FBI report that linked Medico and his corporation to organized crime.

Issue: Is the media privileged to publish defamatory statements that are based on a summary of official government documents?

Rule: Publishing a defamatory but accurate and fair synopsis of an official report or proceeding dealing with a subject of public concern is privileged.

Note: This is an application of the "fair report privilege."

Burnett v. National Enquirer, Inc. (1983)

Facts: The National Enquirer printed a defamatory article about Carol Burnett that was later retracted. Burnett was awarded both compensatory and punitive damages despite a statutory provision that limited damages for "newspapers" to special damages if a timely retraction was printed.

Issue: Do the damage limitations granted in the California retraction statute apply to all newspaper publishers?

Rule: The damage limitations granted in the California retraction statute only apply to publishers of newspapers that engage in the immediate dissemination of news such that verification of accuracy is not always possible.

Waldbaum v. Fairchild Publications, Inc. (1980)

Facts: Waldbaum was fired from his position as president of the second largest supermarket in the country. The defendant wrote an article about his ouster and falsely stated that his company had been losing money during the last year. Waldbaum admitted that the defendant acted without malice and the defendant claimed a privilege.

Issue: When does an official who is not a public official cease to be a private person and become a public figure?

Rule: A person becomes a public figure for limited purposes if the person is attempting to have, or can be expected to have, a major impact on the resolution of a public dispute that has foreseeable and substantial effects on persons beyond its immediate participants.

Pacella v. Milford Radio Corp. (1984)

Facts: Pacella claimed he lost an election because of the defamatory statements that were made by an anonymous caller on the defendant's radio talk show.

Issue: Is a broadcaster liable for defamatory statements made about a political candidate during a broadcast?

Rule: A broadcaster is prohibited from deleting libelous statements of political candidates and therefore is immune from liability for broadcasting such statements. This reflects the strong public policy in favor of encouraging free and open debate on public issues.

CHAPTER 18

Privacy

I. PRIVATE FACTS

A party is liable for publicly disclosing embarrassing private facts about a plaintiff.

A. Embarrassing

The published facts must be very embarrassing to a reasonable person. An extrasensitive plaintiff will not recover.

B. Of No Public Concern

The published facts cannot be of legitimate public concern or they will be privileged under Time v. Hill.

Note: A privilege to disclose private facts may extend to private persons who were formerly in the public eye.

C. Publicized

The information must be publicized to more than a few people.

D. Not of Public Knowledge

The information cannot be a matter of public knowledge.

II. APPROPRIATION

This involves the use of the plaintiff's name or likeness for the commercial advantage of the defendant without receiving the plaintiff's permission or agreement.

A. Invasion

There is no requirement that the defendant invade a private area of the plaintiff's life; it is enough to use the name or likeness without permission.

B. Commercial Advertisements

Usually it is limited to commercial advertisements; for example, if a newspaper uses a picture of a woman next to an article about women as an illustration, no appropriation has been made.

III. INTRUSION UPON SECLUSION

This protects a person's rights to seclusion and solitude in all private affairs. This interest is usually balanced against the First Amendment free speech interest.
A. Reasonable Person
  The intrusion must be objectionable to a reasonable person, not just the particular plaintiff.
B. Personal Gain
  A defendant is liable even if there was no personal gain.
C. Private Place
  The intrusion must be into a private place of the plaintiff.
D. Electronic Surveillance
  This is always considered an unreasonable invasion of a private place. Journalists never have a First Amendment privilege to use electronic surveillance devices.
E. Intent
  The defendant's purpose must be to harm the plaintiff's interests.

IV. FALSE LIGHT

This involves placing a person before the public in a false light, that is, painting an image of the plaintiff that would be objectionable to a reasonable person.
A. False Light Occurs When:
  1. One is said to have views one does not in fact have; or
  2. One is said to have done something one did not in fact do.
B. Intent
  If the published information involves the public interest, a plaintiff must prove that the defendant acted with malicious intent. See Ch. 17.
C. Reasonably Sensitive
  An extrasensitive plaintiff may not recover.

V. DEFENSES

A. Consent
  A plaintiff who consents to an invasion of privacy cannot sue. A gratuitous consent may be revoked anytime before the actual invasion occurs.
B. Defamation Defenses
  The privileges that exist in defamation are also privileges for the invasion of privacy. See Ch. 17, V, C.

Exceptions: Truth and absence of malice are not valid defenses to the invasion of privacy. However, the absence of malice may be a defense if the facts are newsworthy.

VI. DAMAGES

A. Special damages need not be proven.

B. This is a personal right and the action will not survive if the plaintiff dies before the suit is resolved.

C. Corporations cannot recover for the invasion of privacy.

CASE CLIPS

Flake v. Greensboro News Co. (1938)

Facts: A picture of Flake was mistakenly used in an advertisement without her consent.
Issue: Is it a violation of privacy to use a person's picture in an advertisement without permission?
Rule: The unauthorized use of one's photograph in connection with an advertisement or other commercial enterprise gives rise to a cause of action for invasion of privacy.

Factors Etc., Inc. v. Pro Arts, Inc. (1978)

Facts: The plaintiff owned an exclusive license to commercially exploit the likeness of Elvis Presley. The defendant independently marketed a memorial poster shortly after the singer's death.
Issue: Does an exclusive right of publicity transferred during a person's lifetime still remain exclusive after the person dies?
Rule: The right of publicity may be validly transferred during the owner's life to one who may prevent a third party from using the publicity for commercial gain, even after the subject's death.

Zacchini v. Scripps-Howard Broadcasting Co. (S. Ct. 1977)

Facts: The defendants videotaped Zacchini's "human cannonball" act and broadcast it on a local television station without his consent.
Issue: Does the media's privilege to report newsworthy matters extend to a broadcast of an entire performance without the consent of the participant?
Rule: (White, J.) The media privilege to report a newsworthy performance does not extend to filming and broadcasting an entire act when the participant does not consent to the broadcast.

Haynes v. Alfred A. Knopf, Inc. (1993)

Facts: P sued author and publisher for invasion of privacy because book portrayed his personal life and conduct in highly unfavorable but accurate light.
Issue: What standard should apply to the interest in privacy when the account of P's personal life is both accurate and relevant to the subject matter of the book?
Rule: The interest in privacy must cede to the public's interest in newsworthiness when the details of personal life are part of a serious treatment of the topic. Moreover, P's offense and embarrassment at the public

portrayal of personal matters must be reasonable in the circumstance, not whimsical and contrived.

Pearson v. Dodd (1969)

Facts: Pearson and Anderson published articles about Senator Dodd based on photocopies of documents obtained from third parties who had removed the documents from the Senator's office, copied them, and returned them to his files without authorization.
Issue: Is intrusion a form of invasion of privacy?
Rule: Any intrusion into spheres from which an ordinary person in a plaintiff's position could reasonably expect that a particular defendant should be excluded is an invasion of privacy.
Note: Although publication of private material is a form of invasion of privacy, there is no invasion of privacy if the material is of public concern.

Dietemann v. Time, Inc. (1971)

Facts: *Life* Magazine's employees entered Dietemann's home under false pretenses and used hidden cameras and tape recorders to collect data for a story that was later published.
Issue: Does the First Amendment give journalists an immunity from liability for torts committed while gathering news?
Rule: The First Amendment has never been construed to accord reporters immunity from crimes or torts such as invasion of privacy committed in the course of news gathering.

Desnick v. ABC, Inc. (1995)

Facts: ABC sent undercover reporters with hidden cameras posing as patients to eye clinics to record their conversations with attending physicians. ABC believed clinics performed unnecessary cataract operations.
Issue: Does the use of investigative reporting techniques constitute an invasion of privacy?
Rule: There was no invasion of privacy because the reporters entered the clinic during business hours and only recorded their particular consultations with doctors. The same methodology is used to test home buying transactions for discrimination. First Amendment protects tabloid reporting.

Roach v. Harper (1958)

Facts: The plaintiff sued the defendant, her landlord, for "bugging" her apartment. The plaintiff did not show special damages or claim that the defendant published any conversations he overheard.

Issue: May an action for invasion of privacy succeed without proof of special damages and publication?
Rule: Proof of special damages and publication are not necessary to maintain an action for invasion of privacy.

Cox Broadcasting Corp. v. Cohn (S. Ct. 1975)

Facts: A television station violated state laws by revealing the name of a deceased rape victim. The reporter learned the name by looking at the indictments against the rapist, which were on public record.
Issue: Is the publication of public information prohibited by state law actionable on the grounds of invasion of privacy?
Rule: (White, J.) Invasion of privacy cannot be raised for published information already part of the public record because it is protected by the Constitution.

Shulman v. Group W Productions, Inc. (1998)

Facts: Shulman was pinned down in an automobile wreck and required a rescue helicopter. D's crew filmed the entire event and later broadcast it on TV. P sued D for invasion of privacy.
Issue: Does the filming of a newsworthy event constitute an invasion of the victim's privacy?
Rule: Activities designed to collect news material are not immune from legal regulation. An intentional intrusion into the private matters of a person can constitute an invasion of privacy. The intrusion must be "highly offensive to the reasonable person."

Humphers v. First Interstate Bank of Oregon (1985)

Facts: A biological mother sued the estate of a physician who revealed her identity to a daughter she had given up for adoption.
Issue: Is a physician liable for disclosing a patient's confidential information?
Rule: A physician's breach of his patient's confidence is actionable as a breach of confidentiality, but is not a violation of privacy.

Anderson v. Fisher Broadcasting Cos., Inc. (1986)

Facts: Fisher Broadcasting used videotapes of Anderson, recognizable and bleeding after a car accident, in promotional spots for a special news report about a new system for dispatching emergency medical help.
Issue: Is the publicity of nonnewsworthy pictures of a person for commercial purposes an invasion of privacy?

Rule: The truthful presentation of facts concerning a person, even non-newsworthy facts that a reasonable person would wish to keep private, does not give rise to common-law tort liability for mental or emotional distress unless the manner or purpose of the defendant's conduct is legally wrongful.

Sidis v. F-R Publishing Corp. (1940)

Facts: The defendants published an article about Sidis, a former child prodigy who had been out of the public eye for over 15 years.
Issue: Is it an invasion of privacy to report a public occurrence or the contents of a public record after a significant amount of time has lapsed?
Rule: Publishing the happening of a public occurrence or the contents of a public record is not actionable, as long as it is still a matter of public interest, no matter how much time has lapsed.

Street v. National Broadcasting Co. (1981)

Facts: NBC produced a television drama of a famous rape trial 40 years after it occurred. Street, the rape victim, sued the network for libel and "false light" invasion of privacy. The defendant claimed a limited privilege because Street was a public figure.
Issue: Does an individual who was once a public figure lose that status with the passage of time?
Rule: Once a person becomes a public figure in connection with a particular controversy, that person remains a public figure thereafter for purposes of later commentary or treatment of that controversy.

Sanders v. Am. Broadcasting Cos., Inc. (1999)

Facts: An ABC reporter, doing an undercover story, infiltrated a company that had its employees perform psychic readings for people who called a 900 number. She posed as a telepsychic and recorded her co-workers' conversations with callers. She did not have permission to do the recording.
Issue: Does the right to privacy protect workers against undercover intrusion?
Rule: The reporter's right to pursue investigative reporting is greater than the workers' interest in the privacy of their conversations in the workplace. In this setting, employees have a limited expectation of privacy. Moreover, the recordings were not "highly offensive" to the reasonable person.

Cantrell v. Forest City Publishing Co. (S. Ct. 1974)

Facts: Cantrell, the wife of a man killed by a bridge collapse, sued the defendant newspaper for an article it published that contained numerous false and inaccurate statements about the family.

Issue: May publishers be vicariously liable for the actions of their employees on a "false light" theory of invasion of privacy?

Rule: (Stewart, J.) Publishers may be liable for invasion of privacy under the doctrine of respondeat superior for articles written by employees acting within the scope of their employment.

Time, Inc. v. Hill (S. Ct. 1967)

Facts: Time published an article stating that a Broadway play was actually a reenactment of Hill's ordeal when he was held as a hostage several years earlier. Hill sued for portraying him in a "false light."

Issue: Is a publication that erroneously portrays a person in a "false light" liable for invasion of privacy?

Rule: (Brennan, J.) A person is liable for invasion of privacy in "false light" cases only if a plaintiff can prove that the person knew of the falsity or acted with reckless disregard of it.

Hustler Magazine v. Falwell (S. Ct. 1988)

Facts: Falwell, a well-known minister, was the subject of a parody in *Hustler* Magazine, which falsely described his first sexual encounter.

Issue: Must a public figure prove "actual malice" to recover for intentional infliction of emotional distress?

Rule: (Rehnquist, C.J.) To recover for the intentional infliction of emotional distress a public figure must prove actual malice.

Nelson v. Times (1977)

Facts: Nelson sued for invasion of privacy and emotional distress after the defendant published an unauthorized picture of her son in connection with a book review in their newspaper.

Issue: Does the publication of a person's photograph in a publication constitute an invasion of privacy?

Rule: Unauthorized use of a person's photograph in a publication is not an invasion of privacy if it is not an unreasonable intrusion upon the seclusion of a person, an appropriation of a person's name or likeness for financial benefit, unreasonable publicity of a person's private life, or publicity that places a person in a false light.

Note: Invasion of privacy is a personal tort that can only be asserted by the person harmed.

Vogel v. W. T. Grant Co. (1974)

Facts: The defendant informed third parties of the plaintiff's debts to coerce him to pay.

Issue: Is the publicizing of a person's debts to a selected and limited group of people an invasion of privacy?

Rule: Notification of a small number of third parties that a plaintiff did not pay off debts is not sufficient to constitute the publication component of the invasion of privacy tort. However, notification of the general public would be unreasonable and actionable.

O'Neil v. Schuckardt (1986)

Facts: The defendants convinced O'Neil's wife to divorce him because he was not a member of their church. They also told O'Neil's children that O'Neil was not their true father. O'Neil sued for alienation of affections and invasion of privacy.

Issue: Is the cause of action for alienation of affections still viable?

Rule: The cause of action for alienation of affections is abolished.

Roberson v. Rochester Folding Box Co. (1902)

Facts: The defendant used Roberson's picture in its advertising campaign without Roberson's permission.

Issue: Can one who has not been defamed assert an action for the unauthorized use of one's likeness?

Rule: Damages and an injunction are not granted for invasion of privacy by the unauthorized use of one's likeness because allowing such suits would result in a vast amount of litigation.

Note: This decision was quickly overruled.

Tropeano v. Atlantic Monthly Co. (1980)

Facts: Tropeano's picture appeared alongside an article in the defendant's magazine. No other reference to the plaintiff was made.

Issue: Are plaintiffs entitled to compensation if their photographs are published without their permission?

Rule: Plaintiffs can recover for the unauthorized use of their photographs only if the use was deliberate and for commercial gain.

Briscoe v. Reader's Digest (1971)

Facts: Reader's Digest published an article mentioning Briscoe by name and describing a hijacking he had committed 11 years earlier.

Issue: Are reports of past crimes protected by the First Amendment?

Rule: Truthful reports of crimes and those involved are newsworthy and are therefore protected by the First Amendment. However, a report about a reformed criminal who has avoided publicity for a long time serves little public purpose, and is an invasion of privacy.

Nader v. General Motors (1970)

Facts: General Motors attempted to discourage Nader, a well-known consumer activist, from publishing a book criticizing their automobiles.

Issue: Has a person committed an invasion of privacy if the person interviewed a party's acquaintances about the party's personal life, followed the party in public, attempted to entrap the party, made harassing phone calls to the party, tapped the party's phone, or conducted a harassing investigation?

Rule: Wiretapping and eavesdropping comprise a prima facie case of invasion of privacy. Interviewing friends, harassing phone calls, and attempted entrapment are not invasions of privacy. Surveillance is actionable only if the defendant was excessively obtrusive.

Galella v. Onassis (1973)

Facts: Galella, a photographer known for harassing celebrities, was detained because of his attempts to secure information about Onassis.

Issue: May the public's right to know impinge on a public figure's right to privacy?

Rule: Legitimate countervailing social needs warrant some intrusions despite an individual's reasonable expectation of privacy and freedom from harassment.

Hall v. Post (1988)

Facts: News stories described the birth and adoption of a child 17 years previously, asking for information on the whereabouts of the child. The follow-up story identified the child and her adoptive parents. The latter sued the newspaper for invasion of privacy by public disclosure of private facts.

Issue: Can an invasion of privacy be established through the public disclosure of private facts?

Rule: Like the false-light privacy tort, the disclosure tort provides duplicative relief in circumstances in which no falsehood was published. The interest in protecting speech is greater than in recognizing a new tort in North Carolina.

Gilbert v. Medical Economics Co. (1981)

Facts: The magazine *Medical Economics* published an article about two cases of alleged malpractice by the plaintiff. The plaintiff sued for defamation because the article suggested that her malpractice was related to her history of psychiatric and personal problems, and included her name and photograph.

Issue: Does the First Amendment give the press the right to disclose private embarrassing facts about individuals who are not public officials or public figures?

Rule: The press may disclose private embarrassing facts about a private individual if the facts are independently newsworthy or have a substantial nexus (i.e., connection) with a newsworthy topic.

The Florida Star v. BJ.F. (S. Ct. 1989)

Facts: The Florida Star newspaper violated a state statute that made it unlawful to publish the name of a victim of a sexual offense. The newspaper obtained the plaintiff's name from a police report.

Issue: Is a state statute that prohibits the publication of truthful information a violation of the First Amendment?

Rule: (Marshall, J.) Publication of truthful information that is lawfully obtained may be prohibited by a state statute only when the statute protects a state interest of the highest order.

Concurrence: (Scalia, J.) A law cannot be regarded as protecting an interest of the highest order when the law leaves appreciable damage to that supposedly vital interest unprohibited.

Carson v. Here's Johnny Portable Toilets, Inc. (1983)

Facts: Carson, a well-known entertainer, sued the defendants for invasion of the rights of privacy and publicity after they marketed a line of toilets named "Here's Johnny Portable Toilets." The phrase "Here's Johnny" was commonly associated with Carson.

Issue: Is a celebrity's right of publicity invaded if neither the celebrity's name nor likeness is used?

Rule: A celebrity's right of publicity is invaded whenever the celebrity's identity is intentionally appropriated for commercial purposes. Identity is not limited to the celebrity's name or likeness; it includes any characteristic that is clearly associated with the celebrity.

Note: The right of publicity protects against commercial exploitation of a celebrity's identity, whereas the right of privacy protects a person's right "to be let alone."

Hamberger v. Eastman (1964)

Facts: Eastman installed a listening device in the Hamberger's bedroom.

Issue: Can an action be brought in tort for intrusion into one's physical and mental seclusion?

Rule: An action in tort may be brought when an intrusion into one's seclusion is such that it would be "offensive to any person of ordinary sensibility."

Diaz v. Oakland Tribune, Inc. (1983)

Facts: Diaz sued the *Oakland Tribune* for invasion of privacy after the paper had published a story revealing that Diaz had undergone a gender-change operation.

Issue: In an action for invasion of privacy against the news media where there is no evidence of malice, must the plaintiff prove that the facts published were not newsworthy?

Rule: Because the media is free to publish matters of legitimate interest, a plaintiff must prove that the facts published were not newsworthy to prevail in an action for invasion of privacy.

Commonwealth v. Wiseman (1969)

Facts: Wiseman made an explicit film, *Titicut Follies*, about the conditions at a correctional institution for insane persons. The Commonwealth of Massachusetts sought an injunction against the film on behalf of the inmates for invasion of privacy.

Issue: Can a film that depicts matters of public concern be subject to an injunction on the basis of invasion of privacy?

Rule: When interests of individual privacy outweigh matters of public concern, injunctive relief may be granted preventing publication to the general public.

CHAPTER 19

Civil Rights

Tort liability may be imposed when one party violates another party's civil or political rights, for example, barring a party from their right to vote.

Recovery may be through statute or common law.

A person whose procedural due process rights are violated is entitled to recover nominal damages if actual damages cannot be established.

When a constitutional right has been violated, compensatory damages should be awarded for actual and pecuniary losses, but not for the importance of the right itself.

CASE CLIPS

Ashby v. White (1702)

Facts: The defendant, an election official, denied the plaintiff his legal right to vote.
Issue: Does the denial of a lawful right give rise to a cause of action?
Rule: One who has a right must be allowed to enforce that right.

Daniels v. Williams (S. Ct. 1986)

Facts: A civil rights action was brought by the plaintiff, a prisoner, who slipped on a pillow left on a stairwell by a prison guard.
Issue: Has a prisoner's due process right been violated when the negligence of a prison official causes injury?
Rule: (Rehnquist, J.) Negligence by a prison official, although a tort, is not a deprivation of due process under the Fourteenth Amendment.

Davidson v. Cannon (S. Ct. 1986)

Facts: Davidson, a state prison inmate, was beaten by another inmate after he warned prison officials that he had been threatened.
Issue: Can a prisoner recover under the Civil Rights Act for a prison official's negligent conduct?
Rule: (Rehnquist, J.) Negligent conduct by a prison official is not actionable under the Civil Rights Act.
Dissent: (Blackmun, J.) Negligent conduct by a prison official can be actionable under the Civil Rights Act if such conduct can be shown to be reckless or deliberately indifferent.

Memphis Community School Dist. v. Stachura (S. Ct. 1986)

Facts: Stachura, a school teacher, was suspended after he showed sexually explicit pictures to seventh graders. A jury awarded Stachura compensatory damages based on the importance of the violated right.
Issue: How should compensatory damages for the violation of a constitutional right be determined?
Rule: (Powell, J.) When a constitutional right has been violated, compensatory damages should be awarded for actual and pecuniary losses, but not for the importance of the rights themselves.
Concurrence: (Marshall, J.) Compensatory damages should not be based on "the so-called inherent value of the rights violated."

CHAPTER 20

Misuse of Legal Procedure

I. MALICIOUS PROSECUTION

To prevail in a suit for malicious prosecution a plaintiff must prove the following:

Mnemonic: **The Cat Ate My Dog**

A. **T**ermination of the Proceeding in Favor of the Plaintiff
   An acquittal, dismissal, or dropping of charges are all sufficient. However, a plea bargain does not satisfy this requirement.

B. **C**riminal Proceeding Originally Initiated by the Defendant
   1. The defendant must have actively pressed charges and not merely told his story to a law enforcement official who then initiated the proceedings independently.
   2. Police and prosecutors are privileged and, therefore, immune from liability for malicious prosecution as long as they generally act within the scope of their duties.

C. **A**bsence of Probable Cause
   This exists if the defendant did not actually believe the plaintiff was guilty or if a reasonable person would not have believed that the plaintiff was guilty.
   1. Grand Jury Indictments
      This will suffice as prima facie evidence of probable cause. However, a failure of the grand jury to indict is not evidence that there was no probable cause.
   2. Arrest Warrants
      The issuance of an arrest warrant based solely on a police officer's sworn statement is not evidence of probable cause.
   3. Reasonable Mistakes
      If a defendant made a reasonable mistake as to the facts or the law, that mistake will excuse a lack of probable cause.

4. Convictions

A conviction proves probable cause. However, an acquittal will not disprove probable cause because the standard for an acquittal is lower than that for conviction.

D. **M**alicious Intent

The plaintiff must show that the defendant had an improper motive in bringing the proceeding (i.e., not for justice).

E. **D**amages

The plaintiff may recover actual or punitive damages.

II. WRONGFUL CIVIL PROCEEDINGS

The elements are generally the same as for criminal proceedings. However, it is more difficult to show that the defendant lacked probable cause because the standard for probable cause is lower in civil proceedings than in criminal proceedings.

III. ABUSE OF PROCESS

Abuse of process is invoked when the criminal or civil action is asserted to bring about a result other than winning the case (e.g., to harass or force settlement). This tort exists when a party has a valid cause of action but sues for wrongful reasons.

CASE CLIPS

Texas Skaggs, Inc. v. Graves (1979)

Facts: The defendant reported to the authorities that Graves's checks had bounced, despite the fact that she had later paid the checks by money order. Graves claimed malicious prosecution by the defendants after the case was dismissed due to a lack of evidence.

Issue: What are the elements needed to bring a cause of action for malicious prosecution?

Rule: To prevail in a suit for malicious prosecution a plaintiff must demonstrate a criminal prosecution instituted or continued by a defendant, termination of the criminal proceedings in favor of the accused, proof the criminal proceeding was brought without probable cause, malicious intent when the proceeding was instituted or continued, and damages suffered by the accused.

Friedman v. Dozorc (1981)

Facts: Dozorc, an attorney, sued Dr. Friedman on behalf of one of Friedman's patients who had died. When the case was dismissed, Friedman sued Dozorc for bringing a frivolous action.

Issue: Does an attorney owe a duty of care to an adverse party to avoid bringing frivolous claims?

Rule: An attorney does not owe a duty to an adverse party to avoid frivolous suits.

Grainger v. Hill (1838)

Facts: Hill borrowed money from the defendants, using his boat as collateral. In violation of the loan agreement the defendants asked for early repayment of the loan and had Hill arrested when he refused. Hill brought an action for abuse of process, but failed to prove that he obtained a favorable termination in the underlying loan dispute.

Issue: May abuse of process be asserted without proof that the suit in question was brought without reasonable or probable cause?

Rule: One who uses the legal system with ulterior motives may be sued for abuse of process even if the use of the system would otherwise have been legal and the claim meritorious.

Russo v. State of New York (1982)

Facts: Russo borrowed a car from his brother-in-law. When the car was subsequently stolen, Russo impersonated his brother-in-law and reported the theft to the insurance company and the police. A police officer discovered the plaintiff's impersonation and arrested him. The charges were dismissed and Russo sued for malicious prosecution.

Issue 1: What must a plaintiff prove in an action for malicious prosecution?

Rule 1: A plaintiff can recover for malicious prosecution by establishing that (1) the defendant commenced or continued a criminal proceeding against the plaintiff, (2) the proceeding terminated in the plaintiff's favor, (3) there was no probable cause for the proceeding, and (4) the proceeding was instituted in actual malice.

Issue 2: Does the issuance of an arrest warrant by a judge raise a presumption of probable cause that would defeat a malicious prosecution claim?

Rule 2: An arrest warrant is not evidence of probable cause when the warrant was issued because of the defendant's sworn statement, as opposed to an arrest warrant issued after a grand jury indictment.

Bull v. McCluskey (1980)

Facts: Bull, an attorney, brought a malpractice suit against McCluskey, a doctor, on behalf of one of McCluskey's patients to coerce a money settlement. Bull knew there were no grounds for the suit and did not introduce any expert testimony at trial. Bull claimed that he did not act out of malice.

Issue: Is malice an element of an action for abuse of process?

Rule: Malice is not required for abuse of process. Abuse of process involves any suit asserted for a motive other than winning.

Gregoire v. Biddle (1949)

Facts: The plaintiff, a Frenchman, was arrested upon entering the United States for being German. He was detained from 1942 to 1946 despite a ruling by the Enemy Alien Hearing Board that he was French. The plaintiff sued various government officials responsible for his illegal detention for malicious prosecution.

Issue: Is a United States Attorney immune from civil liability for malicious prosecution?

Rule: Department of Justice employees are absolutely immune from civil liability for malicious prosecution.

Melvin v. Pence (1942)

Facts: Pence, a detective hired to follow Melvin, a married man, confronted Melvin when he was with another woman. Melvin instituted proceedings before the state licensing authorities to revoke Pence's license, but Pence won. Pence sued for malicious prosecution.

Issue: Can an action for malicious prosecution arise from an administrative action?

Rule: A suit for malicious prosecution may be brought for the wrongful institution of administrative proceedings, in addition to the wrongful institution of judicial proceedings.

CHAPTER 21

Misrepresentation

I. INTRODUCTION

This addresses the tort of misrepresentation individually and does not discuss it as an element of another tort, which it may sometimes be. Generally, misrepresentation involves false statements that cause pecuniary harm. It usually occurs when two parties enter into a contract where one party is hiding or misstating an important fact that would affect the other party's willingness to enter into the contract if it knew the truth.

II. CONCEALMENT AND NONDISCLOSURE

A. Concealment
   Concealment involves misstating or hiding the truth through words or actions. It must relate to a material element of the agreement between the parties. Materiality is generally determined by what a reasonable person would consider material. However, if the defendant actually knows that some issue is extremely important to the plaintiff, then that issue is material.
B. Nondisclosure
   Nondisclosure occurs in situations where a party withholds information, as opposed to taking an affirmative step such as lying. A party is liable for nondisclosure if:
   1. There is a fiduciary relationship, e.g., attorney-client;
   2. The party withholds new information that makes a previously made statement false; or
   3. The nondisclosing party knows that the other party is mistaken about an essential and material fact.
C. Intent
   1. Intent to Misrepresent
      The intent to misrepresent exists if the party:
      a. Made the statement knowing or believing it to be false.

      b. Implied or stated that the party had greater confidence in the accuracy of its statement than it actually did.

      c. Implied or stated that the statement was based on more solid grounds than it actually was.

  2. Intent to Induce Reliance

  A party's intent to cause a plaintiff to rely on its misrepresentations can be extended to remote persons if the party acts in a way to induce their reliance.

III. BASIS OF LIABILITY

A. Third Parties

A party who makes a negligent misstatement is only liable to the limited group of persons it intends to reach or that it knows its recipients intend to reach.

B. Business

Liability is most often allowed in business relationships.

C. Strict Liability

One may not be strictly liable for a misrepresentation unless:

1. The misrepresentation is made in a sale, rental, or exchange transaction. There must be privity for liability to exist.

2. The misrepresentation is made by a seller of chattels.

IV. RELIANCE AND OPINION

To recover for misrepresentation, a plaintiff must prove that the reliance on the misstatement was justified.

A. Statements of Fact vs. Opinions

Reliance on a misrepresentation as to a fact is almost always justified, unless the relied on representation is obviously false. Reliance on a false statement of opinion is only justified if:

1. the defendant has worked to gain the plaintiff's trust;

2. the defendant is or presents himself to be an expert; or

3. a fiduciary relationship exists between the parties.

B. Puffing

Salespersons are allowed to engage in some puffing as part of their sales pitch even if they somewhat exaggerate the product's attributes.

V. LAW

Historically, statements of law were considered to be opinions. However, the modern trend is to handle statements of law in the same manner as all other statements.

VI. PREDICTION AND INTENTION

A false prediction of future events is considered a statement of opinion, but a false representation of a person's intentions is a statement of fact.

VII. DAMAGES

A plaintiff can recover any damages that were proximately caused by a defendant's misrepresentation. A plaintiff can recover consequential damages, as well as reliance damages, but not nominal damages.

A. Reliance

Reliance damages are damages directly incurred because of reliance on a negligent misrepresentation.

B. Consequential

Consequential damages are damages that indirectly result from reliance on a misrepresentation. A party can recover these damages only if they can be proved with sufficient certainty.

CASE CLIPS

Chandelor v. Lopus (1603)

Facts: The defendant, a goldsmith, sold a gem to the plaintiff after misrepresenting the quality of the stone.
Issue: Is a sale of falsely represented goods actionable as deceit?
Rule: False representation of goods by a seller is not actionable unless the seller made a warranty at the time of sale.

Pasley v. Freeman (1789)

Facts: The defendant lied about a third party's financial status, persuading Pasley to do business with the third party. The defendant did not receive any monetary benefit from his deceit.
Issue: May an action for deceit be asserted against a party who makes false statements for no pecuniary gain?
Rule: An action for deceit can be asserted by one who is injured by the false representations of another even if the false statements were not made for contractual or pecuniary advantage.

Swinton v. Whitinsville Savings Bank (1942)

Facts: Whitinsville Savings Bank did not disclose that the house it sold Swinton was infested with termites.
Issue: Must one disclose material facts if not asked to do so?
Rule: One is not liable for the failure to disclose information that is not requested.
Note: This rule has numerous exceptions.

Peek v. Gurney (1873)

Facts: Peek sued a company's board of directors for concealment of facts and misrepresentation after he relied on their prospectus, which falsely described the company's strong financial position, to buy stock.
Issue: Does a failure to disclose material facts make one liable?
Rule: The mere nondisclosure of material facts, however morally censurable, forms no ground for an action for misrepresentation.

Lindberg Cadillac Co. v. Aron (1963)

Facts: The defendant concealed a cracked radiator when trading in his car to Lindberg Cadillac Co.

Issue: Is one liable for misrepresentation without actually making any fraudulent statements?

Rule: Fraudulent concealment is intentional misrepresentation. One may make a "representation" through actions as well as words.

Griffith v. Byers Constr. Co. of Kansas, Inc. (1973)

Facts: The defendants developed a residential site on land that could not support vegetation and then failed to inform its purchasers. The defendants sold lots to a builder who sold the homes to the plaintiffs.

Issue: Does a vendee have a cause of action for concealment of a material fact against a vendor with whom there is no privity?

Rule: A vendor guilty of fraudulent concealment is liable to a party that is not in privity if that party is a member of a class of persons that the vendor ultimately intended to reach.

Laidlaw v. Organ (S. Ct. 1817)

Facts: Organ contracted to buy tobacco from Laidlaw when Organ received information that its price would soon be going up. Laidlaw asked Organ if he had any information about the future price of tobacco, but Organ did not answer.

Issue: Must a buyer divulge external information about the price of a commodity about to be purchased?

Rule: (Marshall, C.J.) A buyer is under no obligation to divulge information that would affect the price of the commodity about to be purchased.

Derry v. Peek (1889)

Facts: The defendants issued a prospectus that said their railroad was approved by a Special Act of Parliament. Peek made investments based on the prospectus, but the company went bankrupt when it failed to obtain approval from the Board of Trade, as required.

Issue: Is an honest but false representation actionable as deceit?

Rule: The tort of deceit is not applicable when a false statement is made by one who honestly and reasonably believes in its truth.

Note: Under modern law, deceit would be found against a party that makes a statement with no reasonable basis to support it.

International Products Co. v. Erie R.R. Co. (1927)

Facts: The defendant agreed to store the plaintiff's goods. The defendant incorrectly reported their whereabouts and as a result, the goods were not covered by the plaintiff's fire insurance.

Issue: When a party has a duty to give correct information, is a negligent misrepresentation of that information actionable?
Rule: A party that has a duty to provide correct information will be liable for the failure to do so.

Winter v. G.P. Putnam's Sons (1991)

Facts: The Winters purchased *The Encyclopedia of Mushrooms*, a reference guide containing information on the habitat, collection and cooking of mushrooms, distributed by Putnam. They alleged that the book contained erroneous and misleading information, when after relying on the book's directions and eating the mushrooms, they became critically ill.
Issue: Can publishers be held strictly liable for the information provided in their books?
Rule: The doctrine of strict liability does not apply to the ideas and expressions contained in a book. No publisher has a duty as a guarantor of accuracy, unless he were to assume the burden.

Richard v. A. Waldman and Sons, Inc. (1967)

Facts: The plaintiff relied on the defendant's plans to confirm that the house he was buying conformed with the zoning law. The plans were mistaken and the house actually violated the zoning law.
Issue: Is a party liable for an innocent misrepresentation?
Rule: When two parties are involved in a sale, rental, or exchange, an innocent misrepresentation may be actionable if a declarant has the means of knowing, ought to know, or has the duty to know the truth.

Credit Alliance Corp. v. Arthur Andersen & Co. (1985)

Facts: The plaintiff, a credit company, relied on the defendant's erroneous financial analysis of a private company.
Issue: Absent privity of contract, is an accountant liable to a party that relies to its detriment upon a negligently prepared report?
Rule: An accountant is liable to a third party for a negligently prepared report if it was known the reports were to be used for a particular purpose.

Citizens State Bank v. Timm, Schmidt & Co. (1983)

Facts: Citizens Bank lost money when it relied on erroneous financial statements negligently prepared by the defendant, an accounting firm.
Issue: Is an accountant liable for damages to a third party not in privity for a negligently prepared report?

Rule: An accountant is liable to a person injured due to negligently prepared financial statements if the person's reliance is foreseeable.

Ultramares Corp. v. Touche (1931)

Facts: The plaintiff was injured when it loaned a third party money based on an erroneous report from the defendant, an accounting firm.

Issue: Is an accountant liable for negligent misrepresentation to a party where there is no privity of contract?

Rule: An accountant does not owe a duty of care to every party that uses financial statements it prepared and is not liable for errors in such statements unless those errors were intentionally fraudulent.

Note: The rule stated here does not represent the modern view.

Williams v. Rank & Son Buick, Inc. (1969)

Facts: Williams bought a car from the defendant after he was told it was air-conditioned and took it for a test drive. A few days later, Williams discovered that there was no air conditioner.

Issue: Is a person who makes obviously false statements liable to a person who relies on the statements?

Rule: One can recover for reliance on a false statement only if the reliance was reasonable.

Sippy v. Cristich (1980)

Facts: While purchasing a house, Sippy noticed stains on the ceilings, but was told by the real estate agent that the roof had been repaired. One month later, the roof leaked, causing substantial damages.

Issue: Does a party have a duty to investigate the veracity of another's representations before relying on them?

Rule: A party is justified in relying on a statement without investigating its veracity unless the party knows or has reason to know of facts that make the reliance unreasonable.

Saxby v. Southern Land Co. (1909)

Facts: Saxby bought a 120-acre farm relying on the previous owner's erroneous estimation of its size.

Issue: Is a misstatement of opinion actionable as fraud?

Rule: Speculative expressions of opinion are not fraudulent and are not actionable as negligent misrepresentations.

Vulcan Metals Co. v. Simmons Mfg. Co. (1918)

Facts: Vulcan Metals sued the defendants for misrepresentations they made about the "absolutely perfect" condition of their machinery.
Issue: When are false statements made by a seller about a product considered an opinion (i.e., not actionable as misrepresentation)?
Rule: When a buyer and a seller have an equal bargaining position (e.g., a buyer has ample opportunity to examine a product), false opinion is considered nonactionable "puffing."

Hanberry v. Hearst Corp. (1969)

Facts: Hanberry's shoes were slippery and caused her to fall down. She bought the shoes because the defendant, a corporation, had given the shoes its "Good Housekeeping Seal of Approval."
Issue: Is a company that endorses products for its own economic gain liable to those who, relying on the endorsement, buy those products?
Rule: When the purpose of an endorsement is to induce a sale, and an endorser represents to the public that it has superior knowledge and special information concerning a product, the endorser may be liable for both statements of fact and opinion.

Sorenson v. Gardner (1959)

Facts: Sorenson purchased a house from Gardner, relying on his representations that it met all the minimum building code requirements. Sorenson sued on discovering otherwise.
Issue: Is a defendant liable for misrepresentations of law that include implied statements of factual matters?
Rule: A plaintiff who relies on statements implied from a defendant's representation of law can recover if the statements are false.
Note: Statements of law themselves have traditionally not been actionable because they were considered to be opinion.

Stark v. Equitable Life Assurance Society (1939)

Facts: Stark bought an insurance policy from the defendants that provided him a lawyer free of charge in the event of accident or injury. After an accident, Stark was incorrectly told by one of the defendant's agents that he could not recover.
Issue: Is a party who agrees to advise another on a matter of law obligated to act honestly and with due care?
Rule: Although misrepresentations of the law are ordinarily not actionable, when parties volunteer such information they are liable for misrepresentation if they do not give honest and fair advice.

McElrath v. Electric Investment Co. (1911)

Facts: The plaintiff leased a hotel from the defendants after they indicated to him that an electric railroad would soon run nearby.
Issue: Are statements regarding the future intentions of third parties actionable as false representations?
Rule: Generally, false representations cannot consist of promises and conjectures, but must contain existing facts to be actionable. However, if a conjecture was intended to create a belief that it was fact, the statement will be actionable.

Burgdorfer v. Thielemann (1936)

Facts: Thielemann induced Burgdorfer to buy a piece of property by orally promising to pay off its outstanding mortgage over the years.
Issue: Is a suit for deceit defeated because the promise was not enforceable under the statute of frauds?
Rule: An action for deceit is based on a false representation and not on an agreement. Thus, a promise that is not enforceable due to the statute of frauds can be actionable as an intentional misrepresentation.

Hinkle v. Rockville Motor Co., Inc. (1971)

Facts: Hinkle discovered that the new car he bought from Rockville Motors was actually used. He sued for misrepresentation, claiming that it would now cost $800 to make the car as good as new. Rockville Motors argued that the present value of the car was irrelevant, and that Hinkle had to show the value of the car when it was sold to him.
Issue: Must a plaintiff prove the actual value of a misrepresented chattel at the time of sale?
Rule: A purchaser of a chattel is entitled to recover both for "out of pocket expenses" and for loss of the "benefit of a bargain" against a party who induces the purchase of the chattel by misrepresentation.

Selman v. Shirley (1939)

Facts: Shirley intentionally misrepresented the quantity of wood on the land that he sold to the plaintiffs.
Issue: Can a party that is defrauded by misrepresentation recover "the benefit of the bargain?"
Rule: A party that is defrauded by misrepresentation is entitled to recover "the benefit of the bargain" that would have been received.
Note: Benefit of the bargain damages are the difference between what a plaintiff actually paid for the property and what the property is worth.

Price-Orem Investment Co. v. Rollins, Brown and Gunnell, Inc. (1986)

Facts: The defendant was hired by a general contractor to survey a site owned by the plaintiff. The defendant erred in certifying the property's boundaries, and the plaintiff consequently lost money.

Issue: Is a party liable for damages incurred by another who reasonably and foreseeably relies on the party's negligent misrepresentations, despite a lack of privity between the parties?

Rule: Under the tort of negligent misrepresentation, a party injured by reasonable reliance on another's careless or negligent misrepresentation of a material fact may recover damages resulting from that injury when the party who made the misrepresentation had a pecuniary interest in the transaction, was in a superior position to know the material facts, and should have reasonably foreseen that the injured party was likely to rely on the representation.

Johnson v. Davis (1985)

Facts: Johnson knew, but failed to disclose, that there had been problems with the roof of his home, which Davis purchased. In fact, Johnson assured Davis that a prior problem with the roof was minor and had been corrected.

Issue 1: Must a seller of realty disclose latent material defects to a buyer?

Rule 1: Where the seller of a home, new or used, knows of facts materially affecting the value of the property that are not readily observable or known to the buyer, the seller is under a duty to disclose them to the buyer.

Issue 2: Is a seller who affirmatively misrepresents a material fact liable?

Rule 2: A seller is liable for fraudulent misrepresentation if the seller makes a false statement concerning a material fact, intends that the representation induce another to act on it, and a consequent injury by the party acting in reliance on the representation occurs.

Watson v. Avon Street Business Center, Inc. (1984)

Facts: The plaintiff bought a warehouse with a leaky roof. Prior to the purchase, the plaintiff inspected the roof. The seller's agent told the plaintiff it was "a good roof."

Issue: May a buyer who partially investigates the condition of that which is to be bought later maintain a suit for fraud in the inducement?

Rule: A buyer who is directed to sources of information and who personally begins an examination of the facts is charged with all the knowledge that would have been obtained had the examination been conducted diligently and completely. Consequently, the buyer cannot complain about a misleading seller's representation because reliance on the representation would be unreasonable.

Burr v. Board of County Commissioners of Stark County (1986)

Facts: The defendant represented to Burr that a child offered to Burr for adoption was healthy, had a healthy mother, and was born in a city hospital. In fact, the defendant knew the child was born in a mental institution to mentally retarded parents and had inherited mental deficiencies.
Issue: Does the doctrine of sovereign immunity preclude a suit for fraud against a political subdivision?
Rule: If a plaintiff proves each element of fraud, the doctrine of sovereign immunity will not shield a political subdivision from responsibility for the fraudulent acts and misrepresentations of its employees and agents made in the performance of their services.

Aldrich v. Scribner (1908)

Facts: The defendant misrepresented that a plot of land he sold to the plaintiff contained 175 fruit trees. The defendant honestly believed this to be true.
Issue: Is a party strictly liable for false statements, or must the party act with knowledge that the statements are false or with reckless disregard for the truth to be liable?
Rule: A seller of land is strictly liable for untruthful statements that a buyer relies on, even if the seller honestly believed the statements to be true.
Note: This is the majority rule.

Christenson v. Commonwealth Land Title Insurance Co. (1983)

Facts: Christenson sued to recover damages caused by the defendant's negligent acknowledgment of a document that incorrectly indicated that certain properties were available as security to Christenson. The plaintiff and defendant were not in privity of contract.
Issue: Absent privity of contract, may one who negligently makes a false statement be held liable?
Rule: A party with a pecuniary interest in a transaction and in a superior position to know material facts may be held liable for negligent misrepresentation, even in the absence of privity, if the party carelessly or negligently makes a false representation expecting another party to act in reliance thereon, and the other party reasonably does so, suffering a loss.

Williams v. Polgar (1974)

Facts: Williams bought property from Polgar in reliance on a faulty abstract of title produced for Polgar. Williams sued the title company for negligent misrepresentation when he discovered the defective nature of the abstract.
Issue: Is a title company liable to persons it should have foreseen would rely on its title abstract if there is no contractual privity?
Rule: A negligent title company is liable to persons it should have foreseen would rely on its abstracts, as well as those it knew would rely on its abstracts, even if there is no contractual privity.

Lucas v. Hamm (1961)

Facts: Hamm, an attorney, prepared an invalid will. Lucas, an intended beneficiary of the will, sued Hamm for malpractice.
Issue: Is an attorney liable to a party that has suffered damages because of the attorney's improper work, although they were not in privity?
Rule: Third-party beneficiaries who are not in privity with a lawyer may recover for the lawyer's negligence if they belong to a limited, foreseeable class of persons.

Bishop v. E.A. Strout Realty Agency (1950)

Facts: Bishop bought a tract of land for the purpose of opening a camp-site. The defendant realty agency misrepresented to Bishop that the nearby lake was deep enough for camp activities. Bishop did not check the depth of the lake.
Issue: Is a seller's misrepresentation excused by a buyer's failure to examine the property purchased?
Rule: A buyer is not precluded from recovery for relying on a seller's misrepresentations of a matter that is not apparent to ordinary observation.
Note: This illustrates the general rule that a buyer has no duty to investigate before purchase.

Turnbull v. LaRose (1985)

Facts: Prior to consummation of a business transaction, LaRose, a seller, made certain assurances to the plaintiff, a buyer.
Issue: Does an action for misrepresentation lie where a buyer alleges reliance on a seller's opinions, as distinguished from statements of fact?
Rule: A seller's assurances, as distinguished from mere puffing, may be justifiably relied on by a buyer, and thus an action for misrepresentation would lie.

Leyendecker & Associates, Inc. v. Wechter (1984)

Facts: The defendant represented to Wechter that a lot that Wechter subsequently purchased contained 5,800 square feet. In fact, the lot was only 3,389 square feet.

Issue: When a jury finds that there was no difference in the value of property as represented and as received, is a plaintiff precluded from recovering damages?

Rule: Absent a showing of a difference between the value represented and received, a plaintiff may not recover the benefit of the bargain, but may nonetheless recover any actual injuries.

Edgington v. Fitzmaurice (1885)

Facts: The plaintiff invested in the defendant's company, relying on defendant's prospectus that stated the money would be used for new investment. The money was actually used to pay off the company's debts.

Issue: What are the elements of an action for deceit/fraud?

Rule: To prove deceit, the plaintiff must show that the defendant knowingly or recklessly made a false statement with the intention that the plaintiff rely on the statement, and that the plaintiff acted in reliance, suffering some damages.

Adams v. Gillig (1910)

Facts: Adams sold Gillig some land after Gillig had assured her that he would build dwellings on the lot. After the purchase, Gillig constructed a parking garage on the land.

Issue: Is a contract voidable if a defendant misrepresents a material fact?

Rule: Any contract induced by knowing misrepresentation of a material fact is voidable.

Obde v. Schlemeyer (1960)

Facts: Schlemeyer sold a house to Obde knowing that it was infested with termites. Obde had made no inquiries about the possibility of termites.

Issue: Can nondisclosure of a material fact constitute fraud when two parties are dealing at arm's length?

Rule: It is a property seller's duty to inform the purchaser if there are known concealed defects that are not readily apparent, and that constitute a serious danger to property or life.

Ingaharro v. Blanchette (1982)

Facts: Ingaharro bought a house from Blanchette. Blanchette did not inform Ingaharro of problems with the water supply, which Blanchette did not consider serious.

Issue: Can an action for negligent misrepresentation be brought when the seller fails to inform the buyer of a material fact?

Rule: An action for negligent misrepresentation will lie when there is negligent misrepresentation by the defendant and justifiable reliance by the plaintiff. When the defendants honestly believe there is no concealed defect, there is no duty to disclose.

Chatham Furnace Co. v. Moffatt (1888)

Facts: Moffatt leased an iron ore mine from Chatham after Chatham had knowingly used an incorrect survey to assure Moffatt of the value of the mine.

Issue: Can an action for deceit be maintained when the defendant knowingly makes a false statement of fact?

Rule: Fraudulent intent in an action for deceit exists when a party knowingly makes a false statement concerning a matter of fact, as opposed to mere opinion or judgment.

Johnson v. Healy (1978)

Facts: Johnson bought a house from Healy, a builder. Within three years the foundation settled, causing the sewer lines to break. The cost to repair both the sewer lines and the foundation would exceed the value of the house.

Issue: In an action for breach of warranty, can a plaintiff recover damages for the cost to repair, when such cost represents economic waste?

Rule: The general rule for damages in a breach of warranty action is to place the plaintiff in the position he occupied before the injury. However, when the cost to repair represents economic waste, damages should be limited to diminution in value of the property.

Pelkey v. Norton (1953)

Facts: Norton traded in a truck to Pelkey, a car dealer. Norton claimed that the truck was two years newer than it actually was.

Issue: In an action for deceit, may a defendant's fraudulent conduct be excused by the plaintiff's contributory negligence?

Rule: When one intentionally misrepresents facts to another, it is no defense that the other party negligently relied on the misrepresentation.

Corva v. United Services Automobile Association (1985)

Facts: After Corva was involved in a car accident with the defendant's insured, he settled for an amount that he believed to be the limit of the insured's policy. Corva then filed a complaint that the defendant misrepresented the policy limits; the defendants filed a cross-claim against Corva's attorneys based on contributory negligence in failing to verify the policy limits.

Issue: Can a cross-complaint based on negligence be dismissed as a matter of law in an action for intentional fraud?

Rule: The standards of care for justifiable reliance in fraud and reasonable care in negligence are different. Theoretically, one could justifiably rely on misrepresentations but still be negligent for failing to use reasonable care; thus a cross-complaint based on negligence in an action for intentional fraud may not be dismissed as a matter of law.

CHAPTER 22

Interference with Advantageous Relationships

I. INJURIOUS FALSEHOOD

A. Trade Libel

Trade libel is a cause of action against a party who has made false statements concerning a plaintiff's business or product. The plaintiff must prove the following elements:

Mnemonic: **SIPS**

1. False **S**tatement

   The party made a false statement about the plaintiff's property, business, or product.

2. **I**ntent

   The party:

   a. Acted with reckless disregard as to the statement's truth;

   b. Knew the statement was false; or

   c. Acted with malice.

3. **P**ublication

   The statement was communicated to and understood by a third party.

4. **S**pecial Damages

   The plaintiff suffered special damages due to the statement (i.e., pecuniary loss).

B. Slander of Title

Slander of title is an action against a party who has made false statements about a plaintiff's right to property. The elements are the same as for trade libel, except this tort involves property.

For example, Susan falsely claims that she owns Rob's land and causes him damage because a potential buyer of the land backs out of the deal.

C. Defenses to Injurious Falsehood
1. Truth
Truth is an absolute defense.
2. Privilege
A party may raise any privilege that could be raised in a defamation case. See Ch. 17, V, C.
3. Competition by Fair Means
A party is allowed to make generally truthful comparisons between its product and a plaintiff's product.
4. Rival Claimant's Privilege
A party is allowed to challenge a plaintiff's ownership of property if a reasonable person would think that the party may have a possessory interest in the property, even if the party does not actually have one.

II. INTERFERENCE WITH AN EXISTING CONTRACT

This is an action against a third party who induces a party to breach a contract.
A. Elements
1. The plaintiff must be a party to the contract.
2. The third party must induce a party to the contract to breach its contractual obligations to the plaintiff.
3. Intent
It must be shown that the third party:
a. Knew about the contract's existence;
b. Knew its actions would lead to a breach of the contract;
c. Actively interfered with the contract. Merely offering a better price or a better deal is not enough.
4. Damages
The plaintiff can recover for profits lost, any emotional harm suffered, and for punitive damages. The plaintiff, however, cannot recover twice (i.e., from both the breaching party and the inducer).
B. Defenses
1. This tort does not apply to the following contracts:
a. Illegal contracts;
b. Marriage contracts;
c. Contracts terminable at will; and
d. Unenforceable contracts.
Note: All illegal contracts are unenforceable contracts, but not all unenforceable contracts are illegal contracts.
2. Privileges

A party is privileged to interfere with an existing contractual relationship in the following instances:

a. Protection of One's Own Position

A party not trying to develop new business may make statements to protect its existing contract rights.

b. Social Interests

A party may induce a breach if the breach promotes social welfare.

III. INTERFERENCE WITH A PROSPECTIVE ADVANTAGE

This is an action against a party who causes a plaintiff to lose possible future contracts. The elements are basically the same as for interference with an existing contract, except that the party has a greater privilege to interfere.

A. Privilege

A party is privileged to interfere with a prospective contractual relationship when:

1. The party is acting to pursue its own business interests.
2. The party is not merely trying to bankrupt the plaintiff.
3. The party is not acting out of pure malice; mixed emotions are allowed if there is a legitimate business interest involved.
4. The party honestly advises somebody not to deal with the plaintiff (e.g., advice given by a friend or a relative).

B. Interference

Interference with a plaintiff's benefit from prospective non-business-related matters can also be actionable (e.g., if Susan induced Rob's father to leave Rob out of his will, Susan might be liable for tortious interference).

IV. INTERFERENCE WITH FAMILY RELATIONS

This is an action against a party that causes one to lose the affections of a family member.

A. Husband and Wife

A plaintiff who sues a defendant for seducing his or her spouse must prove:

1. The defendant willfully or maliciously seduced the spouse.
2. At the outset, the spouse did not voluntarily accept the seduction.
3. The spouse did not actively contribute to the seduction.
4. The plaintiff was not at fault for causing the spouse to stray.
5. The loss of affection was caused by the defendant's actions.

B. Alienation of a Child's Affections

No cause of action exists against a party that causes a parent to lose a child's affection unless the party:

1. induces the child to leave home. However, causing a child to leave home for marriage purposes is a privileged action.

2. has sexual intercourse with a female child who is a minor.

C. Alienation of a Parent's Affections

There is no recovery available to a child against a third party who causes the child to lose the affection of a parent.

CASE CLIPS

Ratcliffe v. Evans (1892)

Facts: Ratcliffe continued to run the family business after his father died. He sued the defendant for falsely and maliciously publishing an article that implied otherwise, thereby hurting his business.

Issue: What proof is required in an action for malicious interference with business based on a published falsehood?

Rule: In a suit for malicious interference with business based on a published falsehood, a plaintiff needs only to prove a general loss of business; no proof of the loss of any particular customers is needed.

Horning v. Hardy (1977)

Facts: Hardy claimed that he was the owner of property that Horning was about to sell. Horning's purchaser backed out of the sale and Horning sued Hardy in a tort action for injurious falsehood.

Issue: Is a party liable for injurious falsehood when it makes incorrect statements that interfere with the contract of another?

Rule: Parties that make incorrect statements that interfere with the contracts of others are liable for injurious falsehood (also known as disparagement) unless the statements are made to protect the parties' economic interests and are made without malice or negligence.

Bose Corp. v. Consumers Union of United States, Inc. (S. Ct. 1984)

Facts: Bose sued the defendants for product disparagement because of an inaccurate critique of Bose's product in *Consumers Reports* magazine. The defendants argued Bose was a "public figure" and thus they had a privilege because they did not act maliciously.

Issue: Does the rule in defamation actions that false statements be made with actual malice apply to actions for product disparagement?

Rule: (Stevens, J.) Actual malice, or knowingly publishing a false statement or acting with reckless disregard to a statement's truth, must be proved in a product disparagement action.

Testing Systems, Inc. v. Magnaflux Corp. (1966)

Facts: Testing Systems and Magnaflux were competing manufacturers. Magnaflux circulated a false report that the U.S. government found Testing Systems' products to be inferior to Magnaflux's products.

Issue: What are the boundaries of a competitor's privilege to "puff" and make "unfavorable comparisons?"
Rule: False statements of a specific nature that unfairly compare two products are not privileged.

Lumley v. Gye (1853)

Facts: The plaintiff held an exclusive contract for the performance of an opera singer. The defendant, knowing of the plaintiff's contract, maliciously induced the singer to breach the contract.
Issue: Does a party whose contract has been breached because of the malicious intrusions of a third party have a cause of action against the third party?
Rule: One who maliciously induces another to breach a contract is liable for the interference.

Imperial Ice Co. v. Rossier (1941)

Facts: Imperial Ice bought an ice distributing company with an agreement that the former owner would not compete with Imperial Ice. The defendants, another ice distributing company, induced the former owner to breach this clause.
Issue: Is one who induces a third party to breach a contract liable when the inducement is for economic gain?
Rule: One seeking to advance one's own economic interests is not privileged to induce a third party to breach a contract.

Bacon v. St. Paul Union Stockyards Co. (1924)

Facts: Bacon bought and sold livestock in the defendant's stockyards. The defendant wrongfully excluded him from its stockyards and forbade others to employ him.
Issue: Is wrongful interference with employment a tort?
Rule: Wrongful interference with one's employment is actionable as a tort.

Temperton v. Russell (1893)

Facts: The plaintiff refused to stop supplying materials to a building company with which the defendants had a dispute. As a result, the defendants induced persons who had contracts with the plaintiff to break their present contracts and refuse to enter into future ones.
Issue: Is one liable for interfering with another's future contractual relations?

Rule: When one maliciously conspires to injure another by keeping others from entering into contracts with that person, an action will lie for damages.

Tarleton v. McGawley (1793)

Facts: The plaintiff engaged in trade with natives along the coast of Africa. The defendant, claiming that the natives owed him money, shot at them and thus scared them from trading with the plaintiff.
Issue: Is a party liable for improper conduct that results in the loss of another's prospective business?
Rule: One is liable for the intentional interference with another's prospective economic advantage.

Adler, Barish, Daniels, Levin and Creskoff v. Epstein (1978)

Facts: Epstein, a former member of the plaintiffs' law firm, advised clients at the firm that he was leaving and starting his own practice. He also gave them forms to discharge his old firm as their counsel.
Issue: May one limit speech that does no more than propose a commercial transaction?
Rule: It is constitutional to limit commercial speech when the conduct in question is a departure from "recognized ethical codes."

Leigh Furniture and Carpet Co. v. Isom (1982)

Facts: Leigh Furniture sold its business to Isom, but then constantly harassed Isom, his customers, and his suppliers. Isom eventually went out of business.
Issue: What must a plaintiff prove to sustain a cause of action for wrongful interference with prospective economic relations?
Rule: To recover damages for wrongful interference with prospective economic relations, a plaintiff is required to prove that a defendant intentionally interfered with the plaintiff's existing or potential economic relations for an improper purpose or by improper means, causing injury to the plaintiff.

Della Penna v. Toyota Motor Sales, U.S.A., Inc. (1995)

Facts: P engaged in the sale of re-exported Lexus cars to Japan. He bought the cars in the United States from dealers for a little less than the retail price and sold them in Japan at a substantial profit. Toyota, the manufacturer, sought to end this practice by pressuring U.S. dealers not to sell cars to P. Its strategy worked and P sued Toyota for tortious interference.

Issue: Does simple interference wrongfully hinder a business enterprise?
Rule: To recover, P must prove more than interference and demonstrate a disruption of an established business relationship through tortious activity.

Smith v. Ford Motor Co. (1976)

Facts: Smith was the manager of a profitable Ford dealership. He was discharged by the dealership's shareholders after Ford Motors pressured them to fire him.
Issue: May a person bring a suit against a third party who pressured the person's employer to terminate an employment contract?
Rule: One who pressures an employer to terminate the employment contract of another will be liable for malicious interference of a contractual relation.

Richardson v. La Rancherita La Jolla, Inc. (1979)

Facts: La Rancherita, a lessor, tried to prevent the plaintiff from assigning a lease that required La Rancherita's approval of all assignments. The plaintiff engaged in a legal maneuver that technically was not an assignment and La Rancherita intervened.
Issue: When is intentional interference with a contract justified?
Rule: A party who intentionally interferes with a contract in a "good faith effort" to protect its interests is not liable for such interference.

Brimelow v. Casson (1923)

Facts: Brimelow underpaid his chorus girls, forcing them to commit immoral acts out of economic need. Casson persuaded theater owners to cancel their contracts with Brimelow unless wages were increased.
Issue: When may interference with another's contract be justified?
Rule: Interference with a contractual relation may be justified when a third party acts to protect the interest of others and of society.

Duff v. Engleberg (1965)

Facts: Engleberg maliciously influenced his neighbors not to sell their house to the plaintiffs, who were African-American.
Issue: What types of damages may a party recover from a third party who maliciously interfered with a contractual relation?
Rule: A party may recover specific performance, incidental damages, and punitive damages against a third party who maliciously interferes with a contractual relation.

Harmon v. Harmon (1979)

Facts: The plaintiff claimed that his brother fraudulently induced their mother to take the plaintiff out of her will.
Issue: Is it tortious to interfere with one's expectation of future financial gain?
Rule: A person is entitled to recover damages when, "but for" the tortious interference of another, the person would likely have received a gift or a specific profit from a transaction.

Nash v. Baker (1974)

Facts: Nash sued Baker on behalf of herself and her five minor children. She claimed that Baker, a wealthy widow, lured her husband away through monetary inducements and sexual charms.
Issue: Can a child sue a third party who causes the alienation of a parent's affection?
Rule: A child does not have the right to be compensated by a third party for the alienation of a parent's affections.

National Association for the Advancement of Colored People v. Claiborne Hardware Co. (S. Ct. 1982)

Facts: The NAACP organized a boycott of the white merchants of Claiborne County. The boycott was effectuated by the peaceful exercise of First Amendment rights as well as some individual acts of violence. Based on the tort of malicious interference, the merchants were awarded damages for all their business losses.
Issue: Will the exercise of First Amendment rights support an award of damages for malicious interference?
Rule: (Stevens, J.) Although a state may legitimately impose damages for the consequences of violent conduct, it may not award compensation for the consequences of nonviolent, protected activities. Only those losses proximately caused by unlawful conduct may be recovered in an action for malicious interference.

Abrahams v. Kidney (1870)

Facts: The defendant seduced the plaintiff's minor daughter. The daughter became ill afterward and was unable to work for the plaintiff.
Issue: Is compensation for interference with family relations due to seduction limited to losses caused by pregnancy or venereal disease?
Rule: Damages are not limited to those resulting from pregnancy or venereal disease in cases involving interference with family relations arising from a seduction.

People Express Airlines, Inc. v. Consolidated Rail Corp. (1985)

Facts: People Express was forced to evacuate its terminal located within one mile of Consolidated Rail Corp.'s freight yard after a dangerous chemical escaped from one of the defendant's railway tank cars.

Issue: Is a defendant who negligently interferes with a plaintiff's business, causing pure economic losses unaccompanied by property damage or personal injury, liable in tort?

Rule: A negligent party is liable to foreseeable plaintiffs for economic losses proximately caused by its breach of duty to avoid the risk of economic injury.

Mogul Steamship Co. v. McGregor, Gow, & Co. (1889)

Facts: The defendants formed a shipping association, offering a 5 percent rebate to those who dealt exclusively with their group. The plaintiff, a rival shipper, claimed that the defendants were trying to run him out of business.

Issue: Can an action for unfair competition be asserted without proof of ill will or illegality?

Rule: Competitive actions are not actionable unless they are dishonest, intimidating, or illegal.

International News Service v. Associated Press (S. Ct. 1918)

Facts: The I.N.S. and the A.P. were both in the business of gathering and distributing news. The I.N.S. started taking the news gathered and published by the A.P. in one part of the country and publishing it in other parts before the A.P. could publish it there.

Issue: Is it an unfair trade practice for one to distribute information gathered by another party at great expense for one's own profit?

Rule: (Pitney, J.) Information is quasi-property to those who gather and distribute it at an expense for commercial gain. Exploiting another's property before the owner is able to use it is an unfair trade practice.

Dissent: (Brandeis, J.) Knowledge, truth, conceptions, and ideas are free for common use after they have been voluntarily communicated, with the limited exception of material that is protected under patent and copyright law.

Ely-Norris Safe Co. v. Mosler Safe Co. (1925); Mosler Safe Co. v. Ely Norris Safe Co. (S. Ct. 1926)

Facts: The defendant sold safes that were similar in appearance to the plaintiff's brand safe, but were of inferior quality. The similarity caused confusion between the two brands, prompting the plaintiff to sue for unfair competition.

Issue: Can a party recover damages from a competitor who uses deceit to gain customers?

Rule: (Holmes, J.) A party may recover damages for the deceptive actions of a competitor if it can prove actual lost sales.

Katz v. Kapper (1935)

Facts: Kapper forced Katz out of business by selling his goods at a loss and threatening Katz's customers.

Issue: What methods of competition are lawful?

Rule: A threat is unlawful only if it is a threat to do an unlawful act. Competition in business is not actionable, even if it ruins a rival, as long as the methods do not involve wrongful conduct.

Note: When defendants have a legitimate commercial interest a court will generally ignore the presence of malicious motivations.

Wilkinson v. Powe (1942)

Facts: Wilkinson had a contract with dairy farmers to haul milk to Powe's creamery. Powe informed all the farmers that he would only purchase milk hauled by his own trucks, thereby inducing the farmers to breach their contracts with Wilkinson.

Issue: Is a contract right a property right such that an action for intentional interference will lie when a party actively solicits a breach of contract?

Rule: The right to perform a contract is generally regarded as a property right; any interference with contract rights that proximately results in a breach will bring about a cause for an action in tort.

Tuttle v. Buck (1909)

Facts: Tuttle alleged that Buck set up a barbershop with the sole purpose of driving Tuttle out of business.

Issue: Can an action lie when a defendant interferes with the prospective business advantages of the plaintiff for the sole purpose of injuring the plaintiff?

Rule: An action in tort will lie when a party starts a business in opposition for the sole purpose of driving a competitor out of business, with no regard to any legitimate competitive gain for himself.

Baker v. Dennis Brown Realty, Inc. (1981)

Facts: Baker had nearly completed a real estate transaction with one agent from defendant's firm when another agent from the firm "froze out" Baker and cut a deal for his own client.

Issue: Will an action lie against a party who intentionally induces a seller not to enter into a contract with another?

Rule: An action for intentional interference with a prospective contractual relationship will lie when it is found that the defendant purposely caused a seller not to enter into a business relationship with the plaintiff, the defendant's actions were not privileged, and the plaintiff suffered actual damages.

CHAPTER 23

Some Unclassified Torts

I. TORTS "IMPLIED" FROM LEGISLATIVE PROVISIONS

Monetary damages may be awarded for injuries resulting from a violation of the Fourth Amendment, which protects against unreasonable searches and seizures. These damages may be awarded even though a remedy has not been provided for by the Constitution and has not been enacted by Congress; that is, the remedy is judicially created.

II. PRIMA FACIE TORT

The inability of a plaintiff to fit a tort action into one of the classical categories will not prevent recovery for an act that is corrupt by conventional standards or intentional as to its consequences.

III. OTHER TORTS

A breach of contract is ordinarily compensated by contractual remedies. Damages are not imposed in tort unless there is a special relationship between the parties.

CASE CLIPS

Burnette v. Wahl (1978)

Facts: Five minor children sued their mothers for psychological injury caused by the failure of the mothers to perform their parental duties.
Issue: Are parents liable in tort for abandoning their children?
Rule: Parental desertion is not grounds for an action in tort.

Bivens v. Six Unknown Named Agents of Federal Bureau of Narcotics (S. Ct. 1971)

Facts: Acting without a warrant, six federal agents handcuffed Bivens, searched his home, and threatened to arrest his family.
Issue: Does the violation of a party's Fourth Amendment right against unlawful search and seizure give rise to pecuniary liability?
Rule: (Brennan, J.) Monetary damages may be awarded for injuries resulting from a violation of the Fourth Amendment.
Concurrence: (Harlan, J.) Damages may be awarded even though a remedy has not been provided for by the Constitution and has not been enacted by Congress (i.e., the remedy is judicially created).
Dissent: (Black, J.) The judicial creation of a remedy is an exercise of power the Constitution does not give to the Supreme Court.

Transamerica Mortg. Advisors, Inc. (TAMA) v. Lewis (S. Ct. 1979)

Facts: A shareholder sued the managers of a trust for fraud and breach of fiduciary duties.
Issue: Does the violation of the Investment Advisers Act of 1940 create a private cause of action for damages or other relief?
Rule: (Stewart, J.) The Investment Advisers Act of 1940 confers no causes of action for damages and other forms of monetary relief. It limits relief to actions for rescission of investment contracts.
Dissent: (White, J.) No distinctions should exist between legal and equitable relief when recognizing implied private causes of actions.

Reves v. Ernst and Young (S. Ct. 1993)

Facts: Ernst and Young audited a company giving it a value of $4.5 million, when in reality, if valued on a market basis, the company would have been considered insolvent. After also failing to relate the true financial situation to the directors, the company filed for bankruptcy.

Issue: Must one participate in the operation or management of the enterprise itself to be subject to liability under RICO?
Rule: To be liable under the RICO provision, an individual must be involved in directing the enterprise's affairs.

Porter v. Crawford & Co. (1980)

Facts: The defendants, without reason, stopped payment on a check written to Porter, causing the check to bounce and service charges to be assessed.
Issue: Is there recovery in tort for a lawful act?
Rule: One may recover in tort for a lawful act that is performed maliciously and with intent to cause harm to a plaintiff.

Morrison v. National Broadcasting Co., Inc. (1965)

Facts: The plaintiff participated in the defendant's rigged game show believing it to be honest and authentic. When the truth was told the plaintiff, a student, suffered harm to his reputation. Although morally reprehensible, the defendant's actions were not illegal.
Issue: Is there a tort action for damages that are caused by a legal activity that violates moral expectations but does not fit under a recognized tort category?
Rule: The inability of a plaintiff to fit a tort action into one of the classical categories will not prevent recovery for an act that is corrupt by conventional standards or intentional as to its consequences.

Neibuhr v. Gage (1906)

Facts: Gage threatened to falsely testify against Neibuhr unless he sold Gage his shares in Gage's company.
Issue: Is a party injured by duress entitled to the same remedies as one who is injured by deception?
Rule: A party injured by duress is entitled to the same remedies that are available in cases of deceit.

Seaman's Direct Buying Service, Inc. v. Standard Oil Co. Of California (1984)

Facts: Standard Oil refused to fulfill its contractual obligation to sell the plaintiff oil, claiming it was prohibited by government regulations. Standard Oil still refused after receiving government clearance.
Issue: Is there a tort action for breaching an implied covenant of "good faith and fair dealing?"

Rule: A breach of contract is ordinarily compensated by contractual remedies. Damages are not imposed in tort unless there is a special relationship between the parties.

Foley v. Interactive Data Corp. (1988)

Facts: Foley is a former employee of defendant. He alleged that he refrained from pursuing other possible job opportunities and offers because he believed that defendant, as based on its "termination guidelines," would discharge him only for reasons of good cause.

Issue: Do breaches of an implied covenant in employment contracts give rise to actions seeking awards of tort damages?

Rule: The employment relationship is fundamentally contractual, and as such, in the absence of any legislative direction otherwise, contractual remedies should remain the sole available relief for breaches of the implied covenant of good faith and fair dealing in the employment context.

CHAPTER 24

Compensation Systems as Substitutes for Tort Law

I. EMPLOYMENT INJURIES

Worker's compensation does not bar an intentional tort action because harm from an intentional tort is not a risk inherent in the workplace.

A negligent party can obtain limited contribution from a comparatively negligent employer in an amount proportional to the employer's percentage of negligence, but not to exceed the employer's total worker's compensation liability to the employee.

II. AUTOMOBILE ACCIDENT INJURIES

No-fault laws, which compensate victims of automobile accidents without regard to fault, are constitutional because they serve the public policy objectives of speedy adjudication and elimination of unnecessary cases from the judicial system.

CASE CLIPS

Blankenship v. Cincinnati Milacron Chemicals, Inc. (1982)

Facts: Eight employees alleged they were injured by toxic fumes that their employer, Cincinnati Milacron Chemicals, knew about but failed to correct or warn against.

Issue: May an employee bring a tort action for an intentional injury if there is a worker's compensation statute in effect?

Rule: Worker's compensation does not bar an intentional tort action because harm from an intentional tort is not a risk inherent in the workplace.

Martin v. Lancaster Battery Co., Inc. (1992)

Facts: Supervisor adjusted results of medical tests showing that P had been exposed to high levels of lead at work. P later developed diseases related to lead toxicity.

Issue: Does the exclusivity of Worker's Compensation bar an action by a worker for fraud against the employer in these circumstances?

Rule: Employee is entitled to bring a separate action for fraud. Worker's compensation system applies to work-related injuries that arise from the dangers of the workplace. Court further concluded that fraud is not part of the trade-offs that underlie worker's compensation.

Kerans v. Porter Paint Co. (1991)

Facts: Female employee complained of sexual harassment by her supervisor. She filed suit against the employer.

Issue: Does the exclusivity of worker's compensation bar the lawsuit in tort?

Rule: Worker's compensation does not preclude the lawsuit for sexual harassment because it is intended nearly to provide a remedy for worker economic loss, not the psychological indignities suffered by a victim of sexual harassment.

Lambertson v. Cincinnati Corp. (1977)

Facts: Lambertson was injured by a press brake that his employer, Hutchinson Manufacturing, purchased from Cincinnati Corp. The jury found that all three parties were negligent.

Issue: How are comparative negligence and worker's compensation statutes reconciled?

Rule: A negligent third party can obtain limited contribution from a comparatively negligent employer in an amount proportional to the employer's percentage of negligence, but not to exceed the employer's total worker's compensation liability to the employee.

Montgomery v. Daniels (1975)

Facts: The plaintiff filed an action challenging the constitutionality of New York's no-fault automobile accident compensation law.
Issue: Do no-fault compensation laws violate the due process and equal protection clauses of the Fourteenth Amendment?
Rule: No-fault laws are constitutional because they serve the public policy objectives of speedy adjudication and elimination of unnecessary cases from the judicial system.

Pinnick v. Cleary (1971)

Facts: The plaintiff was involved in a car accident and was barred from recovery for mental pain and suffering because he did not meet the requirements of the state no-fault insurance law. He would not have been barred under common law.
Issue: Is a statute that places constraints on the availability of relief for pain and suffering unconstitutional?
Rule: A government has a legitimate interest in speedy adjudication and lessening the burden of litigation in its courts. Legislation that sets objective criteria to avoid speculative and exaggerated claims is constitutional.

Ayers v. Township of Jackson (1987)

Facts: By its operation of a landfill, Jackson Township contaminated its residents' well water. The township was found liable under the New Jersey Tort Claims Act.
Issue: What proof is needed to justify compensation for medical surveillance under the Tort Claims Act?
Rule: The cost of medical surveillance is compensable when expert testimony proves the toxicity of the chemicals, the seriousness of the diseases at risk, and the value of early diagnosis through reasonable and necessary surveillance.

Wright v. Central Du Page Hospital Association (1976)

Facts: The plaintiff challenged the constitutionality of a statutory provision limiting medical malpractice judgments to $500,000.
Issue: May recovery for a specific type of tort be limited by statute?

Rule: Statutorily limiting recovery for a specific type of tort, such as medical malpractice actions, is arbitrary and unconstitutional.

Johnson v. St. Vincent Hospital, Inc. (1980)

Facts: The plaintiff challenged the constitutionality of a statute that required malpractice claims to be submitted to a review panel and set limitations on the damages that could be recovered.
Issue: May a state require malpractice claims to be submitted to a panel and place limitations on the damages that may be recovered?
Rule: A requirement to submit medical malpractice claims to a review panel does not violate the right of trial by jury and access to the courts. Furthermore, a state may have a legitimate regulatory interest in limiting the damages that may be recovered.

Kane v. Johns-Manville Corp. (1988)

Facts: As a result of present and expected suits, the defendant filed a voluntary petition in bankruptcy under Chapter 11. Kane, on behalf of himself and future third parties, challenged the Bankruptcy Court's confirmation of the Plan of Reorganization.
Issue: Does an injured plaintiff have standing to assert the rights of future claimants by challenging a reorganization plan?
Rule: An injured plaintiff lacks sufficient standing to challenge a reorganization plan on the grounds that the plan would violate the rights of future claimants and other third parties.

Ives v. South Buffalo Railway Co. (1911)

Facts: Under the worker's compensation laws, the plaintiff, a railroad employee, was entitled to damages caused by a necessary risk of his employment regardless of fault.
Issue: Are worker's compensation statutes that make an employer liable regardless of fault constitutional?
Rule: No-fault worker's compensation statutes violate an employer's right to due process and, therefore, are unconstitutional.

New York Central Railroad Co. v. White (S. Ct. 1917)

Facts: White sought to recover for damages against the defendant under New York's worker's compensation statute.
Issue: Is a worker's compensation statute constitutional?

Rule: (Pitney, J.) A worker's compensation statute is a valid expression of the government's right to legislate rules concerning the public interest, and thus is constitutional.

Shavers v. Kelly (1978)

Facts: The plaintiff challenged the constitutionality of Michigan's No-Fault Insurance Act because it partially abolished the common law recovery for negligently caused accidents.
Issue: Does a No-Fault Act violate due process by partially abolishing a tort remedy for persons injured by the negligence of others?
Rule: The abolition of a tort remedy for injuries is constitutional if it bears a reasonable relationship to a permissible legislative objective.

Usery v. Turner Elkhorn Mining Co. (S. Ct. 1976)

Facts: Turner Elkhorn Mining challenged the constitutionality of a federal statute that provided benefits for miners suffering from Black Lung disease by creating several presumptions in their favor (e.g., any miner with 10 years of experience who died from a respiratory disease is rebuttably presumed to have died from Black Lung disease).
Issue: Is a statute that creates presumptions unconstitutional?
Rule: (Marshall, J.) A statute is not unconstitutional for enacting presumptions if Congress did not act in an arbitrary or irrational manner.

Duke Power Co. v. Carolina Environmental Study Group (S. Ct. 1978)

Facts: The plaintiffs challenged the constitutionality of the Price-Anderson Act, which limited the total liability for a nuclear disaster.
Issue: Can Congress impose a limitation on liability for an activity that is licensed by the federal government?
Rule: (Burger, C.J.) Limiting liability is an acceptable method for Congress to utilize in encouraging the private development of certain activities.

Industrial Union Department v. American Petroleum Institute (S. Ct. 1980)

Facts: American Petroleum challenged the government's regulations regarding the use of the chemical benzene. The government enacted these strict regulations to limit employees' exposure to benzene.
Issue: Can the federal government place stringent technological and economic limitations on chemical exposure?

Rule: (Stevens, J.) A clearly significant risk of material health impairment must be shown before the federal government can impose the strictest controls on a chemical.

American Textile Manufacturers Institute v. Donovan (S. Ct. 1981)

Facts: The plaintiffs challenged the validity of federal standards that limited occupational exposure to cotton dust claiming that the cost of the standards exceeded their benefits.
Issue: Must safety regulations be justified by a cost-benefit analysis?
Rule: (Brennan, J.) The federal government is not required to establish that the costs of a health-related safety regulation bear any reasonable relationship to its benefits. A feasibility analysis is required as opposed to a cost-benefit analysis.

Matter of Richardson v. Fielder (1986)

Facts: Richardson was killed while he was engaged in a theft at his workplace during working hours.
Issue: Are worker's compensation benefits awarded for injuries caused by an employee's non-work-related illegal activities that occur during the course of employment?
Rule: Worker's compensation benefits can be awarded where an injury to an employee results from an illegal activity during the course of employment when the employer knows about and tolerates the illegal activity.

Harris v. Bd. of Educ. Howard Cty. (2003)

Facts: Employee injured her back while moving boxes during the course of her employment.
Issue: Does the plaintiff need to establish that her injury resulted from "unusual activity" or workplace circumstances?
Rule: Workers' compensation coverage applies once an accidental injury occurs during the course of employment. The plaintiff need not establish that there were unusual events or circumstances in the workplace leading to injury.

Wilson v. Workers' Compensation Appeals Board (1976)

Facts: The plaintiff, a teacher, was injured while driving to school.
Issue: Are worker's compensation benefits awarded for injuries incurred while commuting?

Rule: Worker's compensation benefits are not awarded for injuries sustained while commuting.

Dowdy v. Motorland Insurance Co. (1980)

Facts: Dowdy was injured by a bundle of steel that fell off a loading dock as he prepared to unload his truck. The defendants claimed that Dowdy could not recover damages under no-fault insurance because he was not injured while using a vehicle, as his policy required.

Issue: Does an accident involving a parked car fall within the requirements of no-fault statute?

Rule: No-fault insurance law can be invoked for an accident involving a parked vehicle only if the vehicle was parked in a way that caused an unreasonable risk, the injury was due to equipment permanently mounted on the vehicle, or the injury was sustained by a person who was occupying or entering the vehicle.

Shaw's Case (1923)

Facts: Shaw was injured while at work and began receiving workmen's compensation payments. After a time Shaw went back to work and received money from his employer. The workmen's compensation insurer reduced its disability payments to Shaw based on the amount of money he was receiving from his employer.

Issue: Can workmen's compensation benefits be reduced if an employee is receiving money from an employer?

Rule: Workmen's compensation benefits are based on the extent of an employee's incapacity for work, not on the amount of money paid to him by an employer.

Chapman v. Dillon (1982)

Facts: Dillon suffered severe but nonpermanent injuries in a car accident with Chapman. According to the state no-fault compensation system, no actions would be allowed in tort for nonpermanent injuries.

Issue: Is a nonfault compensation system that removes actions involving nonpermanent issues unconstitutional on the basis of denial of access to courts, due process, and equal protection?

Rule: No-fault compensation systems can remove actions involving nonpermanent injuries. A no-fault system should provide a reasonable alternative to the court tort system, prompt recovery of expenses, and a reasonable, nonarbitrary classification of persons bearing a substantial relationship to the legislative purpose.

311